The Great Warpath

The Great Warpath

British Military Sites

from Albany to Crown Point

David R. Starbuck

University Press of New England · HANOVER AND LONDON

UNIVERSITY PRESS OF NEW ENGLAND, HANOVER, NH 03755

© 1999 BY UNIVERSITY PRESS OF NEW ENGLAND

PRINTED IN THE UNITED STATES OF AMERICA

5 4 3 2

CIP DATA APPEAR AT THE END OF THE BOOK

Illustration credits

Courtesy of the Fort William Henry Corporation: Figs. 1-2, 4-2, 4-4, 4-5, 4-6, 4-7, 4-8, and 5-11.

Courtesy of Saratoga National Historical Park: Fig. 2-15.

Courtesy of Dennis E. Howe: Fig. 3-11.

Courtesy of New York State Library: Fig. 3-30.

Courtesy of Paul Huey and the Bureau of Historic Sites, New York State Office of Parks, Recreation and Historic Preservation: Figs. 5-3, 5-4, 5-5, 5-6, 5-7, 5-8, 5-9, 7-1, 7-2, 7-6, 7-7, 7-9, 7-10, 7-11, and 7-12, and the figures in the boxes on pages 7, 8, 9 and 10.

Courtesy of the New Hampshire Historical Society: Figs. 6-3 and 6-4.

Courtesy of Sarah Kinsella Waite: Fig. 6-16.

Courtesy of Gordon DeAngelo: Fig. 6-18.

Courtesy of Ellen Pawelczak: Fig. 6-20.

Courtesy of Kevin J. Crisman: Figs. 8-2, 8-3, 8-4, 8-5, 8-6, 8-7, 8-8, and 8-17.

Courtesy of the Lake Champlain Maritime Museum and the Vermont Division for Historic Preservation: Figs. 8-9, 8-10, 8-11, 8-12, 8-13, and 8-14.

Courtesy of Mark Peckham: Fig. 8-15.

Courtesy of Joseph W. Zarzynski and Bateaux Below, Inc.: Figs. 8-16, 8-18, and 8-19.

Courtesy of Russell Bellico and Bateaux Below, Inc.: Figs. 8-20 and 8-21.

The National Society Daughters of Colonial Wars
is pleased to have been of help in the publication of this work by
David R. Starbuck, Ph.D.
The Society promotes historical research and the study
of the American Colonial Period from the time of the settlement
of Jamestown, May 13, 1607, to the Battle of Lexington, April, 19, 1775.
It seeks to commemorate the events of that period
and to honor the memory and spirit of those who assisted
in the establishment, defense, and preservation of
the American Colonies.

Contents

Preface

When I was growing up in the Adirondack Mountains of New York State in the fifties and sixties, I was often told that there were no archeological sites in that region—that I would have to go elsewhere if I wanted to be an archeologist. And that was exactly what I did until, twenty years later, I found that most of my research had come to focus upon the eighteenth century and that many of the very best colonial military sites in the United States lay within the region that I had left as a boy. I returned to New York State and began directing excavations at eighteenth-century military sites in 1985 and have been doing so ever since. The area in which I grew up may have seemed uninteresting when I was younger, but during my recent efforts to learn more about America's colonial wars, I have to admit that I cannot imagine a more archeologically rewarding and exciting part of the country than upstate New York and adjacent parts of Vermont.

Some of the information I include in this book has already appeared in articles and chapters elsewhere, but much is new. In any case, it would not have been possible to publish these results in book-length form, and with so many illustrations, were it not for the very generous financial support of the National Society Daughters of Colonial Wars, who offered to help at just the right time. I am greatly indebted to the Daughters, and especially Past National President Harriett Jurgeleit, National President Neoma O'Brien, and Past National Historian Mary Lee Birmingham, for sharing the belief that the history of the colonial wars is woefully neglected in America today, and that a book such as this—written in a popular style—can help to restore public interest in the events and processes that made us a nation over two hundred years ago.

I also wish to thank the Archaeological Institute of America, Long Island Society, and its president, Joseph Lepelstat, and Beatrice Holland, chairperson, The Americas Study Group, for their most kind support of this book. The Long Island Society awards one grant each year to an archeological project somewhere in the world, and their award for 1998 was split equally between preparation of this volume and the acquisition of supplies for our field work at French and Indian War sites in the Lake George area.

The illustrations in this book come from many sources; I especially wish to thank Kevin Crisman of Texas A&M University, Arthur Cohn and Scott McLaughlin of the Lake Champlain Maritime Museum, Joseph Zarzynski and Russell Bellico of Bateaux Below, Inc., Dennis Howe of The Printed

Word, The Fort William Henry Corporation, Mark Peckham, Sarah Kinsella Waite, Ellen Pawelczak, Gordon DeAngelo, the New Hampshire Historical Society, and Paul R. Huey of NYS Parks, Recreation and Historic Preservation. Their generosity with graphic materials they owned or prepared has made this a much more useful and attractive book.

The preparation of a volume such as this requires a great deal of behind-the-scenes work, and here I must gratefully acknowledge the efforts of Phyllis Deutsch, Michael Burton, and Mary Crittendon of University Press of New England for their efforts to keep this book on track over the past year. I also wish to thank the reviewers of this volume, Dr. Mary C. Beaudry of Boston University, Dr. Paul Huey of the New York State Office of Parks, Recreation and Historic Preservation, and Timothy J. Todish of Suagothel Productions Ltd. for many useful comments that have fundamentally altered the orientation of this book and its intended audience. Mary, in particular, firmly reminded us that this book had to live up to its goal of appealing to a broad audience, and not just to historical archeologists.

Finally, my biggest thanks go to all of the field and laboratory supervisors, students, volunteers, site owners, and administrators who have worked with me since 1985, providing the data and many of the interpretations contained in this volume. We often conducted two field projects each summer, with as many as eighty workers on each project, and that means upwards of a thousand professional and avocational archeologists need to be acknowledged here. That presents a bit of a dilemma: I do not want to leave anyone out, yet we cannot afford to add ten pages to this book! Consequently, I here name a partial group, but one that is, I hope, representative: Paul Anderson, Sandra Arnold, Louise Basa, Bruce Batten, Megan Battey, Joshua Blackler, Gerald Bradfield, Herman Brown, Sylvie Browne, Betsey and Mark Brownell, Frank Bump, Peggy Burbo, William Byrd, Debby Campagna Williams, Mary Cassedy, Cathleen Catalfamo, Ann Clay, Deborah Conners, Stephen Coulthart, Joel Dashnaw, Lynn Davis, Barbara and Gordon De Angelo, Michael Deblois, Joseph Delecki, Paul Demers, Frank DeNardo, John Dumville, Marie Ellsworth, Barbara Erwood, John Farrell, Andy Farry, David Ferris, Lachlan Field, Emily Fowler, Linda Fuerderer, Carl Fuller, Paul Gooding, Ben Gworek, Elizabeth Hall, Brett Harper, Fred Harris, Phillip Haubner, Bruce Hedin, William Herrlich, Dennis Howe, the late Antonett Howe, Peggy Huckel, Dick and Mary Janssen, Brad Jarvis, Hans Jensen, Ryan Joyce, Maureen Kennedy, William Ketchum, Philip Keyes, Matthew Kierstead, Doug Kneeland, John Kosek, Andrea LaPan, Leah Larcenaire, Dylan Larke, Cathy Lee, Naton Leslie, Peter Lihatsh, Maria Liston, Christopher Lohr, Louise Luchini, Len Lumsden, Sherry Mahady, George Martin, Ray Matteau, Elaine McGoldrick, Ken McIver, Phil Mead, Jane Mendocino, Gini and Bob Miettunen, Melanie Morehouse, William Murphy, Emily Nichols, William Nikas, Bernard Noble, Colin O'Brien,

S. Paul Okey, David and Nancy Osgood, Dot Osterhout, Scott Padeni, Merle and Bob Parsons, Fred Patton, the late Joan Patton, Ellen Pawelczak, Giovanna Peebles, David Pinkham, Robert Piper, Audrey Porsche, Louise Ransom, Ken Rhodes, Marjorie Robbins, Victor Rolando, Jene Romeo, Matt Rozell, Walter Ryan, Frank Schlamp, Steve Sgorbati, Roland Smith, Gerd Sommer, Dorothy Stanton, Herbert Swift, Judy Symon, June Talley, Don Thompson, Janet Truelove, Sarah van Ryckevorsel, Mark VanValkenburg, Sarah Waite, Carolyn Weatherwax, Dan Weiskotten, Tim Whelan, Linda White, Susan Winchell-Sweeney, Diane Wood, Claudia Young-Palmer, and Janet Zeno. To these archeologists, and to everyone else, thank you for making this book possible.

August 1998   D.R.S.

Chronologies

Chronology of the French and Indian Wars

1689–1697	King William's War is fought between France and the combined allies of Britain, Spain, and the Netherlands
1701–1713	Queen Anne's War is fought between Britain and France
1734–1737	French build Fort St. Frederic on Lake Champlain
1744–1748	King George's War is fought between Britain and France
1754	(July 4) The French defeat George Washington and an army of Virginians in the Battle of Great Meadows at Fort Necessity in western Pennsylvania
1755	(July 9) Battle of the Wilderness (Braddock's Defeat) near Fort Duquesne in western Pennsylvania; the French destroy a British column
	(Sept. 8) Battle of Lake George between the provincials under General William Johnson against the French under Baron Dieskau; the provincials win
	British General William Johnson and Captain William Eyre begin construction of Fort William Henry and Fort Edward
	French begin construction of Fort Carillon (Ticonderoga) on Lake Champlain
	(Sept. 8) French and Native Americans are surprised and slaughtered south of Lake George by a group of provincials, and their bodies are thrown into "Bloody Pond"
1757	(Aug. 3–9) The French under the Marquis de Montcalm lay siege to Fort William Henry; the British, led by Colonel George Monro, surrender and the fort is destroyed
	(Aug. 10) The retreating British column is attacked by Indians attached to Montcalm's army; this becomes known as the "massacre"
1758	(March) Battle on Snowshoes is fought between Rogers Rangers and the French

	(July 8) General James Abercromby's army attacks the French at Fort Carillon; Lord Howe is killed and Duncan Campbell is mortally wounded
	Fort William and Fort Gage are constructed by the British in Lake George
	260 British bateaux are sunk in Lake George to protect them; this is later referred to as the "Sunken Fleet"
	America's oldest intact wooden warship, the radeau *Land Tortoise*, is built and then sunk in Lake George
1759	British under General Jeffery Amherst begin construction of Fort George at the south end of Lake George
	(July) General Amherst's army attacks Fort Carillon, but the French blow it up. The fort is renamed Fort Ticonderoga. The British also capture Fort St. Frederic
	British under Amherst begin construction of His Majesty's Fort at Crown Point
	(Sept. 13) General James Wolfe's army attacks Quebec, and the city surrenders to the British a few days later
1760	(Sept. 8) Montreal is captured by the British
1763	The Treaty of Paris ends the French and Indian War, and with it many of France's claims to North America

Chronology of the American Revolution

1775	(April) Fighting in Lexington and Concord
	(May 10) Ethan Allen and the Green Mountain Boys take control of Fort Ticonderoga from the British
	(May) Fort George is captured by Americans under Captain Bernard Romans
	(June 17) Battle of Bunker Hill (Breed's Hill)
	(Sept. 4–Dec. 21) Americans under Richard Montgomery and Benedict Arnold invade Canada and take Montreal; Montgomery is killed at Quebec City, and the campaign fails
1775–1776	(Winter) General Henry Knox uses oxen and sleds to deliver the artillery from Fort Ticonderoga to Boston; the British are forced to evacuate the city

1776   (July 4) Signing of the Declaration of Independence

(July) Americans begin constructing the fortifications on Mount Independence

(Summer) Americans led by Benedict Arnold construct the first American fleet in Whitehall, N.Y. ("the birthplace of the U.S. Navy")

(October) The British fleet commanded by Sir Guy Carleton is slowed by Benedict Arnold and American ships at the Battle of Valcour Island; then the British return to Canada when they see the strong American force at Mount Independence and Fort Ticonderoga

1776–1777   (Winter) A floating bridge is built across Lake Champlain between Mount Independence and Fort Ticonderoga

1777   (July 6) As a British army commanded by General John Burgoyne approaches, American forces abandon first Ticonderoga and then Mount Independence

(July 7) The British advance guard clashes with the retreating Americans at the Battle of Hubbardton in Vermont

(Aug. 16) A detachment from Burgoyne's army, led by Lt. Colonel Baum, is defeated in the Battle of Bennington by American militia under John Stark

(August) Jane McCrea, an American woman, is murdered and scalped by Native Americans attached to Burgoyne's army

(Sept. 19) Burgoyne attacks American forces in Stillwater, N.Y., at the Battle of Freeman's Farm; both sides withdraw and entrench

(Oct. 7) Burgoyne attacks the Americans for a second time, at the Barber Wheatfield; General Simon Fraser is mortally wounded, and the British retreat north

(Oct. 17) Burgoyne surrenders the British army at Schuylerville (Old Saratoga)

1780   (October) British Major Christopher Carleton conducts raids throughout the Champlain Valley and burns Fort George

1781   (Oct. 19) General Cornwallis's forces surrender in Yorktown, Va., leaving the British with garrisons only in Savannah, Charleston, and New York City

1783   (Sept. 3) The peace treaty is signed, ending the American Revolution

The Great Warpath

Chapter 1

A Most Historic Waterway

General Observations

I WAS BORN in Ticonderoga, New York, and my interest in the archeology of military sites surely comes from having grown up just south of that historic town. My teachers often spoke of the dramatic events that transformed northern New York in the eighteenth century, and it was impossible to go through school in New York State in the 1950s and 1960s without developing a keen interest in the battles and fortifications that made us an English-speaking colony and then an independent nation. While I have never personally served in the military, my fascination with the wars fought on the eighteenth-century American frontier has always been strong.

Unfortunately, there has been a great erosion in the teaching and reading of American colonial history over the past thirty years, and now it is only the older visitors to my annual summer excavations who remember having been taught about Rogers' Rangers or who have read *The Last of the Mohicans*. Earlier generations routinely read novels about colonial warfare, such as *Arundel* and *Northwest Passage* by Kenneth Roberts, but now even World War II has become "ancient history" for some. In a time of cultural diversity and political correctness, many young people learn about other cultures at the expense of learning about their own history. My frustration with this loss of our cultural heritage and identity was one of the reasons I began digging military camps in 1985, and I have been doing so ever since. Throughout this period it has been extremely satisfying to meet and talk with the ever-increasing numbers of diggers and visitors to my excavations each summer. And so this book reflects thirteen years of digging and conducting historical research, all the time lobbying for a new and deeper appreciation of early American military history (see the box "Deciding Where to Dig").

The waterway that runs from the Richelieu River in Canada to Albany, New York (along the border between New York State and Vermont), has the greatest density of eighteenth-century military sites in North America (see figure 1-1). War was waged throughout the 1750s at both the northern and southern ends of Lake George, and the best-known conflicts of the French and Indian War took place within this corridor at a British fort, Fort William Henry, and at a French fort, Fort Ticonderoga. Twenty years later, during the American Revolution, Saratoga achieved fame as the scene of one of the most decisive battles in world history, and John Burgoyne's march from Canada to the Saratoga Battlefield left a trail of British military sites that is hundreds of miles long.

Events and sites such as these were so seminal in shaping the United States of today that I have decided to name this military corridor "The Great Warpath." After all, for about one hundred years, it was precisely that. Still, there are ample British military sites in Canada and other sites running south to Virginia and west to Michigan. Parks Canada has done a superb job in excavating and interpreting many British and French forts, including Fort Chambly, Fort Lennox, the fortifications at Quebec City, and Fortress Louisbourg—the greatest French fortification in the New World.

To the south, one of the best-known early fort excavations was conducted

FIG. 1-1. Eighteenth-century military sites along The Great Warpath. Modified from a map by J. Edens, *Expedition* Magazine, which was based on an original map by David Starbuck.

★ Deciding Where to Dig

I often cringe whenever I'm asked to explain why I decided to dig in a particular spot. Not that it's a difficult question, it's just that giving a complete answer would require several college-length lectures. And, of course, there are no rules governing how much we should dig. Archeologists of the past often dug far too much at forts and battlefields, leaving little behind for future researchers. Now, thanks to the worldwide interest in preserving heritage sites, the scale of many excavations has been cut back. But while sites must not be overdug, at the same time I believe that there is virtually no point in preserving early military sites unless we are prepared to wrest from them every bit of information we can about the people who once lived, fought, or died there.

All archeological sites are steadily deteriorating and thus will become harder to interpret in the future if they are neglected today. Given the actions of collectors and natural forces such as erosion, rust, frost heaves, and tree roots, information is irretrievably lost whenever digging is postponed. The challenge for archeologists and site managers is thus to agree upon the research questions that need to be answered now, through digging, and to decide which sites are better left alone so that future generations of archeologists will be able to study them with better techniques.

In most cases, the first step in deciding where to dig on an eighteenth-century military site is to conduct historical research using officers' orderly books, soldiers' diaries and letters, and contemporary maps and engineers' drawings. This should be accompanied by interviews with property owners and archeologists who have previously worked in the area. Systematically walking over the surface will determine whether any foundations, earthworks, or artifacts are still visible, and identifying and mapping these surface remains go a long way toward defining precisely where to dig.

Various types of remote sensing equipment, such as proton magnetometers, resistivity meters, ground-penetrating radar, and even metal detectors, may also be helpful in predicting what is below the surface, especially when suitable types of soil are present (it is much easier to "read" buried patterns in sandy soil as opposed to clay). However, remote sensing techniques are never a substitute for digging because such techniques merely demonstrate that an anomaly exists below the surface. They rarely reveal exactly what the feature is, and they certainly do not identify the age of the discovery or the types of buried artifacts. A friend described to me several years ago the pronouncement of the director of a military museum that in ten years it would no longer be necessary to do archeology—that remote sensing had made digging unnecessary. But this director utterly missed the mark: remote sensing provides only the most minimal information about possible ditches, pits, burials, hearths, or kilns. Every buried feature could just as easily be a recent, twentieth-century disturbance, and all such finds still need to be exposed and verified before historical interpretations can begin.

Once a dig is underway, there remains the question of exactly how much an archeologist can dig without risking overdigging the site. This is the hardest issue for archeologists to agree on, but I can state emphatically that choosing an arbitrary percentage of a historical site to sample is utterly without value. Archeologists will often dig a set percentage of a large prehistoric site that covers several acres, and to dig 5 or 10 percent of such a site may involve digging hundreds of pits. But when we dig historical sites, often the only way to interpret what really went on is to dig most or all of a cellar hole or activity area. In fact, to dig less than that is actually a form of treasure hunting—merely acquiring some artifacts—because the site's integrity will have been compromised before it has had a chance to reveal useful, new information. Digging too little is pointless, while digging too much is destructive. Striking the necessary balance between these positions usually comes only after years of experience at archeological sites, learning what does and doesn't work.

by the National Park Service at the short-lived Fort Necessity in western Pennsylvania, where George Washington and a British force surrendered to the French in 1754. Even more significant is the long-term research program at Fort Michilimackinac in Michigan, the setting for successive French and British occupations over most of the eighteenth century. Fort Michilimackinac has seen more excavation, and a better publications program, than any other military site in the United States. Both land and underwater excavations (in the York River) have taken place as well at the Yorktown Battlefield in Virginia, where British and American forces brought the revolution to a close in 1781.

These sites and others have witnessed excavations for many years, but it is without doubt the lesser-known (and therefore less-dug) sites that have the greatest value to archeologists today. Because of the public's interest in forts and battlefields, these sites have created special problems for preservationists as they try to balance the desire to interpret with the necessity to leave a portion of each site intact for future scholars to study. The National Park Service, for its part, has wisely reduced its digging of military sites, but collectors continue to destroy much of what is left (see the box "What's Wrong with Treasure-Hunting?"). Also, it is amazingly rare even today for some museums to call professional archeologists when they are about to disturb below-ground remains with modern construction.

While historians have prepared descriptions of the events that occurred at the better-known forts and battlegrounds along The Great Warpath, modern syntheses are few, as are good descriptions of the ruins that have survived to the present day. Together these New York State and Vermont sites represent an unparalleled historic military presence of national significance. The potential for heritage tourism within this region is almost limitless, and visitors who enter the corridor at Albany or Stillwater are able to travel from the Saratoga Battlefield to the site of the vast encampment in Fort Edward, to the several fort sites in Lake George, to Fort Ticonderoga, the English and French forts at Crown Point, and then on to the many forts in Canada (also see the box "Military Sites in Albany"). A host of other military sites, while extremely important, are not yet being interpreted for the public. These include Fort Miller and Fort Ann (just south and just north of

★ What's Wrong with Treasure-Hunting?

Everyone likes getting something for nothing, so perhaps we are all treasure hunters at heart. However, every historical site is literally unique and irreplaceable, and any site that is not carefully dug and documented (and published on afterward) will lose most of its ability to yield information about the past. A great many countries recognize this fact by defining all buried relics as the property of the state and by compensating finders and property owners for artifacts taken from them. Americans have often resisted this belief that the past belongs to everyone, perhaps because of our strong tradition of private property rights. Still, the objects that we discover in yards or battlefields have little meaning if found with a metal detector, dug out with a shovel, and then sold to another collector or dealer.

Collectors of military artifacts sometimes say to me that they have "saved" or "rescued" objects from the ground, implying that they are performing a necessary service. But when they separate the artifacts from their buried context, and sell regimental buttons and buckles to dealers for two hundred dollars or more, they have destroyed forever the information that archeologists could have gleaned from the ground. Not all collectors are this destructive, of course, and several have revealed to me the secret locations of sites that they felt needed to be carefully researched and protected. I am most grateful to these few for their willingness to share their knowledge. One actually took me to the site of a soldiers' camp very close to Fort Gage in Lake George, which prompted the property owner—the Niagara Mohawk Power Corporation—to sponsor an extremely expensive and productive salvage effort at that site in 1996.

Unfortunately, though, it is much more common for collectors to contact me *after* they have finished their digging, once they are sure I cannot stop them. I recall one case when a collector phoned me at 5 A.M. and asked me to accompany him to the blockhouse site he was digging just south of Fort Edward. I was then treated to the sight of gaping holes that had been dug over many weeks, and the surrounding grass was piled high with rusty metal artifacts and bones, the objects that he knew he wouldn't be able to sell. At times like that I am reminded that treasure hunters always put the object —and its monetary value—first, whereas archeologists are chiefly interested in learning something new. I don't want to imply that archeologists can't appreciate the aesthetics of a beautiful artifact, but we need to interpret the objects properly so that we can tell a powerful and interesting story about what people were doing at that site.

Given the present rate of looting and site destruction, I firmly believe that treasure hunters will have destroyed all remaining eighteenth-century military sites within the next generation, or at least those that are on private land and unprotected. Even the best-known, best-guarded sites such as the Saratoga Battlefield and Fort Ticonderoga are under constant attack, and one or two arrests for illegal digging are made at Ticonderoga each year. In the end, the only hope may come from increasing the penalties for those caught digging on state and federal land, and from better educating property owners so that they won't allow nonprofessional digging on private property. But at this moment, the future appears grim for many of the encampments located on private land. All too often, when increased vigilance drives collectors away from one site, they quickly relocate and begin digging at another.

An equally serious problem is that too many archeologists have dug sites without publishing one word on them afterward. This has made some of us the worst treasure hunters of all! There is no difference, in my opinion, between the collector who digs up artifacts to sell, and the archeologist who digs to achieve fame, or a promotion, and then goes on to dig more sites without writing up his earlier work. Collectors do not hesitate to point out to me how unfair and hypocritical it is when they are attacked by "professionals" who are more destructive than they are. In all sincerity, I couldn't agree with them more.

Fort Edward, respectively), and a variety of sites in Whitehall (formerly known as Skenesborough).

Unlike more traditional military histories, such as *The War of American Independence* by Don Higginbotham and *The Continental Army* by Robert Wright, Jr., this book is written from my perspective as an archeologist and anthropologist. I attempt to read the physical remains of each fortification or encampment in much the same way that a historian reads a book. My approach is somewhat different from that of military historians because while I work with historical records, I also deal with the physical survivals from the eighteenth century. I look to see what patterning has survived in the ground, and I ask whether this has new stories to tell. As an archeologist, I would suggest that for many years too few scholars have had new ideas about the military campaigns of the eighteenth century, and too many publications have been a rehash of the strategies employed two hundred years ago at a few of the major battlefields.

What I believe archeology and anthropology can contribute to colonial military history is the story of daily life in the camps, a lively account of what ordinary soldiers did during the 363 or 364 days of the year that they were not fighting. How better to do this than by studying the remains of the encampments from each war? Vast military camps sprang up and seasonally became some of the largest cities in the American colonies. For example, the camps at Fort Edward and Lake George in northern New York State would seasonally become the third-largest cities in America, surpassed only by New York City and Philadelphia.

Can anything new be learned from the soldiers' earthworks, hospitals, huts, their meals, their pottery, their clothing, and the like? I think that studying the ruins of these great encampments is just the sort of stimulus that military scholarship needs in North America. I have had the opportunity to direct excavations at four of the larger military encampments of the eighteenth century, and at several of the lesser ones, and I believe that integrating the soldiers' own written accounts of life on the frontier with an analysis of the physical remains of their camps provides a very stimulating look at the colonial wars. American historical scholarship does not need another reassessment of a hallowed battleground! But the lives of ordinary

★ Military Sites in Albany

While the many Dutch archeological sites in Albany receive a great deal of attention, none of the later British forts or military hospitals is on public display. This is most unfortunate because much of Albany and several of the surrounding communities are underlain by the remains of military structures, and revolutionary war earthworks are still to be seen in several locations. There were long periods, especially during the French and Indian War, when Albany was the only safe location in northern New York State, and when raiding parties from Canada made it hazardous to travel any further north. This was especially true in 1745 when the French attacked and burned Philip Schuyler's estate in Schuylerville.

Unfortunately, these sites in the Albany area are often found inadvertently, during modern construction, and tend to receive attention only as they are being destroyed. The Bureau of Historic Sites, part of the New York State Office of Parks, Recreation and Historic Preservation, and also staff from the New York State Museum, are often called in at the last moment to identify or salvage British military sites in Albany. The leading archeologists from the Albany area, Paul Huey, Lois Feister, Charles Fisher, Karen Hartgen, and others, have all worked with these remains, but what the city of Albany really needs next is a comprehensive, proactive survey that will identify and interpret the rest of the eighteenth-century British military presence before more is lost.

The trench dug along State Street in Albany in March 1973. Courtesy of Paul Huey and the Bureau of Historic Sites, New York State Office of Parks, Recreation and Historic Preservation.

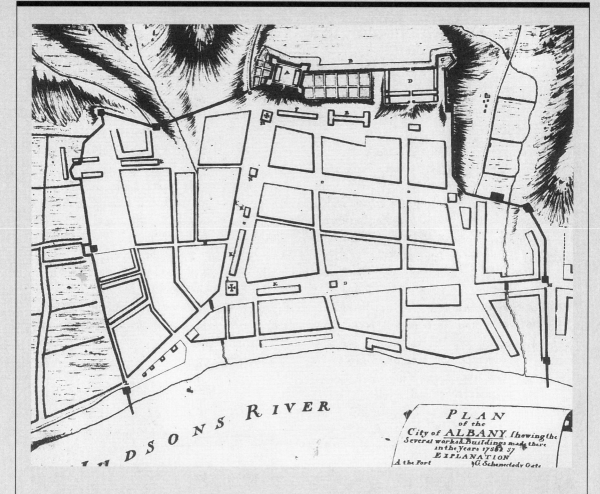

PLAN
of the
City of ALBANY. Shewing the
Several works & Buildings made there
in the Years 1756 & 57
EXPLANATION
A the Fort   G. Schenectady Gate

From the French and Indian War period, one of the most important finds was made in 1973 when the Bureau of Historic Sites worked with the Niagara Mohawk Power Corporation as a trench was dug up State Street in Albany. They uncovered remains of some of the British structures that once stood in the street, including the foundation of a blockhouse (marked "N" in the British map of Albany) at the intersection with North Pearl Street. In the blockhouse they found shell scraps and waste from wampum making, which Paul Huey believes soldiers stationed in the blockhouse were making in their spare time. Nearby, they found a collapsed, wood-walled cellar in the street about where Fort Albany (occasionally called "Fort Frederick") had originally stood. According to Paul Huey, the pine wood was so well preserved that the power equipment could barely go through it. Unfortunately, because this hill was graded down in

A British map of Albany showing military structures erected in 1756 and 1757. This shows as "K" the "Magazines & Stables built by the A.D.Q.M. Gral." "H" indicates the English Church, and "A" is "the Fort" (Fort Albany). Courtesy of the British Museum, CXX1/42, and Paul Huey and the Bureau of Historic Sites, New York State Office of Parks, Recreation and Historic Preservation.

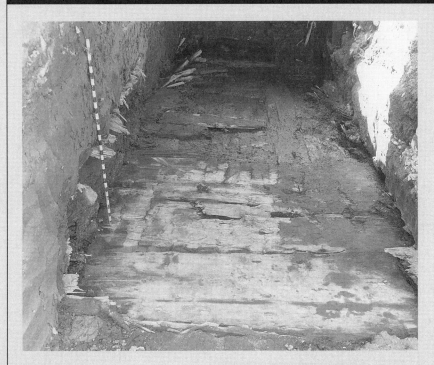

The remains of the wooden cellar at the site of Fort Albany, March 1973. Courtesy of Paul Huey and the Bureau of Historic Sites, New York State Office of Parks, Recreation and Historic Preservation.

Revolutionary war earthworks (1777) on Peebles Island, Waterford, New York. This profile shows the rescue excavation conducted there in 1979. Courtesy of Paul Huey and the Bureau of Historic Sites, New York State Office of Parks, Recreation and Historic Preservation.

the nineteenth century, probably nothing else survives from Fort Albany.

There was an extensive revolutionary war period occupation in Albany, including a large general hospital, but almost nothing has been published and little has been professionally dug. However, this period *is* well represented at Peebles Island State Park, where the Bureau of Historic Sites maintains its conservation facility. In 1979 the route of a waste water line went through a small section of the revolutionary war earthworks, and staff from the bureau were able to excavate a cross-section profile. There also is a well-preserved, clearly defined earthwork redoubt originally built in 1777 that survives at the northwest point of Peebles Island. The bureau sometimes shows this site to the public when it gives tours, and it is a wonderfully intact survival.

Corner of a revolutionary war earthwork redoubt built in 1777 on Peebles Island (1996). Courtesy of Paul Huey and the Bureau of Historic Sites, New York State Office of Parks, Recreation and Historic Preservation.

soldiers as they went to war is a story that is only now starting to be told, increasingly by archeologists and not just traditional historians.

In this book I present a historical and archeological overview of some of the most significant military events and sites along the waterway that runs from Albany to Crown Point, devoting a chapter to each site. Along the way, I discuss the history of each major site, the ruins that have survived to the present day, and what I consider the research potential of each ruin to be. My personal bias is that I believe this region played the most central role in helping the United States to achieve independence from France and then Britain. I also believe that archeological sites are best protected by keeping the public well informed about them. The vast majority of treasure hunters *already* know where the best sites are and have been digging into them for years. It is only with widespread public support and the dissemination of knowledge that we can hope to protect these sites from looting.

But why study the remains of military sites? Isn't a great deal already known from historical documents? Whenever my students ask me this question, I argue that archeology acts as a good check against the historical record, which is notoriously faulty. Also, the use of material culture in combination with documents permits us to explore many themes that simply are not adequately addressed within historical scholarship. Among these are such questions as: What differences existed in living standards between officers and enlisted men? How were the designs of European forts adapted to the American landscape? Was all material culture 'outdated' at military sites on the frontier (that is, were soldiers the *last* to receive the latest fashions and technology)? What was the diet of soldiers on the frontier? Did they eat just salt beef and salt pork, or did they have access to fresh meat and fish? Was it too dangerous to leave the camps to hunt wild game? Did soldiers follow military manuals closely as to how they were supposed to fight and lay out their camps in the field? What construction techniques were used for building forts, blockhouses, barracks, and ordinary living structures like tents, houses, and huts? In this last case, we know that engineers' plans typically have survived only for the largest, most permanent military buildings. The huts, tents, and lookout posts erected by the soldiers are rarely depicted on contemporary plans.

In answering these questions and others, my colleagues in archeology and I are trying to learn more about eighteenth-century military life along The Great Warpath, as well as elsewhere in the United States and Canada. But within the Hudson River, Lake George, and Lake Champlain Corridor, it is clear that only at the Saratoga Battlefield has legitimate archeology been pursued systematically, over a long period of time. Elsewhere, professional archeology goes back only twenty to thirty years within this region, and there are still institutions that choose not to hire competent professionals to do this work. Just over ten years ago, an interpreter at one of this region's reconstructed forts told me that they didn't need archeology because original engineers' plans had survived—an attitude that had already caused many inaccuracies in their reconstruction. They were opening a new part of their fort to the public on that particular occasion, and had never gotten archeological evidence to make their exhibits more accurate.

Military History

The first of the colonial wars between the French and British were King William's War (1689–1697), Queen Anne's War (1701–1713), and King George's War (1744–1748). Little archeology has been done at the sites of these earliest conflicts, although a few forts were being constructed at that time, such as Fort St. Frederic in the Champlain Valley. St. Frederic was built and occupied by French forces between 1731 and 1759 to provide protection for French farmers who were moving into the region; in 1759 they were forced to blow up the fort and retreat because a British army under General Jeffery Amherst was approaching. Extensive digging was conducted there in 1968 by Roland Robbins, and the ruins of Fort St. Frederic are at present owned and interpreted by New York State.

It was not until the 1750s and the last of the French and Indian Wars that The Great Warpath truly earned a reputation as one of the most turbulent settings on the world stage. In the space of a few years, military events transformed what had once been canoe routes and Native American trails into one of the largest population centers in the Americas. Between 1755 and 1777, the whole world followed events in this region, and British newspapers routinely described happenings on Lake George, in Fort Edward, at Ticonderoga, and elsewhere. Long-standing rivalries exploded into war in September of 1755 when the British and French clashed at the south end of Lake George, in what is commonly called the Battle of Lake George (figure 1-2). The British won this initial encounter, and a state-owned park known as Battlefield Park now encompasses this site.

As soon as the battle ended, a fort-building race began. The governor of Canada ordered French forces to start construction of Fort Carillon (Ticonderoga) in 1755, sited where it would overlook both Lake Champlain and the outlet from Lake George. From there, French armies hoped to control travel between Canada and settlements to the south. While Fort Carillon would not have held more than about four hundred men, the surrounding military encampment was spread out over a huge area, creating what is now a vast archeological site. Just before the fort was opened to the public in 1909, some digging was done to find the bases of stone walls, and portions of the fort were rebuilt atop its original foundations. Much later, in 1957, Duncan Campbell spent five weeks exposing the foundations of a storehouse and

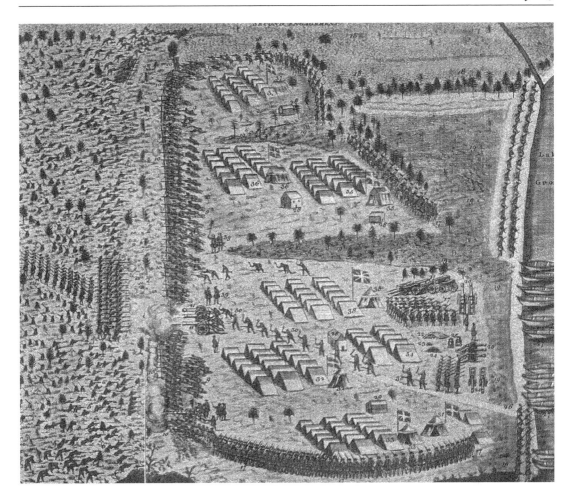

blacksmith shop in the French village that lay between Fort Ticonderoga and the water. This village originally contained a blacksmith shop, a bakehouse, storehouses, a wine shop, a trader's store, and dwellings for civilians. But these covered only a tiny part of the fort's property, and Ticonderoga also has French lines and camps that go on practically forever.

For their part, the British and their engineer William Eyre began constructing two forts along The Great Warpath in the fall of 1755. The smaller was the ill-fated Fort William Henry at the southern end of Lake George, while the main British fort was Fort Edward, located sixteen miles to the south. These were the first forts built by the British in North America using the design of the great French builder of forts, Sebastien Le Prestre Vauban. In other words, this was the first time the British constructed their earth and log forts in the same manner that the French built their more permanent forts, with corner bastions where they could catch their enemies in a crossfire.

FIG. 1-2. "A Prospective Plan" of the Battle of Lake George, September 8, 1755, by Samuel Blodgett. Courtesy of the Fort William Henry Corporation.

Each fort came to a radically different end. Fort William Henry was destroyed during the siege and infamous massacre by the French and Native Americans in August 1757. The slaughter of British subjects under French protection and the desecration of the fort's cemetery were used by the British as a rallying cry for the rest of the French and Indian War, and James Fenimore Cooper's famous novel of 1826, *The Last of the Mohicans*, ensured that this massacre would endure as the most memorable event of the war. It is perhaps the *only* event from that war that is widely remembered in North America today.

While later armies camped on top of the charred ruins of Fort William Henry, it was not until 1952 that archeology began at the fort, directed by Stanley Gifford. The fort was promptly reconstructed on top of its ruins and still stands today as the historical centerpiece of the Fort William Henry Corporation. The digging of Fort William Henry was watched by about sixty-five thousand visitors each summer in the 1950s, and recently a whole new generation of tourists was able to watch the excavations we conducted there in the summers of 1997 and 1998. A few of the recent visitors were, in fact, returnees from the 1950s, eager to see whether archeological techniques had changed in forty-five years.

Just to the south, Fort Edward fared rather differently during the war because it never came under direct attack from the French. This huge supplies base and staging area, together with Rogers Island in the Hudson River, contained the ranking British officers in the North and some fifteen to sixteen thousand men for brief periods during 1758 and 1759. Above the ground there is little to see of old Fort Edward today because it is in a residential neighborhood, making this a difficult site to interpret for the visiting public. Still, teams from Adirondack Community College (ACC) dug into the fort site for two years (1995–1996), and we have discovered many charred beams and postmolds from the fort and its interior structures. And nearby, I have led classes from ACC for six years (1991–1994, 1997, and 1998) on Rogers Island, which was the main base camp for Rogers' Rangers, the colonials who fought in the woods much the way the Native Americans did. Excavations there have exposed huts, barracks, dumps, a latrine, and a smallpox hospital —the earliest military smallpox hospital to be dug in North America.

Of these several French and Indian War sites, Fort Ticonderoga is certainly one of the best known because of the many battles that occurred there, including the British conquest of the fort in 1759, and the later capture of the fort by Ethan Allen and the Green Mountain Boys at the start of the American Revolution. These events have elevated Ticonderoga into an immensely popular attraction that draws many of its visitors from Canada and overseas. Since it was reconstructed, "Fort Ti" has come to symbolize the French settlement of this region, and it actually received as many as a quarter of a million visitors each year in the 1950s. The current annual visitation is more modest, at approximately one hundred thousand.

But there are a host of less famous sites from the colonial wars, too, ranging from the ruins of Fort Saratoga and Fort Hardy in Schuylerville; to Bloody Pond south of Lake George, where a raiding party of Canadians and Native Americans were killed in 1755 and their bodies thrown into a small pond by New Hampshire and New York militiamen; to three later forts that were built in the village of Lake George by the British: Fort George, Fort Gage, and Fort William. Until recently, when work was done at Fort William Henry and the Niagara Mohawk site, only Fort Gage had been professionally excavated, a British fort built immediately after the fall of Fort William Henry. Part of Fort Gage was excavated in 1975 by Lois Feister, Paul Huey, and the Auringer-Seelye Chapter of the New York State Archaeological Association. Unfortunately, this had to be a salvage excavation, necessitated by the construction of a Ramada Inn atop the fort's remains. In this case, modern development caused irreparable harm to one of the region's most significant military sites.

Lake George Village also saw the construction of Fort George, begun in 1759 and then never finished. Still amazingly intact, this was raised in the same location where the Battle of Lake George had occurred four years earlier. A small British garrison was based there between the two wars, and Fort George later became the site of one of the largest provincial hospitals during the American Revolution, receiving thousands of smallpox patients from northern New York and New England. This was the only fort on Lake George to span both wars. A single corner bastion and a few building foundations are visible today, and the site is now owned and managed by New York State. Fort George overlooks the Million Dollar Beach at the south end of Lake George, but the only archeological work ever conducted there was a brief surface mapping project undertaken in 1994. Nevertheless, the ruins of this fort may well be the most intact British military site surviving in the northeastern United States.

Less well known in Lake George is the site of Fort William, a small fort built in 1758. The fort is now located dangerously close to the town's many discount stores (the Million Dollar Half Mile) and treasure hunters have begun to disturb this site; it appears it may be destroyed before research is ever conducted there. Elsewhere, the sites of extensive British and French camps, created by Sir William Johnson and generals Amherst, Abercromby, and Montcalm, underlie practically the entire village of Lake George, and many of these camp sites have already been destroyed by commercial development.

Collectively, these French and Indian War sites are unquestionably the most and the best eighteenth-century military sites in America today, yet from a war that is largely forgotten. In the public's imagination, the Civil

War and twentieth-century wars have all but eclipsed the earlier battles and forts, yet the early sites along The Great Warpath can still aid in historical research and promote heritage tourism, making the eighteenth century come alive for visitors.

But conflict on the frontier of colonial America did not end with the battles of the 1750s and 1760s. Many of the soldiers who had fought as enlisted men against the French returned as officers twenty years later to fight either against or for the British Crown in the 1770s. The coming of the American Revolution led to the creation of many new military sites along The Great Warpath, even while some of the older sites, including Fort George, Fort Edward, and Fort Ticonderoga, continued to be occupied. In the north, construction of the English fort at Crown Point had begun in 1759, thanks to a force of eight thousand men under the direction of General Jeffery Amherst. It subsequently evolved between the two wars into the largest British fort in North America. Even today the ruins of its huge stone barracks buildings look like two-story Georgian mansions. However, a fire in 1773 caused the barracks to burn, the powder magazine blew up, and everything was abandoned by 1777. Now owned by New York State, the vast ruins of Crown Point are unparalleled: the imposing earth walls are crumbling but awesome, and the stone officers' and enlisted men's barracks are well presented and maintained. Staff from the New York State Office of Parks, Recreation and Historic Preservation have conducted many small-scale excavations there, at hut sites and around the barracks, and the archeological potential is enormous.

On the eastern side of The Great Warpath is one of the least disturbed sites of the American Revolution, located in Vermont at Mount Independence, a three-hundred-acre fortification overlooking Lake Champlain and positioned directly across from Fort Ticonderoga at the narrowest point on the lake. The Mount was *the* major fortification built by Americans in the North, in 1776, to withstand a British onslaught from Canada, and this was the first site that opposed General John Burgoyne's army in the summer of 1777. That July, Burgoyne swept the Americans from their outposts at Mount Independence and Ticonderoga, and then a British garrison occupied the site for the next several months before they burned down all of the buildings and retreated. For the next two hundred years, this vast mountaintop was never built upon and then, at the request of the Vermont Division for Historic Preservation, three years of excavations and mapping were conducted there between 1989 and 1992.

More recently, some of the results have gone on display in a striking new visitors' center at the Mount, a most distinctive building shaped like an upside-down bateau. The State of Vermont, in cooperation with Fort Ticonderoga, has chosen a somewhat different way of presenting the past at Mount Independence in that *none* of its many barracks buildings, huts, storehouses, blockhouses, and hospitals has been rebuilt. Everything at Mount Independence is genuine, and nothing is a twentieth-century monument to the past.

Also in Vermont, the Hubbardton Battlefield lies about twenty miles south of Mount Independence and is the only eighteenth-century battle site located on Vermont soil. It was there that American soldiers retreating from Mount Independence clashed with Burgoyne's advance guard on July 7, 1777. This is another site that has a visitors' center operated by the Vermont Division for Historic Preservation, albeit on a modest scale. Some of the first historical archeology in Vermont was conducted there in the 1970s by Beth Bower, followed by excavations I directed there in the 1980s.

Finally, Saratoga National Historical Park, site of the two battles of Saratoga in late 1777, lies close to the southern end of The Great Warpath. The action that was centered in Stillwater and Schuylerville is justly famous, for this was where John Burgoyne's army of seven thousand British and German soldiers was finally halted by General Horatio Gates and twenty thousand American troops. Many of the captured British soldiers never went home after the war and instead settled in the colonies. The park has over a quarter of a million visitors each year, and it is near the spot where many visitors first enter The Great Warpath and decide which additional sites they will visit as they travel north. The battlefield has been the subject of much research and many publications, and archeologists have conducted excavations in the park since the 1940s. Several scholars have worked there, including John Cotter and Edward Larrabee in the 1950s and 1960s, Dean Snow in the 1970s, and most recently I have dug there in the 1980s and 1990s. However, the long-term effect of many collectors, perhaps too many archeologists, and too much plowing has been to reduce radically the archeological research potential of this famous site, and little original fabric from the time of the battles is on display to the public.

In addition to the many land sites that have survived along the sides of The Great Warpath, there are easily hundreds of extant underwater sites, including the remains of many military vessels studied in Lake Champlain by the Lake Champlain Maritime Museum and Texas A&M University, plus the hundreds of vessels (chiefly bateaux) discovered in Lake George by the group known as Bateaux Below. These bateaux were deliberately sunk by the British during the military campaigns of the 1750s, and recently Bateaux Below has discovered America's oldest intact wooden warship, a British seven-sided radeau known as the *Land Tortoise*, perfectly preserved in the cold waters of Lake George.

Why Study or Preserve These Military Sites?

Since the late 1960s, Americans have been taught less and less about the colonial wars of North America. This makes it doubly important not just to know which eighteenth-century military sites have survived, but to use them as a way to learn more about early American culture. A serious problem, though, is that a great many military sites are privately owned, and treasure hunters (and property owners) have been digging into them for years. Regrettably, looters can realize instant profits from the sale of military paraphernalia, and the penalties for illegally collecting on state or federal land are so mild that they do not appear to serve as a deterrent to site destruction.

Nevertheless, many thousands of visitors travel to reconstructed British forts and battlefields in North America each summer, and thousands more enjoy dressing and equipping themselves as eighteenth-century British soldiers. The role of British armies in shaping and creating North America will not be forgotten, and British military sites continue to reveal much information about camp layout, consumption practices, and construction techniques to the current generation of archeologists. These sites are of great benefit to heritage tourism, and to historical scholarship, and hopefully the forts and battlefields of northern New York and Vermont will increasingly receive the respect and the sensitive interpretation that they deserve.

Further Reading

Anderson, Fred. 1984. *A People's Army: Massachusetts Soldiers and Society in the Seven Years' War*. Chapel Hill: The University of North Carolina Press.

Campbell, Lt. Col. J. Duncan. 1958. Investigations at the French Village 1957. *The Bulletin of the Fort Ticonderoga Museum* 10 (2):143–55.

Cooper, James Fenimore. [1826] 1980. *The Last of the Mohicans*. New York: Penguin Books.

Dunn, Shirley W. 1994. *The Mohicans and Their Land 1609–1730*. Fleischmanns, N.Y.: Purple Mountain Press.

Fowler, Barney. 1982. *Adirondack Album*. Schenectady, N.Y.: Outdoor Associates. See the chapters "Goliaths in Green" and "Frontier Forts."

Fry, Bruce W. 1984. *"An Appearance of Strength": The Fortifications of Louisbourg*. 2 vols. Parks Canada, Ottawa: Studies in Archaeology, Architecture and History.

Harrington, Jean C. 1957. *New Light on Washington's Fort Necessity*. Richmond, Va.: Eastern National Park and Monument Association.

———. 1976. The Puzzle of Washington's Fort Necessity. *Archaeology* 29 (3): 178–85.

Higginbotham, Don. 1971. *The War of American Independence*. Boston: Northeastern
    University Press.
Roberts, Kenneth. 1930. *Arundel*. New York: Fawcett Crest.
————. 1936. *Northwest Passage*. New York: Fawcett Crest.
Wright, Robert K., Jr. 1989. *The Continental Army*. Washington, D.C.: Center of
    Military History, United States Army.

Chapter 2

The Turning Point of the Revolution: The Saratoga Battlefield

A YEAR AFTER the Declaration of Independence, British forces were still hoping to bring hostilities to a speedy conclusion in the American colonies. The Continental Army had yet to win a major victory when a force of between seven and eight thousand British, German, and Canadian troops, with perhaps a thousand hangers-on (camp followers, servants, teamsters, and so on), left Canada in the spring of 1777, planning to split the northern colonies as they traveled south along Lake Champlain, Lake George, and the Hudson River en route to Albany. Under the command of Lt. General John Burgoyne, this army expected to receive provisions and Loyalist recruits along the route, and they did not anticipate serious resistance from the less-experienced Continental Army or from militia units. Burgoyne's strategy assumed that a second British army under Sir William Howe would push north from New York City, advancing up the Hudson, and a third British army, under Lt. Colonel Barry St. Leger, was to leave Oswego and travel through the Mohawk Valley, proceeding toward Albany.

While this three-pronged attack upon Albany may have been sound military strategy, the plan quickly unraveled because Howe's army never left New York City, and St. Leger's troops were halted at the Battle of Oriskany, near Fort Stanwix in what is now Rome, New York. Burgoyne thus proceeded south, quite unaware that his force would be alone in September when they encountered American forces in Stillwater at what has become known as the Battles of Saratoga. The events that followed have been intensively documented both in contemporary accounts and many subsequent histories, including Richard Ketchum's new book, *Saratoga: Turning Point of America's Revolutionary War*. Many generations of American historians have referred to the two battles in Saratoga as the turning point of the American Revolution because they prompted France's entry into the war. Historians thus describe Saratoga as one of the twenty or twenty-five most significant battles in world history.

Burgoyne's troops sailed along Lake Champlain, encountering limited resistance at Fort Ticonderoga and Mount Independence, and stiffer resistance in Hubbardton, Vermont, during a brief battle on July 7, 1777. Quite aware of these events, an equally large American force under Major General Horatio Gates had ample time in which to construct defensive earthworks at Bemis Heights on the west bank of the Hudson. This point of high ground, located just north of the small village of Stillwater, was the site of scattered upland farms as well as a tavern belonging to Jotham Bemis. At the time of the battles, the landscape was thus a mixture of woodlots and fields.

Burgoyne's army traveled down the west bank of the Hudson, roughly where Route 4 is today, and on September 19, 1777, the two forces clashed in fields in front of the American position. Known ever since as the Battle of Freeman's Farm, the action proved inconclusive, but the British and Germans remained on the field at the end of the day. The Americans returned to their position, and the British proceeded to construct their own earthworks facing the American lines. These consisted of several large redoubts joined by long earthen and timber barriers that snaked across the landscape. Regimental camps were set up behind these, with a few hundred men in each camp. Many of the officers on each side occupied local farmhouses, while troops were quartered in tents. A typical mess consisted of five or six men who shared a tent and cooked all of their food together in the same kettle. Their most common weapon was the "Brown Bess" musket that fired a 69-caliber ball through a 75-caliber bore.

Digging in for the next three weeks proved to be a fatal strategy for the British and their allies because American forces steadily increased in number as militia units arrived from New York, New Hampshire, Massachusetts, and Connecticut, ultimately swelling the revolutionary side to over twenty thousand men. At the same time, the British were short on provisions. A raiding party led by a Hessian officer, Lt. Colonel Friedrich Baum, had earlier been dispatched to Bennington, Vermont, to procure supplies, but they had been defeated and Baum mortally wounded by New Englanders under John Stark on August 15 at Walloomscoick, New York, in what is now known as the Battle of Bennington. Also, the expected Loyalist sympathizers did not materialize.

Finally, on October 7, a force of about seventeen hundred British and Germans led by Brig. General Simon Fraser marched out to probe the American lines in an area that is now called the Barber Wheatfield. They were met by three times as many Americans, and riflemen led by Colonel Daniel Morgan struck the British from under the cover of woods and halted their advance. General Fraser was among those who were hit, and, after being carried from the battlefield, he died the next morning in the house of the nearby Taylor farm. The British army was forced into retreat. In another six days they decided to capitulate, and then on October 17 they formally surrendered and laid down their arms in what is now Schuylerville. Thus ended the ill-fated British expedition, earning Burgoyne's force the unfortunate distinction of being the first British army in history to surrender upon the field of battle.

Saratoga brought an end to hostilities in the North, France entered the war on the side of the Americans, and all fighting shifted to the southern colonies. In the space of a month, however, the two sides had created what is now a vast archeological site, spread out over thousands of acres and including two battlefields, the foundations of many farmhouses and barns that were occupied during the battle, lengthy defensive lines, and many campsites and redoubts. These sites are now incorporated within Saratoga National Historical Park, a twenty-six-hundred-acre park administered by the National Park Service (NPS) which interprets the landscape based upon its 1777 appearance. Historical maps showing the battles at Saratoga are extremely incomplete, however, and archeology has often been needed to add more detail.

Early Archeology at the Battlefield

The farms that once made up the battlefield areas were acquired by New York State beginning in 1926, and a state park was created there. Later, in 1938, 1,430 acres were transferred to the federal government, and in 1948 an act of Congress authorized the establishment of Saratoga National Historical Park. While much collecting occurred at these farms immediately after the battles ended and then throughout the nineteenth century, it was not until the period of federal ownership that archeologists came in to locate specific sites for the sake of public interpretation. Robert Ehrich worked there in 1940 and 1941 with laborers from the Civilian Conservation Corps, exposing sections of the British and American lines, together with the Balcarres and Breymann Redoubts. Ehrich, as did later archeologists, relied heavily upon a map prepared in 1777 by British Lieutenant James Wilkinson of the 62nd Regiment of Foot, and a major objective of his early excavations was to test the accuracy of Wilkinson's map. During the course of his excavations, Ehrich not only dug along the defensive lines but also located six skeletons at the south end of the Balcarres Redoubt, which he promptly reburied without marking their locations.

In subsequent years National Park Service archeologist John Cotter excavated in the Balcarres Redoubt and on the site of the Neilson farm, one of the farms occupied by American officers. Between 1958 and 1964 Cotter and Edward Larrabee, working independently, both dug sizable portions of the yards surrounding the Schuyler House in nearby Schuylerville. Neither succeeded in locating foundations from the mansion built by General Philip Schuyler in the mid-1760s, a massive structure that had been burned by the

British on October 11, 1777, during their retreat. However, both archeologists exposed wells, outbuilding foundations, root cellars, and ditches, revealing a pattern of intensive property use from the mid-eighteenth century up until the present.

More recently, teams from the State University of New York at Albany, under the direction of Dean Snow, conducted in Saratoga one of the first extensive mapping projects ever to be undertaken at any major historic battlefield in the United States. Between 1972 and 1975 Snow relied heavily upon low level aerial photographs as he prepared a series of base maps that documented roads, earthworks, foundations, and walls at the time of the battles. Snow did considerable digging in order to clarify structural details on his maps, and he excavated within the Balcarres, Breymann, Bemis Heights, and Great Redoubts, as well as along the British fortification wall in the vicinity of the 21st Regiment encampment. He also recovered two human skeletons from within redoubts and excavated within the foundation of the Taylor farmhouse, the site of Simon Fraser's death. The Taylor house was just above the floodplain on the west bank of the Hudson, approximately 170 feet lower than the farms on Bemis Heights.

In spite of the usefulness of past archeological research, much of Saratoga National Historical Park, which now totals 3,406 acres, is still incompletely known. That is why I promptly consented in 1985 when Dick Ping Hsu of the National Park Service asked me to conduct excavations at the site of the American Headquarters, at the Taylor house, and at the Schuyler House in Schuylerville. I was a professor at Rensselaer Polytechnic Institute at the time, and I spent three years digging at these and other sites within the park. Still, even today further excavations are needed, especially within the two battlefield areas—Freeman's Farm and the Barber Wheatfield—to locate more precisely where the action took place in 1777.

History of the American Headquarters

While previous excavators in Saratoga National Historical Park located many of the most distinctive historical features, they clearly had a strong bias in favor of testing the British redoubts. American battle lines were relatively neglected, principally because the NPS did not have the funds to buy large farming areas on Bemis Heights. This changed in late 1984 when those lots that contained the American headquarters, lots 13 and 14 of the Saratoga Patent, were added to the park and became available for excavation and interpretation. This area is just south of Routes 32 and 423, a modern highway that lies approximately on top of the earlier road to Bemis Heights. The Bemis Tavern, in use at the time of the battles, lay a few thousand feet east and downhill from there.

Sometime between 1760 and 1777, a weaver and captain in the Albany Militia, Ephraim Woodworth, leased these fields and proceeded to build a house, barn, and outbuildings. The house was definitely one of the best in the region and was of frame construction, unlike the other farmhouses in the area, which were nothing more than log cabins. Clearly General Gates would have picked one of the best houses available for himself and his officers, and they used it as their headquarters throughout most of the engagement. Also, a later visitor, Benjamin Silliman in 1819, stated that "From the style of the panel-work and finishing the house appears to have been in its day one of the better sort—the panels were large and handsome and the door was still ornamented with brass handles."

The Woodworth family departed when American troops arrived to begin work on their defenses. While this was not the only farmhouse that Gates occupied during the course of the battle, it nevertheless was where the Native Americans on the American side brought British prisoners for interrogation each morning, and where Gates and General Benedict Arnold quarreled after the battle on September 19 because Arnold felt his own division had not received due credit in Gates's official report to Congress. After Arnold stalked out of the Woodworth farmhouse on September 22, he repeatedly defied Gates's authority and so was relieved of his command, only to reappear on October 7 when he heroically led American troops in charges upon the British redoubts.

Some of the primary sources that mention the Woodworth farm note that the American field hospital was situated within the Woodworth barn. The most detailed of these descriptions is a later visitor's account, by General Epaphras Hoyt, who described the mass burials nearby:

> A small distance east of the [Woodworth] house, ast [sic] the time of the battles, stood a barn in which many of the wounded were deposited; but the foundation only remains to mark the spot. [In] The fields . . . adjacent here the bones of many a patriot who died of wounds received in the two actions of the 19th of September and 7th of October, rest in obscurity. My companion pointed out the spot where twenty-eight of these heroes were interred in one grave; and near this spot the veteran Col. Breyman and Sir Francis Clark, Burgoyne's aid-de-camp [sic], mortally wounded and taken prisoners in the second action mixed their remains with their brave conquerors.

Ample evidence further identifies this spot as the location of the hospital. For example, an account cited by John Brandow in *The Story of Old Saratoga* . . . claims that Francis Clark and Gates had an interesting exchange there just before Clark died:

in the field was Gates's headquarters, and up to the right of it was the hospital. Here Gates stayed during the second day's battle, and here he had the heated argument with Sir Francis Clerke [*sic*], a wounded prisoner, over the merits of the questions at issue between the Americans and British.

Yet another reference to the hospital comes in a letter from a young Hessian chaplain, Feldprediger Milius, to his father. The letter, dated November 20, 1777, describes wounded Hessian soldiers being treated in the American hospital before they died and were buried nearby. Sources such as these are strong evidence that the remains of Americans, Germans, and British were all combined within mass burials in the fields of the Woodworth farm, probably within easy carrying distance of the Woodworth barn.

After the battle on October 7, American forces moved north, pursuing Burgoyne's army in its retreat. Bemis Heights, after less than a month of occupation by the American army, ceased to have a military function, and some farmers returned. However, the Woodworth family was not among these, and their farm buildings went into decline. Still, the farm's reputation as the American headquarters, the site where Gates and his officers planned their successful strategy, lingered on, and numerous early-nineteenth-century travelers visited the house and commented on its appearance. In 1819 only one room was still in use, by a cooper and his family, and the end finally came in 1829 when the house was razed. The date of the barn's destruction is unknown.

Benson Lossing visited the site in 1848 and, using information supplied by a neighbor, Charles Neilson, published sketches that included the former house and barn (figure 2-1). In 1924 the Neilson family printed and sold their own map of the Bemis Heights area (figure 2-2), and the two sets of drawings are remarkably similar in showing the headquarters and hospital (farmhouse and barn) side by side, south of the road to Bemis Heights. The Lossing sketches are especially useful in that they portray the headquarters with two stories, doors on the east and south, and with a well just outside the southern door.

The last map to portray the headquarters foundation was also the only one with an accurate scale. This was a map drawn by the surveyor Edward West in May 1926 for the New York State Conservation Commission. It clearly portrays a foundation that is labeled "Remains of Foundation of Gen. Gates Headquarters," and this was the last time the foundation was recorded before it slipped from view beneath the topsoil of the field. As for the hospital, there was no reported sighting of its foundation after about 1820, suggesting that its foundation was not as substantial as that of the headquarters. From this time on, both of the foundations were effectively lost, although a local farmer, Tony Burdyl, described to me how he had plowed up stones and

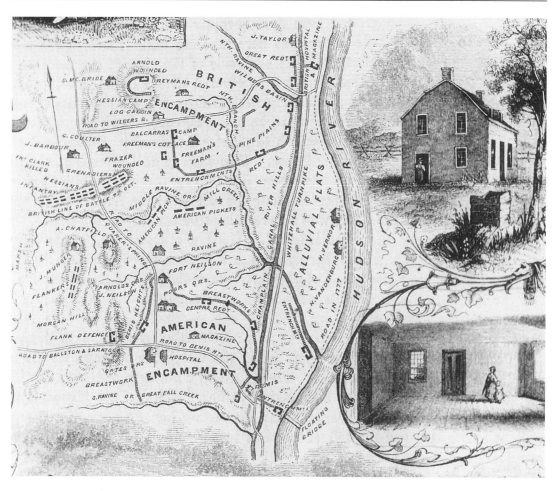

FIG. 2-1. Plan of the American headquarters (left) and views of the Woodworth farmhouse (right). Note the close proximity of GATES HRS and the HOSPITAL to each other. From Benson J. Lossing, 1851, *The Pictorial Field-Book of the Revolution* (New York: Harper & Brothers), p. 46.

bricks in this area before 1951. He also was able to point out where a spring had once been located several hundred feet southeast of this spot. Both documentary and oral history were thus relatively precise in suggesting where, within the field, archeological testing might be helpful.

Discovering the American Headquarters

Archeologists have conducted a great deal of field work at other sites of the revolutionary war era, most notably Fort Stanwix, the New Windsor Cantonment, Morristown and Pluckemin (New Jersey), and Valley Forge. But the Saratoga Battlefield is somewhat atypical in that it contains such a great diversity of military features within its borders. While many of the central battlefield areas had previously been dug by other excavators, the setting of the American headquarters was some distance away, and left relatively un-

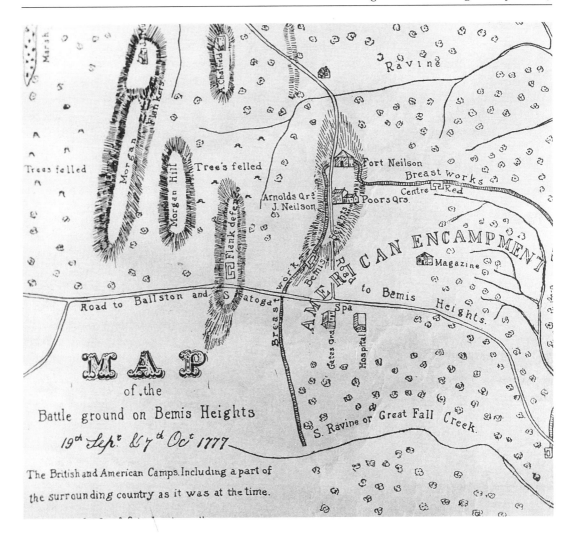

disturbed. The Woodworth farm was clearly tangential to the actual fighting; the officers there were approximately 1.7 miles from the September 19 battle and about 1.3 miles from the October 7 battle. It is tempting to suggest that the general who was referred to as "Granny Gates" by his men picked this setting because it was as far as possible from the actual conflict. Still, the Woodworth farm was in an easily defensible position. Gates was flanked by American units on the north, west, and east, but against his back, to the south, was a deep ravine on Great Fall Creek (figures 2-1 and 2-2). Gates's position could not be outflanked, but neither could he retreat.

Determining the location of the farm buildings that Gates had occupied was given a very high priority by the National Park Service. So when I met with staff at Saratoga National Historical Park in 1984, we decided that the

FIG. 2-2. Detail from "Map of the Battle ground on Bemis Heights 19th Sept. & 7th Oct. 1777." Gates's headquarters and the American hospital are portrayed side by side in the center of the map, just south of the Road to Bemis Heights. Drawn by Charles Neilson. Lith. by J. H. Hall, Albany. 1924.

work to be conducted there in 1985–1986 would have as its primary objective the location of foundations from the Woodworth farmhouse and barn, as well as any associated burials. Still, I had to wonder whether evidence for military occupation would be totally intermixed with debris from 220 years of farm occupation. Because the Woodworth farmhouse had been occupied for ten to twenty years before the battle and for 52 years afterward, I doubted very much that significant numbers of military artifacts would be found inside or surrounding a cellar hole that had been filled in 1829 or shortly thereafter. The barn appeared to be a better candidate for high site integrity because that building had been removed earlier. At the same time, barns often have minimal foundations, making them somewhat more difficult to locate. So I wanted a testing strategy that would look for evidence of other outbuildings or lesser features (such as privies and trash pits)—features that would have been in use briefly, but that might have been made and used only at the time of the military occupation. If I could find items of standard military issue or buttons from uniforms, they would help to confirm whether any foundations found there had been occupied by the military at the time of the battle, whereas the dating of domestic artifacts would confirm whether these had been the Woodworth farm buildings. Also, I wanted to recover artifacts that might prove the presence of officers so that I could contrast them with remains from campsites occupied by enlisted men.

In 1985 we conducted a proton magnetometer survey at five-meter intervals atop the highest rise in the field south of Routes 32 and 423. Unfortunately, this remote sensing technique failed miserably because a high iron content in the soil produced virtually identical magnetometer readings throughout the field. Next we tried to dig shovel test pits (small holes, about sixteen inches across), which were equally fruitless because all of the dirt in the field was clay hardpan that shovels would not penetrate. Finally, I turned to a tractor-mounted power auger to drill some 119 holes at five-meter intervals on a systematic grid, hoping that the presence and/or absence of artifacts would at least establish where human occupation had been most intensive. This technique was a bit more successful, and we found scatters of pottery and bricks in an area where there were lots of woodchuck holes. Curiously enough, we could see that some of the woodchuck holes contained quite a few stones.

We then started backhoe trenching in order to locate foundation walls. In 1985 our first trench located two foundation walls from a single structure (figure 2-3), and both were substantial enough to suggest they were from a house rather than a barn or other outbuilding. At the same time, some seven meters to the south, we began looking more closely at the stones and artifacts that were coming out of the woodchuck holes. I suddenly realized that I was looking into the top of a well shaft—it was the original Woodworth well! A local newspaper, the Troy *Times Record*, entitled one of its articles,

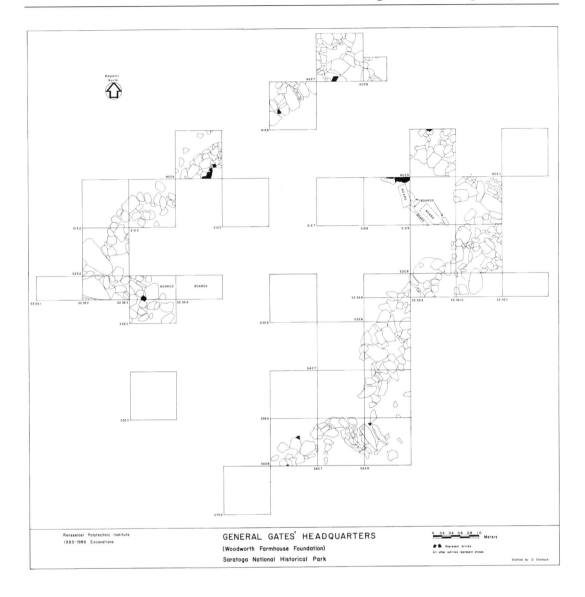

GENERAL GATES' HEADQUARTERS
(Woodworth Farmhouse Foundation)
Saratoga National Historical Park

Rensselaer Polytechnic Institute
1985-1986 Excavations

"Chucks Lead the Way." It was true: the woodchucks *had* been more successful than the archeologists.

Here I want to digress for a moment and state that it was fortunate the woodchucks cooperated when they did because we were having such obvious difficulties in our search that a couple of different dowsers had each volunteered their services and were eagerly telling us where four or five buildings had been and even how deep remains were going to be. Now, while I do not deny that dowsing rods in the right hands have often succeeded in locating water, their ability to find buried foundations or artifacts is questionable.

FIG. 2-3. General Gates's headquarters (the Woodworth farmhouse foundation).

Nevertheless, we were getting desperate, and I actually dug a few holes to check out their "readings." Never again. I am now firmly convinced that the best use for dowsing rods is to decide where to put piles of backdirt from an excavation—because they are guaranteed to find only the most sterile, empty, barren spots on any archeological site!

We were not seriously deterred, however, and kept using the backhoe throughout 1986 as we tried to find the barn foundation. We excavated a total of twenty-four backhoe trenches across the northern part of the field, and most of these we placed just east of the foundation that had already been located. Farm buildings were usually built close together, and both the Lossing and Neilson maps (figures 2-1 and 2-2) showed that the hospital was only a few feet to the east. But to be on the safe side, we also dug trenches across every other point of high ground in the field.

For most of the 1986 season the trenching revealed little, although we found a thin scatter of artifacts about fifty feet east of the first foundation. We also located a long, curving line of stones that looked rather like a French drain, flanking the site on the west, north, and east. Thousands of small, loosely-packed stones lay within a ditch, allowing water to flow downhill more easily than in the surrounding clay subsoil. But in spite of the backhoe trenching, we were totally unable to find evidence for mass burials (or even solitary burials). I could only conclude that bodies had either been removed and reburied elsewhere after the battle was over, or else that the burials had been interred from the start in a more distant field. Perhaps it was just as well that we were unsuccessful because I had started receiving lengthy phone calls from an activist in Albany, who insisted that I had no right to "desecrate" the dead. I of course did not share her views, but our search was difficult enough without having to deal with protesters.

Finally, during the last week of our 1986 season, our backhoe trenches (trenches 21–23) exposed small clusters of stones only about forty to fifty feet east of the first foundation. These arrangements of stones surrounded the area in which we had located the artifact scatter several weeks before. While we did not find continuous foundation walls, this was certainly not surprising. Many barns have their weight supported only at the corners, and virtually all of the artifacts we had found were inside the outline created by the four clusters of stones. In the end, I have no doubt that these two foundations were from the headquarters and the hospital, confirming the maps drawn by Lossing and Neilson, but finding them in the field of clay was truly a nightmare.

The American Headquarters (Woodworth Farmhouse)

We dug a total of thirty test pits and one backhoe trench (trench 1) in the vicinity of the American headquarters, but only eighteen pits within the cellar hole itself. The tops of the foundation stones were at the base of the plowzone, about a foot below the surface of the field. At a depth of sixteen to eighteen inches, the homogeneous gray clay changed to a layer of brick fragments and foundation stones, underlain by a dense layer of artifacts that ranged in depth from twenty-six to thirty-two inches. This zone contained a great many animal bones, clam shells, pottery sherds, tobacco pipes, and much building material. The zone bottomed out at about forty inches, at which point boards and smaller bits of wood and charcoal were scattered over the sterile clay hardpan that lay underneath.

The artifacts in the bottom of the cellar hole did not date any later than 1829, and a great many dated to at least twenty years earlier. Most were probably thrown into the open cellar within a few years after the removal of the house, or else during the years of its final decay when only a single room was occupied by a cooper and his family.

The northern and eastern walls of the cellar now measure approximately eighteen feet long, the southern wall about twenty-two feet, and the western wall about twenty-four feet. Allowing for some slumpage of the foundation stones, the house when intact probably measured about twenty feet on a side. Although Lossing's 1851 sketch showed doorways on the eastern and northern sides, as well as two stories and two chimneys (figure 2-1), not enough had survived for me to prove this archeologically. We found relatively few bricks in the cellar hole, and this probably means that nearly all intact ones were salvaged and taken elsewhere at the time the house was razed. Still, there were slightly higher numbers of bricks just inside the center of the western wall, so I believe that a fireplace and chimney may have stood there. In keeping with National Park Service guidelines, we exposed all four corners of the foundation but left much of the interior intact for the benefit of future archeologists (see figure 2-3).

The American Field Hospital (Woodworth Barn)

The search for the American hospital was a greater challenge because barns often have minimal foundations; some are even built directly upon the surface of the ground. This meant that traces could be so slight that we might not recognize the remains of a barn even if we were digging through it. In 1985 several of our auger holes turned up building debris, but it did not appear to have any particular orientation. This bit of refuse, plus the available historical maps, helped us narrow down the location of the hospital. But we still had to blanket the area between 16 and 115 feet east of the headquarters foundation with backhoe trenches before we finally found small clusters of stones that appeared to be the remains of a building. Moderate numbers of artifacts, chiefly pottery and animal bones, were in the open space inside the stones. These covered an area about twenty feet north-south by sixteen feet east-west, downslope and directly east of the headquarters foundation. The stones occurred only as corners, and there was no evidence for complete walls there. While the evidence is not wholly conclusive, our best guess is that this was an impermanent structure, with its weight carried upon corner posts.

We excavated a small area only and found no artifacts that suggested either a barn or a hospital. This could have been a shed or workshop, but the facts suggest otherwise: (1) this was nearly as large as the house foundation that was exposed; (2) this was exactly where Neilson and Lossing placed the barn; and (3) backhoe trenching revealed virtually no evidence for foundation debris anywhere else in the vicinity of the farmhouse. The absence of medical artifacts was of course disappointing, but if the barn had stood for twenty or thirty years after the battles, there would be no reason to expect doctors' implements (or amputated body parts!) inside or near the remains of the building.

The Woodworth Well

As I mentioned, the well was discovered in 1985 by woodchucks. A woodchuck hole exposed stones on the eastern side of the well, which made it easier to find and then excavate this tantalizing feature. I had never dug a well before, but the prospect of good preservation made it well worth the effort. During 1985 and 1986, we found that the uppermost six feet were completely filled with stones, while the next two feet were a mixture of earth and stones. We then halted the dig so that we could comply with OSHA (Occupational Safety and Health Administration) regulations and installed a five-foot-high section of culvert, twenty-four inches in diameter, within the upper part of the well shaft (figure 2-4).

Safety requirements prevented us from completing the well during 1985, and we covered its top—and filled in all of the surrounding pits—with hay bales for the winter. When the dig resumed in 1986, we first removed the bales, and in doing so we discovered to our horror that we had created an ideal home for every snake in the field. Two to four snakes dangled from the bottom of each hay bale we pulled out, and I watched and listened as several snakes splashed into the well water below. Like Indiana Jones, archeologists sometimes have to go where the snakes are to make the best discoveries!

Below the eight-foot level, water was pouring into the well, and we had to wet-screen all of the dirt to recover the artifacts. This proved quite difficult because there was a fair amount of clay inside the well, and it left every object obscured with a thin gray coating. Fortunately, though, organic material such as seeds, nuts, and bones were beautifully preserved in this oxygen-free, peat-like environment. In addition to the clay and many stones, much of the matrix below eight feet consisted of matted grass. Below five feet, the walls of the well became slightly out-flaring, but the diameter of the well measured thirty-four inches along most of its descent. It bottomed out on bedrock at a depth of thirteen feet and one inch, at which point the bottom was slightly basin-shaped where the original diggers of the well had cut some fifteen to eighteen inches into the bedrock. The only datable artifacts I

FIG. 2-4. The Woodworth well, after a culvert was inserted in 1985 to prevent collapse.

FIG. 2-5. The handle and
bottom from a wooden
bucket, excavated from the
Woodworth well.

FIG. 2-5. The handle and bottom from a wooden bucket, excavated from the Woodworth well.

found inside the well were small sherds of whiteware and redware, probably all post-dating Gates's occupation of the farmhouse. In addition, the well contained literally thousands of bones from small mammals (skunk, squirrel, and woodchuck) that had fallen in (I will forever have visions of skunks and squirrels playing tag on the rim of the well and every so often taking a false step). Some of the more distinctive artifacts from the bottom of the well included pieces of a wooden bucket, part of a red earthenware bottle, a whetstone fragment, part of the frame of a pair of eyeglasses, great numbers of cherry pits, squash seeds, and hickory nuts (figures 2-5 and 2-6), and even a single fragment of peanut shell. Nothing there was clearly from the time of the American Revolution; it had, rather, the appearance of debris that had accumulated naturally from the surface of the field, with grass, stones, and small animals occasionally falling in, until a farmer filled in the last several feet with stones all at once to make it easier to plow the field.

The well was also full of boards, which I placed in a solution of polyethylene glycol (PEG) to stabilize them. We next used the technique that archeologists call "water separation" in order to remove charcoal, seeds, and bones from the gooey matrix of clay and grass in the bottom several feet of the well. And this wasn't easy: pouring the clay into water ensured that *everything* from the well ended up with its own coating of clay.

FIG. 2-6. Artifacts excavated from the Woodworth well. Top (left to right): a red earthenware bottle neck, a whetstone fragment, and a fragment of an eyeglass frame. Bottom: cherry pits, squash seeds, and hickory nuts.

The French Drain at the Woodworth Farm

The most unusual feature at the American headquarters was a lengthy, stone-lined drain that curved around the two foundations, acting as a trap for water originating on the north, west, or east (figure 2-7). We exposed sections of this with backhoe trenches, revealing what looked like a very large horseshoe, curving for more than 202 feet. Round field stones had been laid into a ditch, two and three stones deep and two to six stones wide. While rather crude, this French style of drain, through which water is allowed to percolate between stones, was massive and ambitious. The small numbers of artifacts found within the surrounding ditch were all from the nineteenth century, clearly post-dating General Gates. In fact, this drain is quite similar to what John Worrell has termed a reverse French drain at the Stratton Tavern site in Northfield, Massachusetts, used to channel water around that farmstead throughout the nineteenth century.

The Artifacts Found at the American Headquarters

We recovered the most artifacts from the cellar hole of the headquarters building and only a very few in the hospital area or around the well (see figures 2-8 to 2-12). Evidence for firearms included just six musket balls, two pieces of cannister shot, one butt plate, one trigger guard, a possible "worm" and a possible musket tool (both badly rusted), and three gunflints (figure

FIG. 2-7. The French drain protecting the Woodworth farmhouse and barn. This view (facing south) shows the drain as exposed in trench 9, on the eastern side of the site.

2–8). One of these flints was a French style gunflint, whereas the others were cruder gunspalls. Only the cannister shot was convincingly from the military occupation of the site; everything else could easily have come from civilian uses. Oral tradition holds that collectors went to Saratoga for years following the battles, and it may be that the Woodworth farm was picked over as thoroughly as the rest of the battle sites. In fact, one of the more shocking stories still told by staff at the park is that shopkeepers in Troy would pay boys for artifacts they found at the battlefield, but if they found any human bones, they were "to throw them into the woods."

The most common ceramics we excavated from the headquarters cellar hole were plain creamware and pearlware, followed by redware, white salt-glazed stoneware, porcelain, delft, and very small amounts of Jackfield and whiteware—all quite predictable wares to find on a rural farm in upstate New York in the late eighteenth and early nineteenth centuries. While some of these could have been in use at the time of the battle, or even during the earlier Woodworth occupation, the vast majority of the ceramics were left there by the final occupants of the house at the turn of the century.

In addition, the cellar hole contained a few hundred fragments of tobacco pipe stems, most of which dated from the late eighteenth century and had a

FIG. 2-8. Evidence for firearms at the Woodworth farm. Top: a butt plate and a trigger guard. Bottom: musket balls, cannister shot, a "worm," a musket tool, and gunflints.

bore diameter of ⁴⁰⁄₆₄ inches. Curiously, there also was a unique ceramic cube (about 1⅛ inches on a side) with small projections on three out of the nine surfaces (see figure 2-9). This was probably a child's toy or a gaming piece.

The preservation of metal artifacts was extremely poor inside the damp cellar of the headquarters, and much of the metal was building hardware (many hundreds of hand-wrought nails, smaller numbers of cut nails, and nearly a dozen hinges). But personal items included some sixty-five whole or fragmentary metal buttons, manufactured chiefly of white metal (twenty-nine), brass (twenty-seven), and bronze (seven); one set of cuff links, octagonally shaped and made of cast bronze; and fourteen buckles or buckle fragments, consisting of brass and copper alloy shoe buckles and iron harness buckles (see figures 2-10 and 2-11).

Metal tools and kitchen implements were also common in the cellar, including a surprising number of bone-handled table knives and two-tined forks (figure 2-12), a complete spoon, a spoon bowl, and several fragments from cast-iron cooking pots or kettles. Many artifacts were rusted beyond recognition, but some of the more interesting pieces included a thimble and a brass furniture escutcheon plate (figure 2-9); the brass spigot from a barrel; and the complete blade (7¼ by 11½ inches) from a large spade.

We found a total of eight coins in or around the cellar hole on the headquarters site. The most recent, a large cent dating to 1809 (found at a depth of twenty-eight inches within the fill of the cellar), accords well with a cellar that would have been filled in prior to (or in) 1829. The earliest coins in the

FIG. 2-9. Miscellaneous small finds from the American headquarters. Top: chert biface, quartzite projectile point, chert projectile point, ceramic toy or gaming piece. Bottom: bone gouge, brass furniture plate, thimble, bone handle.

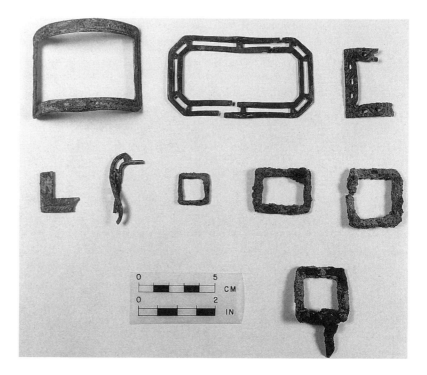

FIG. 2-10. Buckles excavated from the American headquarters.

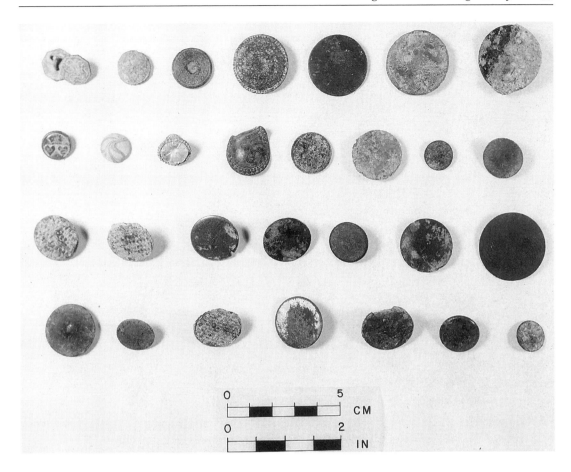

assemblage were two British half-pennies (both undated), followed by a New Jersey copper cent (1787), a Massachusetts copper cent (either 1787 or 1788), and four large cents (dating to 1798, 1800, 1800, and 1809).

FIG. 2-11. Metal buttons excavated from the American headquarters.

We examined a total of 6,262 bones from the house, barn, and drain, and bones were especially rich within the headquarters cellar. We excavated most of these from the center and southeastern part of the cellar, just above the bottom flooring. All body parts were represented, although limb extremities and teeth were so common that Barry Gray, one of my students, argued that the Woodworth cellar hole was used as a garbage dump for "butchering waste" rather than the remains of food consumption. Nevertheless, there were plenty of meaty parts, with many butchering marks from sawing and chopping. There is no evidence that any of these bones represented meat consumed by the American army. It is more likely that they represent waste thrown into the cellar either just before or just after the house was taken down.

Pig, cow, and sheep bones were the most abundant, but deer, turkey,

FIG. 2-12. Bone-handled knives, forks, and a spoon excavated from within the headquarters foundation. All are common eighteenth-century types.

chicken, and fish were also represented (see table 2-1). A great many of the bones were from immature, domesticated animals, suggesting that most of the animals had been slaughtered just as soon as they neared full-growth, probably in the fall so that they would not have to be fed through the winter.

The headquarters cellar hole also contained a considerable quantity of worked bone, including the many bone-handled knives and forks already mentioned, a single five-holed bone button, a bone gouge (figure 2-9), and other bone handle fragments. We also recovered a total of six wood buttons from the headquarters, together with several boards at a depth of about forty inches in both the northeastern and southwestern corners of the foundation. These lay directly atop the sterile clay underlying the site, and from their placement beneath all of the trash deposits, I am reasonably sure that they were floor boards within the original Woodworth farmhouse. Throughout the cellar there were numerous bricks and a great many plaster fragments and window panes, but fragments of bottle glass or tablewares were extremely rare.

Table 2-1
Faunal Remains from the American Headquarters,
Saratoga Battlefield (House, Barn, and Drain)

Identifications	Number of elements	% of sample	Min. no. of individuals
Fish	9	0.14	1
Bird	310	4.95	
Chicken	120	1.92	3
Turkey (wild)	25	0.40	3
Duck	7	0.11	1
Mammal	4,540	72.50	
Mouse	1	0.02	1
Eastern wood rat	16	0.26	2
Muskrat	6	0.10	1
Woodchuck	85	1.36	3
House cat	10	0.16	1
Dog	1	0.02	1
Pig	697	11.13	13
Deer	24	0.38	1
Sheep	147	2.35	2
Cow	250	3.99	3
Horse	13	0.21	1
Human	1	0.02	1
Totals	6,262	100.02	38

Adapted from a table in Gray (1988:18).

Some Final Thoughts on the American Headquarters

Years of farm occupation made it difficult to identify any military remains from the American headquarters. We found no evidence of burials, or short-term features pertaining to the battles, or any evidence of doctors or officers. Given the brevity of the military occupation in the farmhouse and barn, this is not surprising. Still, we found good evidence for what upland farms along the Hudson would have looked like when they housed American and British officers in the late eighteenth century.

If indeed from fifty to one hundred troops on both sides died in the American hospital and were buried within these fields, the next generation of archeologists must still locate the burials and any associated amputation pits. While we dug a great many backhoe trenches on the high ridges close to the headquarters, the more distant fields still need to be checked for burials. More thorough testing in the hospital area might yield medical supplies and help determine exactly when the barn was taken down. Finally, I believe that further digging west and south of the headquarters foundation could reveal whether additional Woodworth outbuildings once extended in these directions. The fact that the French drain curves far to the west strongly suggests that it was flanking and protecting an additional building or activity area on the western side of the farmhouse. This would have been a most unusual farm site if it had no other sheds or workshops nearby.

History of the Schuyler House

Since 1950, when the National Park Service acquired the Philip Schuyler estate in Schuylerville, New York, the property has been on exhibit to the public as part of Saratoga National Historical Park (see figure 2-13). It is the eighteenth-century history of the property that is of greatest interest to historians today, although the prehistoric remains found there suggest that Native American populations traveled along the northern edge of the property on Fish Creek (also known as the Fish Kill) as early as the fourth millennium B.C.

Historical records indicate that Johannes Schuyler first built there some time after 1720, and by 1745 his son, Philip Schuyler (uncle of General Philip Schuyler), had constructed approximately twenty houses, most of them on

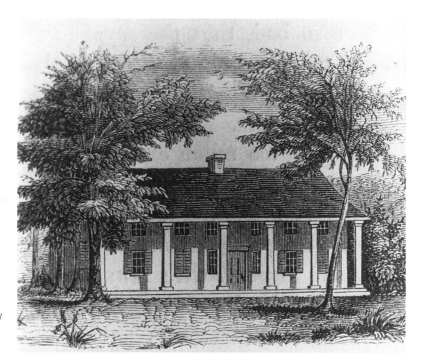

FIG. 2-13. "General Schuyler's Mansion." From Benson J. Lossing, 1851, *The Pictorial Field-Book of the Revolution* (New York: Harper & Brothers), p. 74.

the southern side of Fish Creek. The main house was constructed of brick and had a cellar. Nearby Philip built a sawmill, a blacksmith's house, and an unknown number of barns and stables. Fort Saratoga was located about three-quarters of a mile south of this first Schuyler house, and there were perhaps two hundred people in the community. Unfortunately, a treasure hunter discovered and extensively looted the site of Fort Saratoga over ten years ago. Afterward, the irate farmer who owned the land admitted that he had not been able to understand why the collector kept returning to dig in his field for a year or more, while claiming that he "wasn't finding anything."

It was on November 28, 1745, that French and Native American raiders led by Paul Marin attacked, and most buildings (including the Schuyler house and Fort Saratoga) were burned to the ground. Between 12 and 15 people who had taken refuge in the cellar of the house were burned to death (including Philip Schuyler), 103 were taken prisoner, and others escaped. Despite years of searching, I have not been able to find the foundation, but historian John Brandow claimed that the cellar was rediscovered when the Champlain Canal was widened in 1855. A location on the side of the canal would correlate with a statement by Nathaniel Sylvester in 1878 that the original house stood twelve rods east of the lilac bushes that now grow alongside the 1777 Schuyler house. The cellar on the side of the canal was dug in 1895, and the foundations and the fireplace inside were totally removed. If this was the site of the first Schuyler house, my search for it has been in vain.

It appears that from 1745 until 1763 no buildings stood on the Schuyler grounds, but the British built Fort Hardy at the nearby mouth of Fish Creek in August 1757 (this fell into disrepair after the Treaty of Paris in 1763). After the Treaty of Paris, life here on the frontier became much safer, and large numbers of settlers moved into the area. In fact, the population increased from about two to three hundred people in 1763 to twelve hundred people by 1767. Young Philip Schuyler (figure 2-14), who had inherited his uncle's lands, came here to live in about 1763, and two sawmills were built between 1763 and 1765. Schuyler subsequently constructed a home in 1767 and a flax mill around 1768, and he actively encouraged settlers to move here. Lumber became the chief product of this community, which sent products to Albany and New York City. After 1775 the American army became Schuyler's chief customer, and his personal estate grew to a total of about twenty-four buildings (seven barracks buildings north and seventeen structures south of Fish Creek).

During the first year of the war, Schuyler was promoted to the rank of major general, but his estate stood in the way of Burgoyne's army when the British arrived in Schuylerville (Old Saratoga) in September 1777. Burgoyne's soldiers cut down extensive fields of wheat and corn and proceeded to use Schuyler's grist and sawmills. The British vandalized Schuyler's home

FIG. 2-14. Portrait of General Philip Schuyler. From Benson J. Lossing, *The Pictorial Field-Book of the Revolution* (New York: Harper & Brothers, 1851), p. 38.

considerably in the weeks before October 10, 1777, when orders were issued that led to the burning of his house, mills, and other outbuildings. Schuyler reported that the *only* building not destroyed was his upper sawmill, although a privy associated with the main house also survived the fire. Lossing later stated that this property had a value of twenty thousand dollars.

Schuyler's house, the centerpiece of this estate, consisted of a central, rectangular residence with two rectangular wings extending from either end of the primary structure. While no contemporary paintings have been found, a 1791 sketch by John Trumbull shows three chimneys rising from the ruins. Much later, John Brandow portrayed the center of the house with three stories and the wings with two stories. His conjectural view includes Grecian columns on the front of the house.

More recently, historian Stephen Strach has argued that the house was Georgian in style and had glass-paned windows and wallpaper. Based upon contemporary maps, chiefly the "Plan de la Position de l'Armée sous les Ordres de son Excellence le Lieutenant Général Bourgoyne à Saratoga dant sur la Retraite de Fremanns Ferme," Strach has further argued that *each* of the three sections of the house measured 125.5 by 62.5 feet. If correct, this would

FIG. 2-15. "Plan of the Position which the Army under Lieutenant Gel. Burgoine took at *Saratoga* on the *10th* of September 1777 and in which it remained till the Convention was Signed (16 October)." From the archives of Saratoga National Historical Park. Used by permission.

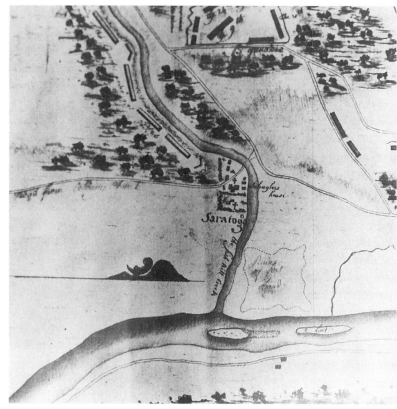

FIG. 2-16. Northern elevation of the 1777 Schuyler house, showing the kitchen wing.

have made it the largest house in all of the American colonies! East of the house, stretching toward the Hudson River, was a large formal garden that was portrayed on contemporary maps (figure 2-15). Edward Larrabee has noted that this appeared on a circa 1837 map as "an oblong garden, fenced or walled, with twelve garden beds separated by walks. One of the beds, near the center of the garden, has a circular walk."

After the British had reduced his estate to ruins, Schuyler hurriedly put his upper sawmill back into operation, turning out planks, and a third main house was next constructed on the property (figure 2-16). Historical sources suggest that this took between seventeen and thirty days (in November 1777), perhaps with minor assistance from some of the artificers in Gates's Army. The third Schuyler house was built atop an already existing foundation, but all historical sources agree that this was *not* the foundation of the earlier mansion.

For example, John Brandow has written that the "house stood about twelve rods southeast of the present one." If accurate, this would place the burned mansion just beyond the present National Park Service boundary fence, on the edge of a modern New York State maintenance facility. Also, in 1819, Benjamin Silliman described passing "the ruins of General Schuyler's house, which are still conspicuous." This, of course, would have been impossible if the third house had been built atop the ruins of the second. General Epaphras Hoyt, visiting the battle sites in 1825, mentioned observing the third Schuyler house, "standing *nearly* on the site of General Schuyler's, burnt by Burgoyne" (italics added). And *The Standard Daily* of October 17, 1877, stated that the existing Schuyler house is "northwest of the site of the burned building of 1777." These and other historical sources thus support that the second mansion, burned by Burgoyne's army, was either south or southeast of the present-day Schuyler house.

After the British surrender, other buildings on the estate were gradually rebuilt, some on their former foundations, and a kitchen wing was added onto the main house around 1780 (figure 2-16, left). General Schuyler spent the later years of his life residing at his mansion in Albany, treating his Schuylerville property as a summer residence. He died in 1804. His son, John B. Schuyler, managed the estate from 1787 until 1795 but added no new buildings. His grandson, Philip Schuyler II (son of John B. Schuyler), lived there from 1811 to 1837; during that time he erected a cotton mill on Fish Creek, built a carriage barn east of the main house, and promoted the 1821–1822 construction of the Champlain Canal that ran just east of the main house.

In 1820 the houses north of Fish Creek officially took the name of Schuylerville. (In 1783 a road had been opened to the area known today as Saratoga Springs.) The estate subsequently passed out of the Schuyler family's hands when the Panic of 1837 forced Philip Schuyler II to sell. In 1839 the Schuyler house and grounds were purchased by George Strover, who lived in it until his death in 1886. Strover's descendants lived there until 1946. Since March 30, 1950, the property has been owned and interpreted by the National Park Service.

Early Archeology at the Schuyler House

It is easiest to interpret the Schuyler estate on the basis of its four periods of occupation, namely the prehistoric period, the French and Indian War, the revolutionary war, and the postcolonial period. Several excavations sponsored by the National Park Service attempted to define each of these periods and their attendant structures. To this end, John Cotter excavated there in 1958, 1959, and 1964; Jackson Moore in a proposed parking area in 1959; and Edward Larrabee in 1959 and 1960. Each of these projects located foundations and considerable sheet refuse, but the intensity of occupation and the size of the overall estate made thorough coverage of the property extremely difficult.

In 1958 and 1960 Cotter and Larrabee successfully exposed a "Burned Structure," located about ninety feet southeast of the present Schuyler house, that measured twenty-two feet wide by thirty-nine to forty-three feet long.

Larrabee believed this dated from 1788 to 1798, although Steve Strach has argued for an earlier date (pre-1760) based upon the presence of early Dutch tiles and pottery. Larrabee also noted the presence of a buried foundation and artifacts just north of the Schuyler house, inside the modern-day service road. John Brandow identified a large woodhouse and slave quarters in this same location, and Larrabee discovered that buildings appeared there in maps of 1777, 1820, and 1837. By 1857 this building had been removed.

Larrabee further identified a rectangular barn foundation, roughly thirty by forty feet, just inside the woods on the eastern side of the property. This had appeared in maps of 1820 and 1837 and had been identified as a barn in 1853. Until very recently there also was a mid-nineteenth-century tenant house that stood north of the present Schuyler house, overlooking Fish Creek. This was finally dismantled in 1963, and the foundations were studied by John Cotter to determine whether it had been built atop the remains of a still earlier building. (A building had appeared there in maps of 1777 and 1820.)

In addition to these major structures, Larrabee and Cotter excavated a privy and dry well just northwest of the current privy house; two possible root or vegetable cellars; one well; and scattered traces of stone walls or foundations some 80 to 140 feet northeast of the Schuyler house. Moore's work in the parking area was somewhat less successful: though he hoped to locate the remains of dormitories that had housed bondservants and slaves before the revolution, he discovered instead the remains of a relatively recent apartment house.

The remains throughout the Schuyler yards suggest an intensive eighteenth- to nineteenth-century use of the property, but the number of features still falls far short of the two dozen structures estimated for the time of General Schuyler's occupation. In fact, the inclusion of structures from the French and Indian War and postcolonial periods probably raises the number of original features (foundations, wells, and privies) to forty or more. Clearly, only a very small proportion of the property has been inventoried archeologically or is ready for thorough public interpretation.

Recent Archeology at the Schuyler House

Given the incompleteness of our knowledge of the Schuyler property, I spent six weeks in the summer of 1987 directing excavations in the yards surrounding the 1777 Schuyler house. My hope was to locate the foundations of buildings that had been burned by the British in 1777, which would allow us to interpret the layout of the estate in the late eighteenth century. Though I most wanted to locate the site of General Schuyler's burned mansion, be-

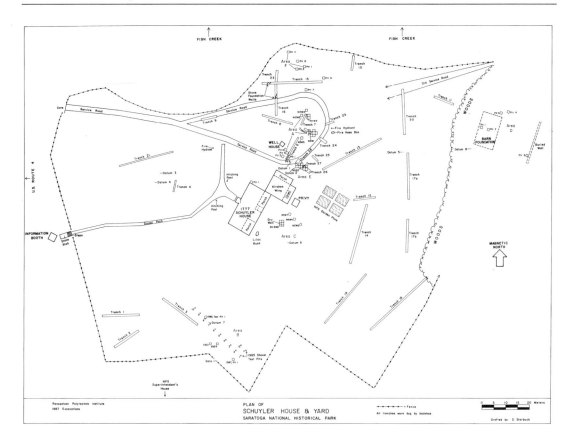

FIG. 2-17. Plan of the
Schuyler house and yards,
1987 excavation.

cause it had been the centerpiece of daily life on the estate during Philip
Schuyler's residence, locating traces of the other two dozen burned buildings
was just as important.

Our excavation strategy was shaped by the considerable size of the surviving estate, the small size of possible outbuilding sites, and the rather inconclusive results from a magnetometer survey we had conducted in 1985.
Digging shovel test pits on a grid would have produced some information
about the limits of sheet refuse, but I did not believe it would help much in
locating foundations, trash pits, or privies. I decided instead to rely heavily
upon backhoe trenches to locate foundations, and then to dig one-meter-
square test pits to expose individual features and artifact concentrations. We
could expose and examine stratigraphic profiles for anomalies most quickly
this way, and lengthy trenches ensured that we would hit foundations rather
than inadvertently jump over them.

We placed some twenty-eight backhoe trenches throughout the Schuyler
yards, taking care to avoid modern utility lines as well as the root systems of
the locust trees that blanketed the yard on the western (front) side of the
house (figure 2-17). Our 1987 work also deliberately avoided all areas of the

southern yard that were close to the house. This zone had been heavily trenched by Edward Larrabee and appeared too disturbed to justify any further digging.

As the work proceeded, the backhoe trenches revealed foundation remains and dense artifact concentrations running north from the current Schuyler house to the fence abutting Fish Creek. We found the foundation remains of three structures north of the Schuyler house, as well as evidence for a very sizable prehistoric occupation from the Late Archaic and Middle Woodland Periods. It was not surprising to find that the Schuylers had created their estate on the side of a creek where Native Americans had fished for thousands of years. Past studies by National Park Service archeologists had never even mentioned the prehistoric occupation in the yards, however; in their eagerness to highlight the Schuylers, they had virtually ignored the evidence for native peoples.

In all cases, prehistoric artifacts were thoroughly mixed with eighteenth-through twentieth-century artifacts, although deeper soil layers tended to have exclusively prehistoric materials. Historical artifacts of all periods were densest both within the building foundations and close to the Schuyler house.

We placed a single test pit against the northwest corner of the Schuyler

FIG. 2-18. Plan of Schuyler yard, area E, burned foundation and possible French drain.

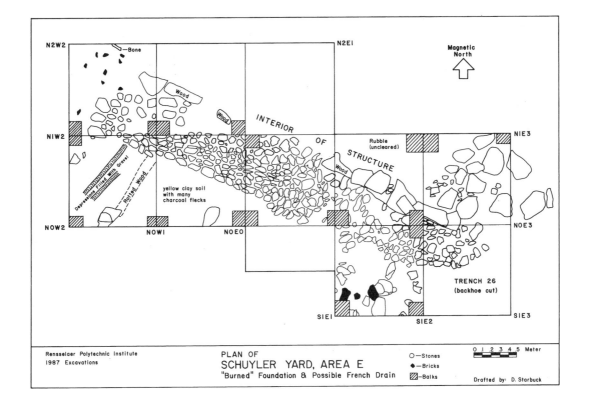

FIG. 2-19. The possible
French drain in area E (facing east-southeast).

house, looking for signs that the 1777 house had been placed atop an earlier
foundation, but we found no evidence of this. While most of the building
foundations and artifacts in the Schuyler yards post-dated the revolutionary
war, we nevertheless discovered the foundation of a burned building about
sixteen feet northeast of the kitchen wing on the Schuyler house (see figures
2-18 and 2-19). As our test pits exposed one side of this foundation, they revealed the many small stones of a French drain that had run along the southern side of the building. This was surrounded by a matrix of much charcoal,
burned earth, and burned (or melted) artifacts. These included many burned
pipe stem fragments, much melted glass and warped pottery sherds, and a
noticeable scatter of animal bones. We were finding material that was totally
unlike any of the other artifact concentrations we had encountered in the
Schuyler yards, and many of the artifacts (while very shallow) were clearly of
eighteenth-century origin. I am sure that this was all that survived from one
of General Schuyler's buildings that was torched by the British in 1777; a
much more extensive excavation is needed to determine the exact function
and extent of the building.

Artifacts Found at the Schuyler House

The historical artifacts we recovered in the yards around the Schuyler House include buttons, pottery, buckles, a pewter spoon, a fragment of cast-iron pot, forks, a knife, gun sights, a gunflint, musket balls, and even a hammerhead. While undramatic, these are the artifacts that would most likely be found in the yards surrounding a house that had been occupied from 1777 until the present. Still, nothing there is Dutch, nothing would have been in use while the first Schuyler house was standing, and the only artifact we excavated in 1987 that clearly dated to 1777 is an exploded fragment of cast iron, a piece of mortar shell that must have landed in the Schuyler yards during the battle. Interestingly, Chinese export porcelain, almost nonexistent in the ruins of the Woodworth farm (the American headquarters), was incredibly common in the yards of the Schuyler house, affirming that the Schuyler estate was far wealthier than the neighboring farms. If the ceramics that were owned by the Schuylers were consistently more expensive, then greater access to elite goods may be reflected in other artifact categories as well.

Some Final Thoughts

When we excavated the Schuyler yards in 1987, we discovered only one outbuilding that dated to the revolutionary war period and that was probably burned at that time. Our inability to find better evidence for outbuildings from the American Revolution, and from the French and Indian War, may partly stem from the fact that some of the buildings had insubstantial foundations. But we never did find any traces of the mansion that Burgoyne burned in his retreat. The digging in the late 1950s, coupled with our 1987 excavation, strongly suggests that neither of the original Schuyler houses was ever located within the current yards of the property owned by the National Park Service. And I do not feel that a pit must be placed *directly* into one of those structures to discover its presence; rather, the sheet refuse and ancillary features that surround such mansions ordinarily extend outward far enough that just hitting some of the trash should prove that the mansion is nearby. Because only two *burned* outbuildings have ever been discovered on this property, and only very small quantities of eighteenth century artifacts, I believe that most of the missing structures must have been located farther to the east and southeast. Because this property was severely disturbed by the Champlain Canal and the construction of the New York State maintenance facility, and is now heavily overgrown with vines and brush, I suspect that evidence for the rest of the Schuyler buildings destroyed by the British will never be found.

Still, I believe that archeologists need to do a lot more with existing, known parts of this estate, and future exhibits and tours should take full advantage of the locations of already-discovered outbuildings. We reburied everything that we exposed with our digs, but the positions of the burned structures, wells, root cellars, and other features in the yards of the Schuyler house all need to be interpreted on the surface of the yard so that visitors can get a better sense of the range of activities that went on *separate from* the primary Schuyler dwelling. A walking tour could show visitors the outlines of each one of these features and offer graphic representations (or three-dimensional models) of what each outbuilding might originally have looked like. This was a grand estate. In fact, it was one of the greatest in all of the American colonies, and it ought to be presented in a way that helps visitors appreciate the scale and vision of the Schuyler family's home on the Hudson River.

Further Reading

Brandow, John Henry. 1900. *The Story of Old Saratoga and History of Schuylerville.* 2d ed., 1919. Saratoga Springs: Robson and Adee.

Burgoyne, John. 1780. *A State of the Expedition from Canada, as Laid Before the House of Commons by Lieutenant-General Burgoyne* . . . . 2d ed. London.

Cotter, John L. 1957. Archeological Data, Neilson House. Manuscript on file at Saratoga National Historical Park.

———. 1958. Report of Schuyler House Archeological Investigations, July 23–27, 1958. Manuscript on file at Saratoga National Historical Park. 5 pp.

Ehrich, Robert. 1942. Progress Report on the Archeological Program of Saratoga National Historical Park. Manuscript on file at Saratoga National Historical Park.

Elting, John R. 1977. *The Battles of Saratoga.* Monmouth Beach, N.J.: Philip Freneau Press.

Hanson, Lee H., and Dick Ping Hsu. 1975. *Casements and Cannonballs: Archeological Investigations at Fort Stanwix, Rome, New York.* Publications in Archeology 14. National Park Service, Washington, D.C.

Ketchum, Richard M. 1997. *Saratoga: Turning Point of America's Revolutionary War.* New York: Henry Holt and Company, Inc.

Larrabee, Edward M. 1960. Report of Archeological Excavations Conducted at Schuyler House, Saratoga National Historical Park, Schuylerville, New York from June 8 through June 29, 1959. Manuscript on file at Saratoga National Historical Park. 89 pp., maps and plates.

Lord, Jr., Philip. 1989. *War over Walloomscoick: Land Use and Settlement Pattern on the Bennington Battlefield—1777.* Albany, N.Y.: New York State Museum Bulletin no. 473.

Lossing, Benson J. 1851. *The Pictorial Field-Book of the Revolution*. New York: Harper Brothers.

Luzader, John. 1973. *Historic Structure Report. Bemis Heights. September 12 to October 8, 1777 (Neilson Farm)*. National Park Service, Denver Service Center.

———. 1975. *The Saratoga Campaign of 1777*. National Park Service, Washington, D.C.

Milius, Feldprediger. 1777. Letter, Feldprediger Milius to his father, November 20, 1777. Manuscript on file at Saratoga National Historical Park.

Moore, Jackson W. 1960. Archeological Investigation of the Schuyler House Parking Lot Area. Manuscript on file at Saratoga National Historical Park. 3 pp., maps and plates.

Snow, Dean R. 1972. Report on the Archaeological Identification of the Balcarres and Breymann Redoubts, Saratoga National Historical Park. 1972 Investigations. Manuscript on file at Saratoga National Historical Park.

———. 1973–1974. Report on the Archaeological Investigations of the American Line, The Great Redoubt, and the Taylor House, Saratoga National Historical Park. Manuscript on file at Saratoga National Historical Park. 28 pp.

———. 1977. *Archaeological Atlas of the Saratoga Battlefield*. Department of Anthropology, State University of New York at Albany.

———. 1981. Battlefield Archeology. *Early Man* 3 (1):18–21.

Starbuck, David R. 1986. Saratoga National Historical Park Archeology Progress Report—1985. Manuscript on file at Saratoga National Historical Park. 113 pp.

———. 1987. The American Headquarters for the Battle of Saratoga: 1985–1986 Excavations. Manuscript on file at Saratoga National Historical Park. 44 pp.

———. 1988. The American Headquarters for the Battle of Saratoga. *Northeast Historical Archaeology* 17:16–39.

———. 1989. Saratoga National Historical Park Archeology Progress Report—1987. Manuscript on file at Saratoga National Historical Park. 69 pp.

Stone, William L. 1895. *Visits to the Saratoga Battle-Grounds 1780–1880*. Port Washington, N.Y.: Kennikat Press. Reissued 1970 by Kennikat Press.

Strach, Stephen G. 1986. The Saratoga Estate of General Philip Schuyler: 1745–1839. An Interpretive and Historical Grounds Survey. Philadelphia: Eastern National Park and Monument Association.

Sylvester, Nathaniel Bartlett. 1878. *History of Saratoga County, New York with Illustrations and Biographical Sketches of some of its Prominent Men and Pioneers*. Philadelphia: Everts and Ensign.

Wilkinson, James. 1816. *Memoirs of My Own Times*. 3 vols. Philadelphia: Abraham Small.

Wilkinson, Lieutenant W. C. 1777. *The British Position near Freeman's Farm, September 19–October 8, 1777, by Lieutenant W. C. Wilkinson, 62nd Regiment of Foot*. Map on file at Saratoga National Historical Park.

Worrell, John. 1980. Scars upon the Earth: Physical Evidence of Dramatic Change at the Stratton Tavern. In *Proceedings of the Conference on Northeastern Archaeology*, edited by James A. Moore, 133–145. Research Reports 19. Department of Anthropology, University of Massachusetts, Amherst.

Chapter 3

The Third Largest City in America: Fort Edward and Rogers Island

Introduction

*T*HE MOST INTACT of the French and Indian War sites along The Great Warpath is easily Rogers Island, a fifty-acre island that lies in the Hudson River about forty miles north of Albany. This location has long been referred to as the Great Carrying Place because Native Americans and then soldiers had to leave their boats to portage around rapids in the river. But in the 1750s, the island and adjacent Fort Edward, a three-bastioned log fort constructed on the east bank of the river, became home to one of the largest British military installations in the American colonies (figure 3-1). Men who later became prominent in the American Revolution were stationed there, including Philip Schuyler, Israel Putnam, and Paul Revere. While the diaries left behind by soldiers as they camped in Fort Edward make few references to women, the camp no doubt also contained a small number of wives and camp followers.

In addition to thousands of British regulars or Redcoats, the fort and island were garrisoned by provincial companies from the colonies of Massachusetts, New Hampshire, Connecticut, New York, and Rhode Island, all eager to drive the French back into Canada. Without question, the most exciting of the provincial forces were the irregular soldiers or Rangers who devised radically new tactics for fighting on the American frontier. While there were several other companies of Rangers who fought in the northern colonies, it was Rogers' Rangers and their charismatic leader, Major Robert Rogers, who earned the most fearsome reputation during the French and Indian War. They were frontiersmen from New Hampshire and elsewhere who traveled on snowshoes, fought from behind trees, dressed in green for camouflage, and sometimes sawed off the ends of their musket barrels so they could travel lighter and faster. They attacked Native American and

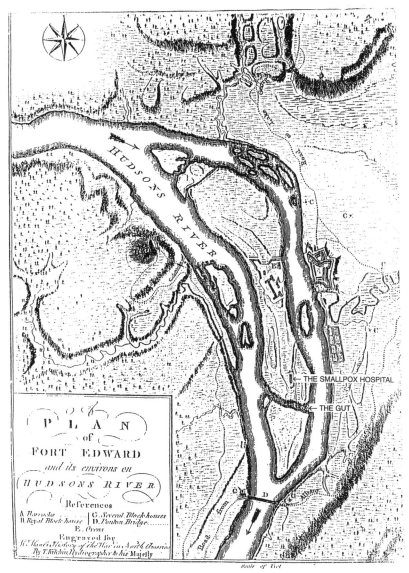

FIG. 3-1. A Plan of Fort Edward and its environs on Hudsons [*sic*] River. Engraved for Thomas Mante, 1772, by T. Kitchen, hydrographer to His Majesty. (Labels "THE SMALLPOX HOSPITAL" and "THE GUT" have been added.) Catalog of Kings Maps, British Museum.

French settlements in the far north, including their famous raid upon the Abenaki village of St. Francis in October of 1759 (chronicled in Kenneth Roberts's book *Northwest Passage*). And they were the most celebrated "Indian-fighters" of the mid-eighteenth century precisely because they adopted the fighting tactics of their foes, combining them with the most suitable of European tactics. They were the inspiration for the "light infantry" concept in the British army.

Rogers' name was soon given to the island because for two and a half years (between 1757 and 1759) Rogers Island was the principal base camp for his

Rangers. While camped on the island, Rogers wrote down a series of Ranging Rules in 1757 that instructed his men in the principles of forest warfare. Military forces still study their fighting tactics today, and experts on this period, including John Cuneo, Burt Loescher, Tim Todish, and Gary Zaboly, have carefully documented their methods.

However, the centerpiece of this military installation was Fort Edward, the largest British fort in the American colonies at that time. Supplies that originated in Albany were sent up the Hudson River in late spring and summer to Fort Edward. Men and supplies were portaged to Lake George, and then bateaux and whale boats carried the British armies north to attack the French at Fort Carillon at the south end of Lake Champlain. During several years in the late 1750s, armies of fifteen and sixteen thousand British regulars and provincials regularly made Fort Edward, and then Lake George, the third largest cities in the American colonies. Even after the construction of Fort William Henry, Fort Edward continued to be strategically important because the French and Native Americans could easily bypass Lake George by traveling down South Bay and Wood Creek, striking deep into British territory.

The encampment in Fort Edward functioned for several years as a huge supply depot and hospital site, briefly seeing additional use during the American Revolution twenty years later. The hospital function was especially critical. Rogers Island and Fort Edward had the largest concentration of hospitals in northern New York, and sick and injured soldiers were sent there from other military camps. On the island there were a smallpox hospital and general hospitals, there were other hospitals inside the fort, and there were even hospital rooms inside many of the barracks buildings (see the box "Military Hospitals"). Among those who died in one of the hospitals was Major Duncan Campbell of the famed Black Watch, the Scottish Highland regiment that suffered devastating casualties during the British assault upon Ticonderoga in 1758. Campbell is now buried in Union Cemetery in Fort Edward, next to the remains of Jane McCrea, the young woman who was killed and scalped twenty years later as Native Americans transported her to her Tory sweetheart.

Frontier camps such as the one in Fort Edward tended to be short-lived, however, and when the Treaty of Paris ended the French and Indian War in 1763, the supply base on Rogers Island had already been abandoned. The fort itself was evacuated in 1766, but it was briefly reoccupied by a small American garrison early in the revolutionary war. The officers who went there during the Revolution included Benedict Arnold, Henry Knox, General Howe, and John Burgoyne. The site then passed into oblivion, and for the next two hundred years the modern village of Fort Edward slowly grew over the ruins of the fort.

A residential neighborhood sits astride the fort today, while the southern

★ Military Hospitals

Health care in eighteenth-century America was radically different from today's, and one of the greatest contrasts was in the role played by hospitals. The eighteenth-century hospital was a rarity, except in urban settings such as New York and Philadelphia where the poor needed inexpensive, readily accessible health care and could not afford to get it at home. In most cases, though, physicians saw patients in their homes, and only travelers needed medical facilities of a more institutional nature.

However, there was one category of hospital that appeared with some frequency in the second half of the eighteenth century: the military hospitals that treated soldiers and officers in the field. Historians have often pointed out that these hospitals had such a high mortality rate that soldiers may have had a better chance of recovering if they remained in huts and barracks with their comrades. These hospitals, most of which were in use for only a few months, the space of a single campaign, ranged from mobile "flying hospitals" to the more permanent regimental hospitals and "general hospitals" that housed substantial numbers of patients with fevers, dysentery, infectious diseases such as measles, and injuries of all types. Military doctors typically owned a medicine chest that might include such therapeutic instruments as scalpels, amputation knives and saws, lancets and other bloodletting instruments, forceps, scissors, bullet probes, and bullet extractors. Medicines were so difficult to obtain during both the French and Indian War and the American Revolution that physicians often spent more of their time searching for medicines than doing any actual healing.

A final type of military hospital was somewhat more specialized: the smallpox hospitals that isolated highly contagious patients. Soldiers who contracted smallpox in the eighteenth century were typically sent to central hospital facilities, such as Fort George in Lake George, New York, where as many as three thousand soldiers lay dying in July 1776. There was no standard design for hospitals, but military hospitals of the 1750s and 1770s appear to have been little more than large, open barns that provided patients fresh air and perhaps a bed of straw.

Unlike urban hospitals for the poor, military hospitals were not built for permanence; many were of post construction and unlikely to have left substantial structural remains behind. Also, the medicines or medical instruments hospitals used were sufficiently rare that archeologists are unlikely ever to find much medical trash in the associated dumps. Still, the search for a relatively intact military hospital site is well worth the effort, and I believe that archeologists may have the best chance at the hospital complex at Fort George. The very largest smallpox hospitals of the American Revolution were constructed there, as well as a general hospital established in 1777. Fort George may provide the last opportunity to find the intact foundations, dumps, and medical supplies needed to interpret the American military's medical procedures of the late eighteenth century.

Further Reading

Gillett, Mary C. 1981. *The Army Medical Department 1775–1818*. Washington, D.C.: Center of Military History, United States Army.

Saffron, Morris H. 1982. The Northern Medical Department 1776–1777. *The Bulletin of the Fort Ticonderoga Museum* 14 (2):81–120.

Starbuck, David R. 1990. The General Hospital at Mount Independence: 18th Century Health Care at a Revolutionary War Cantonment. *Northeast Historical Archaeology* 19:50–68.

———. 1997. Military Hospitals on the Frontier of Colonial America. *Expedition* 39 (1):33–47.

Wilbur, C. Keith, M.D. 1980. *Revolutionary Medicine 1700–1800.* Chester, Conn.: The Globe Pequot Press.

———. 1987. *Antique Medical Instruments.* West Chester, Pa.: Schiffer Publishing Ltd.

part of Rogers Island is still open, undeveloped land. In 1959, after people had sporadically collected artifacts for years, this part of the island was purchased by Earl Stott, whose father had once worked on the walls of Fort Ticonderoga as a stone mason. Earl wanted to save the island from development and promptly commenced digging on the island, hoping to rebuild many of its structures someday. Over the next thirty years, he attracted many hundreds of volunteer workers to dig with him on the island, all drawn by his love of history and, especially, his passion for Rogers' Rangers. They excavated huts, over a dozen fireplaces, and many thousands of artifacts, the most distinctive of which was a combination pocket sundial and compass, in excellent condition, found inside a fireplace in 1965. Without question, though, the best-known event during this period was a Boy Scout camporee, held in 1961, at which time some four hundred Boy Scouts gathered on the island for a "Rogers' Rangers Weekend." They were issued spoons, their scoutmasters were handed shovels, and the big dig was on. The only stipulation was that all finds be turned over to Earl for his collection.

I had heard about Earl many times from collectors and archeologists, but the first time I met him was after a lecture I gave at Saratoga National Historical Park in 1985. After my talk, Earl walked up to me, pulled out a change

FIG. 3-2. A canteen taken from a treasure hunter's trench on Rogers Island and subsequently conserved by Nancy Demetteneyre of the New York State Office of Parks, Recreation and Historic Preservation.

purse, and then poured a few hundred Spanish and English coins into my hand. I stood there speechless as he identified himself, but Earl Stott had that effect on people! A few years later, Earl sold the island to developers, and in the winter of 1990–1991, the new owners asked me to direct a research project for them. I agreed, not knowing that I would be digging on the island, and elsewhere in Fort Edward, for the next eight years. Unfortunately, even during the short transition period to the new owners, a treasure hunter was allowed to trench on the island, and backhoeing exposed several badly rusted canteens (figure 3-2).

Huts and Related Sites

It was in early 1991 that I moved to a house at the northern end of Rogers Island, and that summer I began directing archeological teams from Adirondack Community College, which became the main sponsor of our research. Since that time, over the course of six field seasons (1991 to 1994 and 1997 to

FIG. 3-3. Remains of an eleven-foot-square hut discovered on Rogers Island in 1991. (The staining and vertical planks have been outlined with yarn.) The remains of fireplaces are visible in the bottom center and the right rear (facing east).

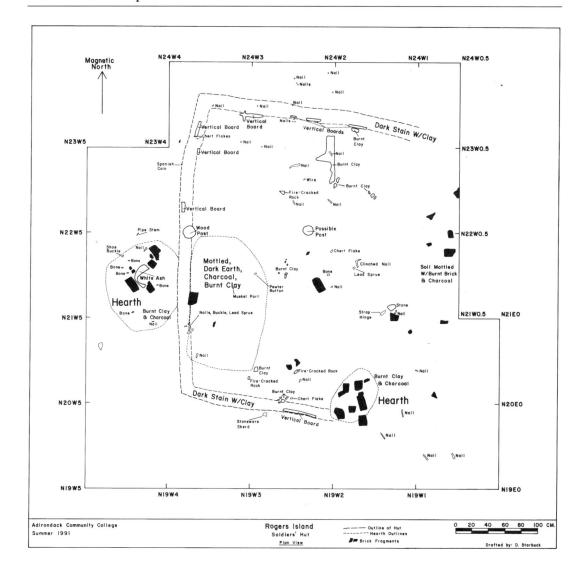

Adirondack Community College
Summer 1991

Rogers Island
Soldiers' Hut
Plan View

—————— Outline of Hut
--------- Hearth Outlines
◆▪ Brick Fragments

0   20   40   60   80   100 CM.

Drafted by: D. Starbuck

FIG. 3-4. Plan view of the hut in figure 3-3.

1998), we have exposed the remains of several huts on Rogers Island and other, more specialized sites. One of the best-preserved examples of these is a soldiers' or Rangers' hut that we unearthed in 1991–1992. One of our veteran diggers, Sarah van Ryckevorsel, found the remains of several vertical wood planks that had once been part of the walls, and then she found scattered bricks and ashes from two fireplaces. Inside the outline formed by the planks, she found traces of an earth floor, compressed by soldiers' feet into a very hard surface. Between five and ten soldiers or Rangers would have lived inside this small building that measured eleven by eleven feet (figures 3-3 and 3-4). Scattered atop this living floor she discovered burned bits of bone, burned clay, nails, lead sprue, a silver shoe buckle, and even a piece of Spanish cob money.

At the end of the 1991 season, we believed that we had reached the bottom of the hut and its contents, but just to make sure we returned the next year and went deeper into the underlying soft sand. This time the excavator in charge, Cathy Lee, an experienced digger from Atlanta, Georgia, unexpectedly discovered, a bit further down, caches of musket balls and gunflints, as well as broken knives, forks, spoons, wine bottles, and fragments of butchered, burned bone. In just one cluster, she found forty-five musket balls (figure 3-5) of just the right diameter to be fired from a British Brown Bess musket. More common, though, were clusters of nine or ten musket balls, along with a few gunflints, which would have been the ideal number for a soldier to carry with him on one of his campaigns into the north country.

About thirty meters northwest from this hut, we excavated a large, post-type building in 1991–1992 that measured greater than ninety feet long by thirteen feet wide. The crew working in this area found a series of postholes positioned at eight-foot intervals around the perimeter. Given the temporary nature of this style of construction, we concluded that this long, narrow building was probably a storehouse. Some of the large, square postmolds still contained the rotting bases of posts, while other postholes contained trash, placed there after the posts had been removed. In addition to nails, bits of animal bone, and sherds of pottery and porcelain, we made two unusual discoveries: the amputated finger bones (phalanges) from a human hand (figure 3-6) and an intact tin bucket (figure 3-7). We knew that amputations often occurred at early military camps, but I still wasn't quite prepared to see fingers thrown out with the garbage!

At the end of the 1992 season, supervisor Dan Weiskotten was trenching north from this possible storehouse when he suddenly encountered the stain from a large latrine or necessary. Wanting to expose it carefully, we waited until 1993 and then opened it up, revealing a deep pit that measured roughly eight feet long by four feet wide (figure 3-8). This was to become the richest feature we ever dug in the town of Fort Edward, for it was full of literally thousands of artifacts, including two felling axes (figure 3-9), many buttons, buckles, musket balls, and butchered animal bones. Cow, pig, and fish bones abounded, suggesting that the soldiers had ample supplies of fresh meat and fish. We even found several bone buttons, possibly from women's clothes, or from men's undergarments. The Learning Channel series *Archaeology* filmed the dig into the latrine and was fortunate enough to capture Sarah van Ryckevorsel as she exposed one of the axes. She little realized that two hours of filming would result in about five seconds on the air. At the bottom of the feature the crew found some gray clay that they placed in a plastic bag and labeled "human excrement?" Curiously enough, this was the find that visitors asked to see for the rest of the summer.

FIG. 3-5. A concentration of forty-five musket balls found underneath the dirt floor of the hut in figure 3-3.

FIG. 3-6. Human phalanges (finger bones) discovered inside a posthole.

FIG. 3-7. A tin bucket, eight inches tall and eight inches in diameter, discovered inside a posthole.

FIG. 3-8. (Right.) Excavating the bottom of a soldiers' latrine, outlined against the yellow subsoil.

FIG. 3-9. (Bottom left.) Felling axes found in the latrine; both have undergone conservation.

FIG. 3-10. (Bottom right.) The fireplace and nails inside a possible officers' hut, on the western edge of the barracks complex.

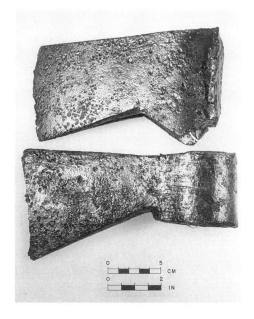

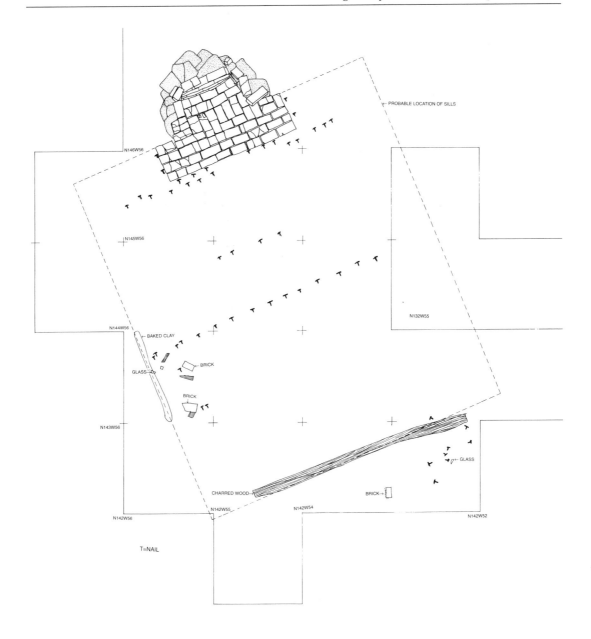

N146W56

N145W56

N144W56

N143W56

N142W56

N142W55

N142W54

N132W55

N142W52

← PROBABLE LOCATION OF SILLS

← BAKED CLAY

GLASS →

BRICK

BRICK

CHARRED WOOD →

BRICK →

← GLASS

T=NAIL

FIG. 3-11. Plan view of the hut in figure 3-10. Drawing by Dennis E. Howe.

Elsewhere, on the western edge of the main barracks complex on Rogers Island, we discovered in 1993 the outline of a small, well-built house that still contained the traces of a wood floor with the floor nails and sills *in situ*—there were three rows of nails rising vertically inside the foundation, where floor boards had been nailed down onto the joists underneath (figures 3-10 and 3-11). The complete outline of the building measured eleven by eleven

FIG. 3-12. (Left.) A cache of melted lead sprue and musket balls, lying within earth that has been fired a bright red; located within the barracks complex.

FIG. 3-13. (Right.) Evidence for burning inside one of the soldiers' dumps on Rogers Island.

feet, and inside were the remains of a well-preserved brick fireplace. But because there had been a solid floor, we found no artifacts underneath. Based on its quality and permanence of construction, this may have been an officers' dwelling, although it may also have been built for year-round habitation.

Throughout our research on Rogers Island, we found military dumps, badly disturbed fireplaces, and reddened earth in almost every area we dug. The reddening of the soil was most often caused by the casting of lead into musket balls: we frequently found small traces of lead sprue mixed in with the staining (figure 3-12). We have even found evidence of a large fire in the middle of one of the dumps, where I believe the soldiers were deliberately burning garbage (figure 3-13). But what we *really* wanted to find was evidence of hospitals and of the large, permanent, barracks buildings. In the fourth year of searching, in 1994, we finally discovered both.

The Smallpox Hospital

Our efforts to discover the smallpox hospital on Rogers Island were significant because amazingly little is known about early smallpox hospitals. Before us, no archeologists had ever dug an early smallpox hospital in the United States. There were no cures for smallpox in the 1750s, so we did not expect to find any medical evidence at the site. The sick probably lay on straw, waiting to die. Twenty years later, during the revolution, soldiers infected themselves with smallpox by scratching material from the pustules of a patient into their own skin. By developing a mild case, they subsequently became immune. In fact, in 1777 George Washington went so far as to order that the Continental Army be inoculated against smallpox. But it was not until 1796 that Edward Jenner began vaccinating with the cowpox virus, injecting material from the cowpox lesions of dairymaids into the arms of his patients, which ultimately led to the eradication of the disease.

On May 31, 1757, a soldier living on Rogers Island, Jabez Fitch, wrote in his diary that he and twenty men had been ordered to construct a smallpox hospital on the southern part of the island: "I was ordered To Go with 20 Men & Build a Hospital on ye Loar End of ye Island To Put those that Had ye Small Pox intoo." It was thrown up so quickly that we did not expect to find substantial foundations, and given its location on a very sandy island, we assumed that no stone had been used in its construction. Still, since later additions were made to the hospital, it could have grown into something more permanent.

The diary of another soldier, Luke Gridley, indicated that on June 17, "one of the men taken with the smallpox May 30th died of it." Then on June 25, "one of our men taken with small pox." Then on June 28, "six men taken with smallpox." On July 2, "six men taken with smallpox." On July 4, "the number of men that have the smallpox in the hospital . . . is 101." And on July 19, "one man and one woman died."

Jabez Fitch in particular cited many cases of smallpox in his diary, named some of the victims, and gave the dates when they arrived at the hospital and when they died. According to journal accounts, smallpox victims died between seven and eleven days after the onset of a high fever. Fitch even mentioned one soldier who survived smallpox only to die of camp distemper (October 20, 1757): "Last night Sgt. Jackson died in the smallpox hospital after he had a long confinement there & had recovered of ye smallpox he died of the camp distemper October 10."

As far as I can tell, the smallpox hospital on Rogers Island was in continuous use for a couple of years, having at least one hundred patients at times. Soldiers were sent to the hospital once they were covered with the tiny pustules, and many hundreds died there of the virus. Contemporary diaries indicate that their friends often went to the hospital to visit them; clearly there was little awareness of how the contagion worked. The smallpox hospital appeared on just one historical map, centered atop a modest terrace at the south end of Rogers Island, as far as possible from the barracks complex (see figure 3-1). Structures such as this needed to be built on high ground because

FIG. 3-14. (Top left.) Fascine or brush-clearing knife discovered in the dump just east of the small-pox hospital.

FIG. 3-15. (Top right.) Close-up of the fascine knife; a maker's mark (LL or LE) appears just to the right of the ferrule.

the island periodically flooded in the springtime, and soldiers sometimes drowned inside their tents during surprise floods. Even today, the central and southern parts of Rogers Island flood every spring, leaving only small patches of high ground jutting out of the Hudson River.

There is only one high terrace at the south end of Rogers Island today, so we were able to pinpoint our excavation area quickly. But discovering traces of this ephemeral building was another matter. I assigned teams to the hospital search for three years. They found a few stains in the sand that quickly faded in the hot summer sun; an extensive dump along the east edge of the terrace, which we thought might be from the hospital; a 1751 Spanish silver real (minted in Mexico City), a massive brush (or fascine) knife (figures 3-14 and 3-15), gunflints, and other artifacts. But nothing specifically suggested a hospital. There were a few small bits of glass medicine bottles, but these are everywhere on eighteenth-century military sites. In 1992 we had an all-women team searching for the hospital who, in their zeal to make a real breakthrough, nicknamed themselves "the commando girls." It may not have been politically correct, but they unquestionably had more enthusiasm than all of my other diggers.

During the following summer one of our best field supervisors, Matthew Rozell, made it his personal goal to find the smallpox hospital, no matter how long it might take. He knew he was getting close when his team discovered the hospital dump, but they found only the same types of artifacts that had been found in all residential areas on the island: buttons, knives, a spoon bowl, gunflints, and more. No one thing proved the existence of a hospital. To do that, we knew we had to find traces of the building itself. And,

FIG. 3-16. The palisade stain that borders the small-pox hospital on the north.

since no one had dug an eighteenth-century smallpox hospital before, we could not easily make predictions about how the building had been laid out.

The breakthrough came in the summer of 1994 as Rozell began exposing long, linear stains filled with dark earth and containing charcoal flecks and lots of rosehead nails. Unlike the crews of earlier summers, Rozell's kept the stains covered at all times and so was able to prevent them from drying out in the sun. One stain ran for over 130 feet north-south on the western side of the terrace and was about a foot wide (figure 3-16). Initially, we interpreted this as a spot where logs may have lain on the ground and then disintegrated; at the south end of this stain, Matt's team discovered both the blade from a spade and the faint traces of a wood handle that had rotted away (figure

FIG. 3-17. The blade from a
spade found in the palisade
stain from the smallpox
hospital.

FIG. 3-18. Plan view of the
1757 smallpox hospital on
Rogers Island.

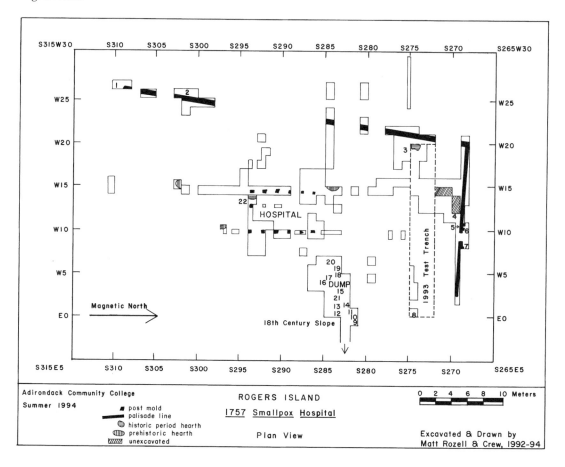

3-17). At the northern end of this stain, he then found a right-angle corner, where the stain turned and continued due east. At first, we thought they had found the outline of the smallpox hospital, but the stain was still continuing east after fifty-eight feet; it was simply too wide for a building that had been quickly thrown up by a handful of soldiers.

We finally decided that these stains must, in fact, be the remains of palisade lines (vertical logs set into ditches) that provided outer boundaries for the hospital complex on the northern and western sides of the terrace. The dump that Rozell had discovered earlier appeared to establish an eastern limit for the hospital complex, and on the south, the terrace dropped down to the river. Activities associated with the smallpox hospital were thus bounded quite tightly on all four sides.

In the middle of the northern palisade stain, Rozell discovered a three-foot-wide gap. After speculating that this might be evidence for a doorway or gateway, he actually found a key just outside the opening. The excavators then cut across the stain, to look at the vertical profile it left in the ground, and they found it to be a deeply-dug trench, basin-shaped at the bottom. Most likely the soldiers had set their posts into this trench.

After locating the four outermost limits of the hospital zone, Rozell's team returned to the center of the terrace, where later in 1994 they began to expose large, square postholes, regularly spaced at five-foot intervals, forming two rows that were fifteen feet apart. The sides of the building were exactly parallel to the western palisade wall, and the hospital was positioned midway between the palisade and the dump on the eastern edge of the terrace. Rozell had enough time to expose six postholes on either side of the building, and I have little doubt that he had finally found the smallpox hospital (figure 3-18). Also, our historical records do not indicate that any other building was ever constructed at this end of the island.

We never did find the answer to *why* there would have been palisade walls on two sides of the hospital. Were these built as a wind break, or perhaps so that soldiers in the more northerly huts and barracks would not have to watch their suffering comrades? Still, after four years of searching, we finally had solid traces of the building itself. In the future, it will be important to find traces of the other, more generalized types of hospitals that were built on the island. The dump from a general hospital would more likely leave behind medical supplies and amputated body parts, which are not to be found—as we have shown—in the remains of a smallpox hospital.

The Barracks on Rogers Island

While Rozell was working at the site of the hospital in 1994, just over half of our crew was excavating in the barracks area over a thousand feet to the north. This was another part of Rogers Island where we had worked for three years with only mixed success. Part of our problem was that the Hudson River channel had been deepened for navigation early in the twentieth century, and the heavy clay dredge had been spread to a depth of ten to twenty feet over the remains of the barracks buildings. While this had slowed down looting over the years, it also made it extremely hard, even with power equipment, to expose more than a little bit at a time.

Underneath the dredge, we found the remains of smallish huts, probably constructed there before the large British barracks went up in 1757–1758. We knew where treasure hunters had ripped out many fireplaces, and we had found tent pegs, but we had utterly failed to find clear evidence of the largest buildings on the island: mammoth, two-story barracks, each measuring hundreds of feet long, with outside staircases and central fireplaces. We knew from contemporary maps that nearly all of the barracks were constructed in two long north-south lines, with each building abutting other barracks buildings to either the north or the south. Contemporary British

FIG. 3-19. A schematicized outline of the barracks building and fireplaces discovered on Rogers Island in 1993–1994.

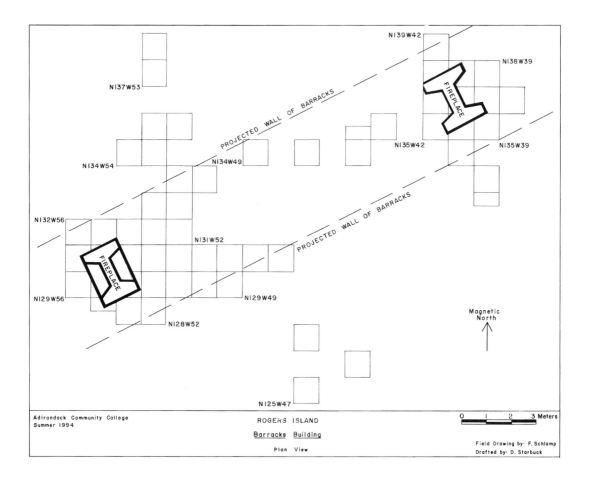

ROGERS ISLAND

Barracks Building

Plan View

Field Drawing by: F. Schlamp
Drafted by: D. Starbuck

FIG. 3-20. The base from a two-sided barracks fireplace of bricks and mortar, discovered in 1994.

engineers' drawings showed that only two barracks ran east-west *across* the island, at the northern and southern extremes of the complex. Regular British soldiers lived in the barracks, separate from the provincial soldiers, and their officers probably lived in small houses between the barracks rows (such as the eleven- by eleven-foot house we had already exposed).

In 1993 we had discovered a large fireplace base of brick that we believed might have once stood inside a barracks building, but not enough of the site was exposed to be sure. Our 1994 excavations revealed what we were seeking: a second massive brick fireplace base, about forty-five feet from the first. The two were perfectly in line with each other, with occasional stains running between the two (see figure 3-19). Each fireplace was two-sided, opening on both the east and west. So, not only were we looking at the interior of *one* barracks building, but it was one of the two east-west buildings. This was exactly the sort of evidence we were looking for, because by locating the ends of this building, we could closely predict where every other barracks had originally stood on the island. And, because collectors in the past had exposed fireplaces just north of where we were working, we now had discovered what was probably the foundation from the *southernmost* barracks building.

The barracks fireplace that we had exposed in 1993 had few artifacts around it, except for the wood handle of a probable brush knife. But the fireplace discovered in 1994 (figures 3-20 and 3-21) was absolutely caked with

FIG. 3-21. Plan view of the barracks fireplace in figure 3-20.

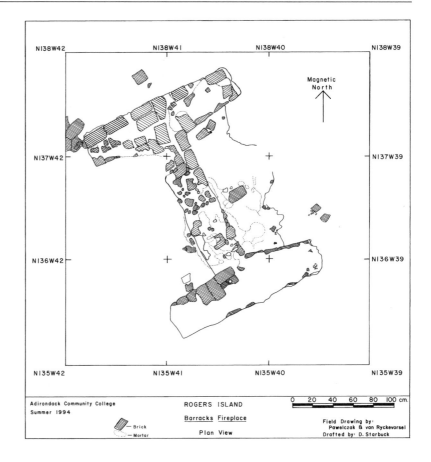

N138W42   N138W41   N138W40   N138W39

Magnetic North

N137W42   +   +   N137W39

N136W42   +   +   N136W39

N135W42   N135W41   N135W40   N135W39

Adirondack Community College
Summer 1994

ROGERS ISLAND

Barracks Fireplace

Plan View

0   20   40   60   80   100 cm.

Brick
Mortar

Field Drawing by:
Pawelczak & van Ryckevorsel
Drafted by: D. Starbuck

trash. Deep charcoal stains lay within both fireplace channels, along with mortar, ash, clay pipes, musket balls, cuff links, gunflints, hundreds of butchered bones, a piece of Spanish cob money, sherds of delft, melted lead sprue, and many tiny pieces of lead shot. This must have been a barracks where British regulars had practically wallowed in their own trash, unwilling even to take their garbage outside of the building. Given the depth of the charcoal in the eastern fireplace channel, we discovered that soldiers kept scraping out the ashes and charcoal, creating a basin that went eight to nine inches *below* the brick sides of the fireplace.

After we discovered the barracks building, our work was suddenly put on hold because Rogers Island was put up for sale by its owners. We did not return for two years. In 1997 and 1998, a new owner, Rogers Island Resorts Ltd., invited us back, and we watched as they hired contractors to remove hundreds of tons of dredge from atop the barracks' site, taking a vast area down to the original ground level. This unexpected development enabled us to find a host of small pits and dumps all around the ruins of our first barracks, and in 1997 we found the outline of another hut (figure 3-22), this one

FIG. 3-22. A hut site, out-lined with string, discovered in 1997 next to the remains of a barracks.

measuring seven and a half by nine feet and containing many gunflints, musket balls, lead sprue, and two frogs (scabbard holders) (figure 3-23). We were even more successful in 1998 when we discovered another eleven-by-eleven-foot hut site and a sixteen-by-sixteen-foot foundation, probably the remains of an officers' building.

The digging on Rogers Island could go on forever, given its richness, though that would destroy what remains of these sites. Still, under other cir-

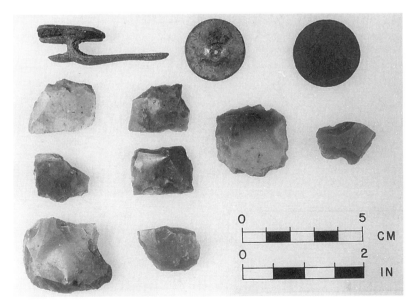

FIG. 3-23. Gunflints, a frog (top left), a button (top center), and a British coin (top right) found inside the 1997 hut (figure 3-22).

FIG. 3-24. Unrefined
stoneware excavated from a
soldiers' dump on Rogers
Island. Upper left: the rim
from a chamberpot; lower
right: the mouth from a jug.

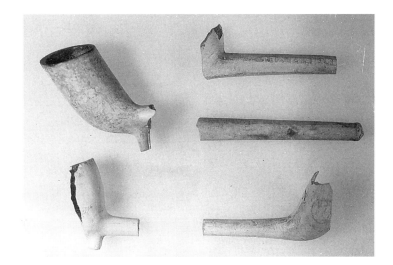

FIG. 3-25. Tobacco pipes
found in various locations
on Rogers Island.

FIG. 3-26. Cuff links, buttons, and a thimble discovered on Rogers Island.

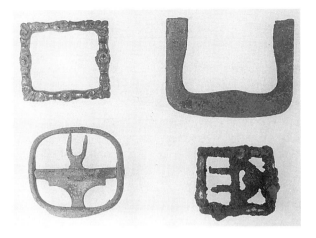

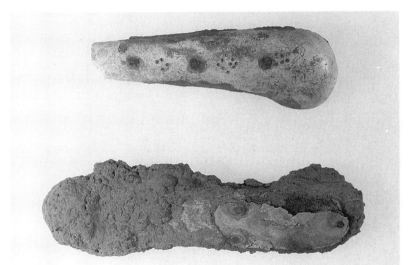

FIG. 3-27. (Top left.) Several buckles discovered on Rogers Island.

FIG. 3-28. (Top right.) Spanish silver coins found in the barracks: a "cob" and a four-real piece.

FIG. 3-29. (Left.) A bone knife handle (top) found in a possible officers' dump and a complete folding knife (bottom) found in the barracks. The rather elegant knife handle has several copper inlays.

cumstances we would like to be able to discover some of the barracks rooms that were adapted to hospital usage and to find the ends of our barracks building so that we could follow the long north-south rows of barracks up the length of the island. We also would like to make more systematic comparisons among the artifact types found in each of our huts, our several dumps, and our one barracks building. We have found such large samples of artifacts in many parts of the island that we hope to be able eventually to compare the material culture of American soldiers or Rangers with British officers and soldiers (figures 3-24 to 3-29).

The Excavation of Fort Edward

Fort Edward was the largest British fort of the French and Indian War but, like Rogers Island, it failed to achieve fame because no major assaults occurred there, nor was there a massacre as in the case of Fort William Henry. Yet this fort was relatively permanent by British standards, and it represented a serious commitment to driving the French out of northern New York. It was a log fort, surrounded by a ditch (or moat), and the dirt from the ditch was thrown up to create embankments. On top of the embankments were pickets that rose up for another twelve feet or so. While a fort of earth and logs may sound rather impermanent compared to coastal forts of stone, it was intended to last for only a few seasons on the frontier, which the British hoped would be enough time to defeat the French.

It must be noted, however, that Fort Edward was not simply a way station for armies passing through. Before the French and Indian War, the only substantial forts in North America were built by the French, and these were imposing, bastioned fortifications of the type designed by Sebastien Le Prestre Vauban. And they were built to last, like Fortress Louisbourg in Nova Scotia. British forts, on the other hand, were little more than log stockades, easily overrun by a determined enemy. This changed in 1755 when Sir William Johnson ordered Captain William Eyre to build Fort Edward and Fort William Henry. Fort Edward, the more substantial of the two, was built in the form of a square with three corner bastions (figure 3-30).

Fort Edward subsequently housed many of the leading British officers in North America. General Daniel Webb was placed in charge of the troops there in 1757, and General James Abercromby arrived in 1758 on his way to attacking Fort Ticonderoga. Abercromby's attack failed, but the following year General Jeffery Amherst gathered an army at Fort Edward and successfully conquered Ticonderoga. British officers stayed at Fort Edward in relative comfort, but after the fall of Fort William Henry, its tactical significance increased when it became the northernmost British fort on the Hudson River/Lake George waterway. The number of buildings constructed inside the fort continually increased until 1758, and larger British armies arrived each summer until the final conquest of Ticonderoga. The only attack upon Fort Edward was a minor skirmish, on July 23, 1757, when the French under Joseph Marin de la Malgue attacked the outworks and about a dozen men were killed.

Construction of Fort Edward cost £14,604, and the buildings inside included a blacksmith shop, a powder magazine, a guardhouse, provision sheds, the casemates, an East Barracks (160 feet by 18 feet), a West Barracks (110 feet by 18 feet) which also contained a hospital, an officers' barracks, and more. The barracks were two stories high; the height of the ground floor was six feet ten inches, and the second floor was six feet six inches.

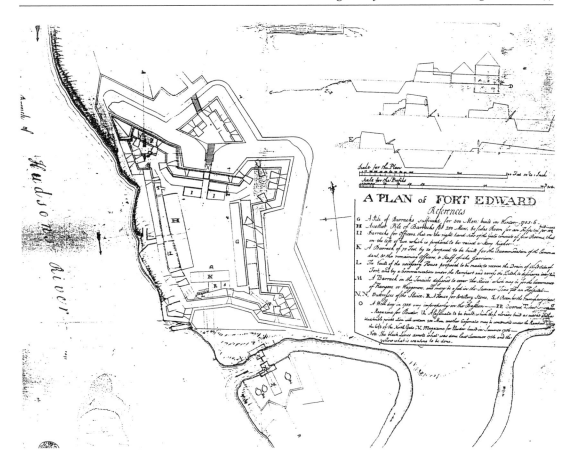

A PLAN of FORT EDWARD

References

In 1759, after General Amherst's victory over Fort Ticonderoga, the garrison in Fort Edward was greatly reduced. The fort then lasted through the American Revolution, with a fairly small garrison, and was probably abandoned at the end of 1777 or soon afterward. Sometime in the nineteenth century, the casemate rooms were filled with sand; the first houses were built on top of the fort in the mid-1800s; and we know from William Hill's *Old Fort Edward Before 1800* that at the end of the nineteenth century, some local property owners were systematically digging up their lawns, looking for artifacts to sell. The only surface traces of the fort today, after the passage of another one hundred years, are portions of the moat and a few timbers eroding out of an earthen bank at the edge of the Hudson River.

Given the number of colonial forts that have been excavated over the years, it is perhaps surprising that Fort Edward has seen so little research. However, most of the dozen or so families that now live on top of the fort have stories to tell about what was found under their yards, or in their cellars, when their houses were originally constructed. In fact, when first excavated, nearly every cellar hit fireplaces or large, burned timbers from the fort. For-

FIG. 3-30. A colored plan of Fort Edward, showing what was built in the summer of 1756 and what remained to be done; it was drawn on a scale of 50 feet to an inch; with profiles on a scale of 20 feet to an inch. Crown Collection of Photographs of American Maps, New York State Library.

tunately, while the various owners of the fort site kept out most treasure hunters over the years, they were wonderfully receptive when, on behalf of Adirondack Community College, I asked for permission to conduct excavations in their yards in 1995 and 1996. During these two field seasons, we dug test pits throughout several of the lawns that cover the fort, and our excavations found enough charred timbers to define both the eastern and western edges of the fort, including the approximate locations of both the East and West Barracks.

In 1995, we conducted a small amount of digging inside the dry moat around the fort, which once had measured from twenty-five to sixty feet wide and ten to fifteen feet deep. We then began intensive digging inside what we believe was the East Casemate room, a well-protected room under the ramparts on the east side of the fort. Typically, casemate rooms provided ample protection during any bombardment. In the yard of Richard and JoAnne Fuller, we found what was clearly the site of a below-ground room, with charred logs at different levels, running to a total depth of about seven feet (figure 3-31). This was a nightmare to dig because all of the deposits were fine sand, and sometime in the nineteenth century this dug room had been filled in with very loose gravel fill. We kept shoring up the walls with sheets of plywood, braced with two-by-fours, but every time it rained, the sand and gravel came pouring down into the bottom of our trenches. We found eight-inch-square beams in several locations, but we finally had to stop at seven feet because one of the property owners was afraid that a neighbor's house was about to slide into the hole! However, by coring deeper into the sand, we

FIG. 3-31. Burned timbers exposed inside the East Casemate of Fort Edward.

recovered evidence that the floor of the casemate room was only about one foot deeper than we had been able to go, making the subterranean room a total of eight feet deep.

On the western side of the fort, alongside the Hudson River, we failed to find clear evidence of a casemate room, but over the course of two seasons we found destroyed fireplaces and intact wood beams running north-south parallel to the river and only several feet from the river's edge (figure 3-32). These extended for over 125 feet, with pockets of artifacts buried alongside, and this part of the fort is now owned by Neal Orsini who operates a bed and breakfast atop the fort. Here we found deep ash concentrations, deep timbers, Spanish cob money, clusters of musket balls and lead sprue, and the stains from ditches and postmolds (figure 3-33). Based on historical maps from the 1750s, we believe that the longest stains, running east-west, line up with the sallyport that ran to the river on the western side of the fort. Perhaps most important, the supervisor over this area, Matt Rozell, noticed that there were three destroyed fireplaces in a row, running north-south down the western side of the fort, each 34 feet from the next. These fireplaces had probably run down the center of the West Barracks, but plowing and local collectors had taken a severe toll, and we simply could not be sure.

We also dug in 1996 in the front and rear lawns of a house that lies atop the southeast corner of the fort. We knew before we started that a past owner of the house had discovered beams from the fort in the cellar roughly thirty years ago, at a depth of about six feet below grade. He was so excited at the prospect of becoming an "archeologist," that he had hooked up a motorized conveyor belt to carry dirt out of his cellar! At any rate, we assumed the house straddled a deep casemate room. We dug in the cellar, where we reex-

FIG. 3-32. (Bottom left.) The remains of wood running north-south along the western edge of Fort Edward.

FIG. 3-33. (Bottom right.) The dark stain indicating a trash pit (top) and an east-west palisade ditch (bottom) inside the ruins of Fort Edward. Note the postmolds (round stains) inside the ditch.

FIG. 3-34. The outline of
soft, decayed wood inside
the remains of Fort Edward.

posed beams running east-west; and we exposed a corner of the casemate constructed with a mortise and tenon joint, as well as additional beams that were running north-south. The wood was very soft and punky, and the timbers were about fifteen inches wide. We then dug in the front yard, where we found the casemate continuing to run north, with the wood ranging from three to seven feet in depth (figure 3-34). The interior of this room was filled with extremely loose sand that required shoring as the walls constantly collapsed. At the bottom, two yards below the present ground surface, we found wood, spikes, a flattened musketball, and a layer of boards that almost certainly had been the floor of the casemate room.

Conclusions

In eight years of digging on Rogers Island and at the site of Fort Edward, we have examined the remains of huts, dumps, a possible storehouse, a latrine, a hospital, at least one barracks building, and one or more casemate rooms. We discovered that an eleven-foot-square module appears to be the most common hut size. We learned that delft and unrefined stonewares are the principal ceramic types that were used by the soldiers, although small quantities of porcelain and white salt-glazed stoneware were also used, probably by the officers. Tobacco pipes were in common use everywhere (with a bore diameter of ⁵⁄₆₄ inches), but wine bottles were relatively scarce. Most of the gunflints we found were of French origin—very few were British—and most of the musket balls recovered were intended to be used in the British Brown Bess musket, although we found many small pieces of buckshot as well. We found that fresh meat (beef and pork) was extremely common; and we were surprised to discover how frequently British half-pennies and Spanish one-half reals were dropped all over the island. In fact, there are many more coins on Rogers Island than at any other military site I have studied. Also, during the 1994 field season we finally succeeded in locating the remains of a small-pox hospital, the first to be dug at any eighteenth-century military camp.

It now is essential that the remainder of the island and the fort be protected—any further digging at this time would destroy what is left of these invaluable sites. Conducting artifact analysis and conservation on the thousands of excavated artifacts is critical, and we also still need to make comparisons between the lives of the ranking officers in the fort and what may have been a less-structured lifestyle on Rogers Island, where most of the colonials lived. This is a truly remarkable site, and it needs to be managed carefully to ensure that it provides the most information to future generations of scholars.

Further Reading

Cuneo, John R. 1988. *Robert Rogers of the Rangers.* Ticonderoga, N.Y.: Fort Ticonderoga Museum.

Fitch, Jabez. 1966. *The Diary of Jabez Fitch, Jr. in the French and Indian War 1757.* Publication no. 1. Fort Edward, N.Y.: Rogers Island Historical Association. 2d edition, 1968.

Gridley, Luke. 1907. *Luke Gridley's Diary of 1757 While in Service in the French and Indian War.* Hartford, Conn.: Acorn Society.

Hill, William H. 1929. *Old Fort Edward Before 1800.* Fort Edward, N.Y.: privately printed.

Loescher, Burt Garfield. 1946. *The History of Rogers Rangers.* San Francisco: printed by the author.

———. 1969. *Rogers Rangers: The First Green Berets.* San Mateo, California: printed by the author.

Rogers Island Historical Association. 1969. *Exploring Rogers Island.* Publication no. 2. Fort Edward, N.Y.: Rogers Island Historical Association. 2d Edition, 1986.

Starbuck, David R. 1994. The Rogers Island Archaeological Site: Transforming Myths into Strategies for Interpreting and Managing a Major Encampment from the French and Indian War. In *Cultural Resource Management*, edited by Jordan E. Kerber, 243–260. Westport, Conn.: Bergin & Garvey.

———. 1995. (ed.) *Archeology in Fort Edward*. Queensbury, N.Y.: Adirondack Community College.

———. 1997a. America's Forgotten War. *Archaeology* 50 (1):60–63.

———. 1997b. Military Hospitals on the Frontier of Colonial America. *Expedition* 39 (1):33–45.

Todish, Timothy J. 1988. *America's* First *First World War: The French & Indian War 1754–1763*. Ogden, Utah: Eagle's View Publishing Company.

Chapter 4

The Scene of the Massacre:
Fort William Henry

O<small>N</small> A<small>UGUST</small> 10, 1757, a small log fort at the southern tip of Lake George was the scene of one of the most notorious and brutal massacres in colonial American history. The British and provincial garrison of Fort William Henry, under the leadership of Lt. Colonel George Monro, had just surrendered to a force of at least ten thousand French regulars, Canadians, and Native Americans under the command of the Marquis de Montcalm. Escorted by no more than a few hundred French regulars, the British and provincial prisoners started the sixteen-mile march south toward safety, the site of Fort Edward where a large British garrison would protect them. While on the military road south of Lake George, Native Americans from a number of tribes suddenly attacked them, and scalped and killed many, literally tearing the uniforms off the backs of the terrified soldiers. Few dared to defend themselves from the assault as Indians hacked them with tomahawks, took scalps, and dragged prisoners away to Canada.

These horrific events inspired one of the first great American novels, James Fenimore Cooper's 1826 *The Last of the Mohicans*. The story has had such a lasting impact because the slaughter at Fort William Henry was unquestionably one of the most controversial events of the French and Indian War and one of the most ruthless massacres in eighteenth-century America.

These events, and those that led up to this slaughter, are superbly described in the book *Betrayals* by Ian Steele, who has revealed how the massacre was the unfortunate outcome of a series of betrayals: Colonel Monro felt betrayed by his commanding general, Daniel Webb, who held five thousand soldiers in reserve in Fort Edward and did not send them to relieve Fort William Henry; the British felt betrayed by Montcalm and the French because their surrender and safe conduct to Fort Edward had been violated; the French felt betrayed by the Native Americans who had slaughtered the defenseless British and provincial prisoners; and the Native Americans felt betrayed by the French because they did not receive sufficient booty after the surrender of the fort.

While Hawkeye and many of the other characters in Cooper's novel were entirely fictional, the setting of the action in *The Last of the Mohicans* was the actual northernmost British outpost in the interior of colonial America. Fort William Henry, named in honor of the son of King George III, had been constructed by the engineer William Eyre on the orders of William Johnson, the prominent major general and King's agent from the Mohawk Valley. Built immediately after the Battle of Lake George in September of 1755, the fort was positioned so as to block any further advance of French forces from Canada. Even more important, it had to withstand attacks from the French positions at Fort St. Frederic and Fort Carillon, just thirty-five miles to the north.

For the French, though, Fort William Henry was a British intrusion into the lake and drainage basin that Samuel de Champlain had first claimed for the king of France, which the Jesuit Isaac Jogues had named "Lac St. Sacrement" in 1642. Lake George thus became a disputed waterway between two great empires, and this small picketed fort with thirty-foot-thick walls of pine logs and earth, with beach sand packed in between the cribbing, was virtually the front line of British defenses.

Sporadic raids and fighting between the two colonial powers escalated into all-out war in August 1757, when the Marquis de Montcalm and an army of French and Native Americans variously estimated between ten and fourteen thousand laid siege to the British fort and its garrison of about twenty-three hundred men. The end came swiftly, but the terms of capitulation were generous: the British and Americans were allowed to leave under French escort, having promised not to fight against the French for the next eighteen months.

Their heroic defense of the fort had lasted just six days, and constant bombardment by French artillery had pounded the log fort into submission. But after the surrender, on August 9, some of the sixteen hundred Native Americans from thirty-three different tribes attached to Montcalm's army entered the fort. As they searched for booty, they killed, scalped, and in at least one case beheaded the sick and wounded soldiers who had remained inside the casemate rooms. A young French Jesuit eyewitness, Père Pierre Roubaud, described the scene:

> I saw one of these barbarians come forth out of the casements, which nothing but the most insatiate avidity for blood would induce him to enter, for the infected atmosphere which exhaled from it was insupportable, carrying in his hand a human head, from which streams of blood were flowing, and which he paraded as the most valuable prize he had been able to seize.

Events further deteriorated when Native Americans dug up some of the bodies in the British military cemetery and began scalping the corpses, many of whom had died from smallpox. One of the smallpox victims who was scalped was Richard Rogers, brother of the famed Ranger leader Robert Rogers. As the Native Americans took blankets and uniforms from the dead, many contracted smallpox, which they carried home to their villages in Canada; and thousands of native people subsequently died in a smallpox epidemic.

On August 10, Native American allies of the French, feeling disappointed with the few scalps they had collected, attacked the retreating British and provincial column, killing and scalping men, women, and children while the French did little to protect their prisoners. This event is portrayed with horrible effectiveness in *The Last of the Mohicans*, although in real life there was no Magua (the Huron warrior who led the attack) and Colonel Monro did not die in the massacre. Rather, Monro and his fellow British officers were prisoners in the French camp at the time of the massacre. Monro died three months later in Albany, New York, from apoplexy. The soldiers' families, camp followers, blacks, mulattos, and even Native Americans who had fought on the British side were attacked and killed or dragged away to the enemy camp. Ian Steele has estimated that no more than 185 soldiers and civilians were actually killed in the massacre, but the terrified survivors clearly believed that the number of those slaughtered had been far greater; even ninety-four years later, historian Benson Lossing claimed that "fifteen hundred of them were butchered or carried into hopeless captivity." Many prisoners were taken into captivity in Canada, where some were adopted into Native American tribes, some were sold into slavery, and others were eventually ransomed and returned home.

The atrocities had been unusually brutal, even for a period when *all* sides, British, French, and Native Americans, practiced scalping and slaughtered innocent civilians. It was a blemish upon Montcalm's reputation that captives under his protection had been murdered. So, after removing the cannons and stores from Fort William Henry, he burned it to the ground on August 11 and 12 and had his men level the charred timbers with picks and shovels. Some historical sources claim that the bodies of the massacre victims were immolated on a great funeral pyre atop the remains of the razed fort, but this has never been proven. And so Montcalm's army returned to Fort Carillon, and Fort William Henry vanished just two years after it had been constructed, a victim of the French and Native American army that had claimed the region for New France. Later armies camped on this spot (Abercromby in 1758 and Amherst in 1759); workmen constructed boats there in 1776 and 1777; and General George Washington tethered his horse on the site of the ruin in August 1783, noting that "there is a lot of history under this ground."

After the French and Indian War (1754–1763) ended, the battle at Fort William Henry might have been forgotten were it not immortalized in

★ The Role of Women at Military Camps

I often am asked whether archeology has revealed any evidence about women or children at military encampments. Regrettably, there is no ready answer because there are very few artifacts we can be positive that women used or wore, and few references to women or children appear in military journals and orderly books. The low visibility of women within what were predominantly male camps derives in large measure from the low status given to female activities. Nearly all military orderly books and diaries were written by white males, and so perhaps it is no wonder that most of these historical sources either pretend that women did not exist or that because most were "camp followers" they need not be taken seriously. Nevertheless, women accompanied British and American forces on most campaigns. Walter Blumenthal, in fact, has demonstrated in *Women Camp Followers of the American Revolution* that far more women traveled with British armies than with American militia or Continental forces.

History presents these women in several ways:

1. As loyal wives who were accompanying their husbands;

2. As victims, such as Jane McCrea, who was killed and scalped by Native Americans in Fort Edward, New York, while trying to reach her fiancee, a Loyalist soldier;

3. As larger-than-life heroines who fought alongside their husbands (these women we now recognize under the generic name "Molly Pitcher");

4. As nurses who worked in the hospitals;

5. As camp workers who washed clothes or sewed and repaired tents, uniforms, and other clothing;

6. As a colorful mixture of sweethearts, mistresses, and prostitutes, some of whom had rather unsavory reputations.

Contemporary sources strongly suggest that while women were tolerated, they were insufficiently appreciated within military encampments of the eighteenth century. Officers sometimes complained about the rations that women consumed and claimed that the women slowed down armies as they traveled. Still, this was more than counterbalanced by the fact that women performed activities that the soldiers were reluctant to undertake. Women unquestionably earned the partial rations (usually half-rations) that they received and—except at times of actual combat—may well have worked harder than many of the soldiers did. Rather than draining resources or hurting discipline, they contributed to a clean and well-kept camp.

Contemporary sources also suggest that the familiar appellation "camp follower" is inadequate to describe the variety of roles in which women found themselves. Many appear to have been respected because of their loyalty to husbands or lovers; others were much sought after because of the services they performed; and still others were despised as prostitutes and were driven from camp if found to be unmarried. However, all were such a prominent feature of camp life that it is surprising that historical sources have not dealt with them in greater detail.

There remains the question of whether archeologists might find objects on military sites that could be distinguished as belonging to women or men. In most cases it would appear that men and women were using and sharing virtually the same material culture, and so it is not easy to determine the sexual identities of the people who used the camp kettles and pottery, for instance.

Still, some objects clearly—or probably—were used by women. For example, toy tea sets sometimes were used by girls, and pins were used as fasteners by women, although occasionally their undergarments had buttons made from bone or materials such as peach pits. Other items likely to have been used by women include small shoe buckles; earrings; hook eyes (often indicative of women's undergarments); sad irons (clothes irons); sewing needles and thimbles (although male tailors also used these); and small silver-plated or brass rings, which occasionally were worn by women, but also were used as trade items for exchange with Native Americans. Women's undergarments used many snaps and drawstrings, but these are practically invisible in the archeological record.

Archeologists need to search more systematically for gender-specific artifacts and for military contexts in which women are known to have lived and where their artifacts can be isolated from those of men.

Further Reading

Blumenthal, Walter Hart. 1952. *Women Camp Followers of the American Revolution*. Philadelphia: George S. MacManus Company.

DePauw, Linda Grant. 1975. *Founding Mothers: Women in America in the Revolutionary Era*. Boston: Houghton Mifflin Company.

Kopperman, Paul E. 1982. The British High Command and Soldiers' Wives in America, 1755–1783. *Journal of the Society for Army Historical Research* 60:14–34.

Mayer, Holly A. 1996. *Belonging to the Army: Camp Followers and Community during the American Revolution*. Columbia: University of South Carolina Press.

Starbuck, David R. 1994. The Identification of Gender at Northern Military Sites of the Late Eighteenth Century. In *Those of Little Note*, edited by Elizabeth M. Scott, 115–28. Tucson: University of Arizona Press.

Cooper's adventure classic. The novel and movie adaptations have shaped and become our most powerful images of colonial American warfare. Few people living today, however, realize how significant the massacre at Fort William Henry was in shaping British and American attitudes toward Native Americans. Contemporary accounts of the brutality were especially gruesome, as evidenced in the following eyewitness description by Major Israel Putnam:

> The fort was entirely demolished; the barracks, out-houses, and buildings were a heap of ruins; the cannon, stores, boats, and vessels were all carried away. The fires were still burning, the smoke and stench offensive and suffocating. Innumerable fragments, human skulls and bones, and carcasses half consumed, were still frying and broiling in the decaying fires. Dead bodies, mangled with scalping-knives and tomahawks in all the wantonness of Indian fierceness and barbarity, were every where to be seen. More than one hundred women, butchered and shockingly mangled, lay upon the ground, still weltering in their gore. Devastation, barbarity, and horror everywhere appeared, and the spectacle presented was too diabolical and awful either to be endured or described.

The 1950s Excavations

In the mid-1850s the Fort William Henry Hotel was built atop the former gardens of Fort William Henry, north of the fort site; and in 1872 ownership

FIG. 4-1. "Site of Old Fort William Henry, Lake George, N.Y." The surface of Fort William Henry in 1910. The Fort William Henry Hotel is in the background (visible through the trees), and a newly-built gazebo is on the right. The top of the fort's original well is faintly visible on the left, among the trees. Reproduced from the Collections of the Library of Congress.

of the fort site was conveyed to the Lake Champlain Transportation Company, which, in turn, became affiliated with the Delaware and Hudson Railroad Company. The D&H built a new hotel on the site of the old one in 1911, but the ruins of the fort itself now lay within a grove of tall pine trees (figure 4-1), where it remained largely undisturbed until 1952. Even the famous collectors William Calver and Reginald Bolton, who acquired artifacts from nearly all of the prominent military sites in New York State, appear not to have dug at Fort William Henry, although they dug at the nearby site of Fort George. In fact, until 1952 no professional excavations had been conducted at any fortress site on Lake George or Lake Champlain. Duncan Campbell's investigations within the French village at Fort Ticonderoga did not occur until 1957, and the first professional work in the Lake George area, a salvage excavation at the 1758 site of Fort Gage, did not occur until 1975.

The fort's ruins had often been visited by guests from the hotels nearby, and the outline of the fort was still quite visible in 1952, when Harold Veeder,

FIG. 4-2. The 1950s excavation, as charred timbers were being exposed. Courtesy of the Fort William Henry Corporation.

an Albany real estate broker, formed a stock company of investors and bought the ruins. The fort had never been built upon, and vague outlines of the dry moat and of diamond-shaped bastions were visible on the surface, along with a few depressions. Historical records had already verified that it was a bastioned fort, the type made popular by Sebastien Le Prestre Vauban, the eminent French designer of forts, and it contained barracks for the soldiers and living quarters for civilians. A deep dry moat surrounded the fort on three sides (a steep slope was on the fourth), and it was possible to enter the fort only by crossing a bridge that spanned the moat.

After the French burned the fort in 1757, the log walls caved in, and sand from the earthworks spread over the ruins and buried much of it by several feet. A few pits were excavated on this sandy promontory in late 1952, and then intensive trenching to find the original construction levels began in the spring of 1953 and lasted through 1954 (figure 4-2). Stanley Gifford, assisted by his wife Ruth, was hired by the Fort William Henry Corporation to direct the excavation. His experience in working on both prehistoric and historic sites in central and eastern New York went back to the early 1930s.

Gifford's project objectives were straightforward: to dig as much of the fort site as possible before the middle of 1954, by which time the developers wanted the fort totally rebuilt. Attempting to locate original floor levels, the bases of stone walls, and the boundaries of the fort, he employed dozens of workmen, who dumped the dirt from their wheelbarrows into a giant sifting

FIG. 4-3. The southwest
bastion of the reconstructed
fort in the fall of 1993, rebuilt atop the remains of the
original 1755–1757 fort. Lake
George is in the back-
ground on the left.

machine. Unfortunately, Gifford's field records subsequently burned during
a fire inside the West Barracks of the reconstructed fort in 1967. All that has
survived is a popular history booklet he wrote about Fort William Henry,
and a few small field notebooks stored today at the reconstructed fort. As a
result, we can describe how he conducted the excavation only through newspaper accounts, photographs, surviving artifacts, and some oral history. Also,
we cannot quantify the excavated artifacts because many of them have vanished from the fort's collections since the 1950s. Certainly one of the most
famous of these was one of Robert Rogers' own powder horns that was
stolen from a display case. Fort William Henry is but one of many museum
villages and historic site recreations where it is extremely difficult to recon-
struct excavation details now that principal archeologists have long since
departed or died. Similar efforts to put order into old notes and collections
have been made at Plimouth Plantation, Colonial Williamsburg, and elsewhere, but often with limited success.

Back in 1953, Gifford's crew proceeded with their work just barely ahead
of the loggers and construction workers who were rebuilding the walls, corner bastions, and barracks (figure 4-3). The public was present to view every
aspect of the dig, and sixty thousand visitors took guided tours of the excavation during the first year. Gifford successfully unearthed stone- and
brick-lined casemate rooms that had been built underneath both the east

and west sides of the fort. It was there, below the level of the fort, where women, children, and the sick were sheltered in times of battle. And it was there that the Native Americans under Montcalm's command had commenced their slaughter of the sick and injured soldiers.

One of Gifford's more interesting discoveries was a layer of black sand that showed where the British Lord Jeffery Amherst had burned over the surface of the ground and covered it with beach sand in 1759. Fastidious about sanitation, Amherst sterilized the site before he was willing to let his army camp on top of the ruins. Elsewhere, Gifford completely excavated the site of the northwest bastion, which suffered most of the impact of the French bombardment. He also excavated a huge crater at the southeast corner of the parade ground, though from photographs of his excavations, he seems to have barely touched the rest of the parade ground.

The reconstruction of Fort William Henry was completed in 1956. But even after Gifford had departed, small archeological excavations continued until 1960 under the direction of other staff at the fort. The process of rebuilding was reasonably accurate because detailed written descriptions and measurements of the fort were available, along with copies of the 1755 construction plans of the fort that were housed in the British Archives, the Canadian Archives, the Library of Congress, and the New York State Education Department. Still, the original architectural plans would have been of little value to the reconstruction without archeology to pinpoint each structure and interpret the activities that went on inside. We should not, indeed, assume that William Eyre's engineering plans were followed exactly in 1755: during excavation and reconstruction workmen found, for example, that the measurements of one bastion were off from the original plans by fourteen feet.

Contemporary architectural drawings reveal that the fort was laid out with four bastions, four curtain walls, and four barracks. The soldiers had built the North and South Barracks of logs and planks two stories high, and the East and West Barracks with one story underground and two stories above ground of logs. The parade ground lay at the center of the fort, and a powder magazine lay underneath the northeast bastion. Gifford excavated the remains of many of the buildings and earthworks, and his excavations within the relatively intact East Barracks exposed many logs that were charred only on the outside, with the inside of the wood still solid. Underneath the brick floor of the East Barracks, inside the remains of a casemate that had been used as a hospital, Gifford found five human skeletons in 1957 (figure 4-4), one of which had eight musket balls intermingled with the bones. These may well have been the remains of some of the aforementioned sick and wounded soldiers who were killed by Native Americans on August 9, when Père Roubaud described an attacker leaving the fort carrying a human head.

FIG. 4-4. Five victims of the massacre were found in a casemate room underneath the brick floor of the East Barracks in 1957. Some of the skulls were broken, possibly from tomahawk blows, and eight musket balls were found intermingled with the bones of one individual. The process of conserving the bones was recorded in a local newspaper account: "First, the bones are exposed to air on a hot dry day for two to three hours. When they reach the peak of hardness, a light cellulose solution is painted on, and then depending on the air, two more coats are painted on, each coat heavier than the other . . ." (*The Glens Falls Times*, Aug. 6, 1957). Courtesy of the Fort William Henry Corporation.

The Military Cemetery

Historians estimate the death toll in Lake George between 1755 and 1757 to be as high as eight hundred or one thousand. Understandably, one of the main goals of Gifford's 1953 excavation was to find the fort's cemetery, unmarked on any plan, but believed to have been located just outside the walls of the fort. The soldiers and civilians buried in the cemetery would most likely have died from smallpox, dysentery, and other diseases, gunshot and knife wounds, and occasional skirmishes (including an unsuccessful attack upon the fort by an army of French and Native Americans in March 1757). Perhaps a few were buried there during the early stages of the siege in August 1757, but I doubt that those who died later in the siege, or during the subsequent massacre, could have been buried there because the cemetery is in an exposed location outside the walls of the fort.

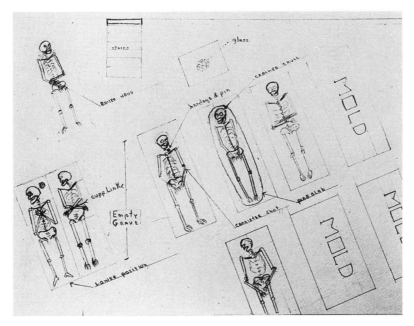

FIG. 4-5. A field sketch of the skeletons in the military cemetery, drawn on July 29, 1954. Seven of the skeletons had been exposed by this date, and three more (identified as MOLD) had been pedestaled and were awaiting excavation. A cuff link attached to a bit of cloth was found at the wrist of one skeleton (left); another skeleton (left center) was accompanied by a bandage and pin, and a musket ball was embedded near the left elbow (figure 4-7); and another skeleton (center) was laid on a pine slab. Courtesy of the Fort William Henry Corporation.

Because Lake George is on the north side of the fort, Gifford conducted grading operations outside the south wall, revealing a number of oblong stains with dimensions of about two and one half by six feet each. He dug around each stain, creating a series of pedestals, and as he dug into these, he uncovered human skeletons at depths of about four to five feet (figures 4-5 and 4-6). He had located a corner of the burial ground. While he excavated only ten grave shafts, his additional test holes placed within the parking lot west of the reconstructed fort brought up more bones. Gifford guessed that at least another two to three hundred skeletons lay underneath, but he made no effort to expose them.

Gifford's task was simplified a bit when an unheated log building was constructed around the ten skeletons in late 1953 to house the open graves and to permit the archeologists to work into the winter. Lake George winters can be fierce, and each one of the recently unearthed skeletons in the military cemetery was given a custom-built electric blanket by General Electric during the winter of 1953–1954. GE engineers surrounded each skeleton with heating cables and covered the remains with special composition paper blankets stretched on a framework of hardware cloth. Thermostats kept the air surrounding the bones at a constant forty degrees Fahrenheit so they would not suffer damage from freezing during the cold winter months.

From examining the bones, Gifford concluded that the soldiers had been buried hastily without coffins, although one was found lying on what appeared to be a slab of pine bark. Most of the bodies must have been wrapped in a blanket or nothing at all; their uniforms were typically reused by other soldiers. A few had cuff links near the wrists, but none had buttons that would suggest a uniform coat. Each corpse lay in an extended position with its legs straight and its arms straight along its sides, and most were Caucasian males in their late teens and early twenties. Some of the bodies had limbs missing, appropriate for a time when shattered or infected limbs were amputated. Gifford recognized that one of the soldiers had been buried with his feet tied together because there were traces of rope in the sand. Curiously, one of the skeletons was even missing its head. One skeleton still had a musket ball imbedded in the vicinity of its left elbow (figure 4-7), another had a musket ball lodged in its neck, while others had skull fractures that appeared to have come from tomahawk blows. One grave contained a chert projectile point, while another skeleton still had the traces of a bandage around its neck, held in place by a hospital pin.

These skeletons, combined with the human bones found scattered inside the ruins of the fort, made up a total find for Gifford and his colleagues of over thirty soldiers who had died at Fort William Henry. It was impossible to assign names or ranks to any of the dead, and even now we cannot say which skeletons were British and which were American provincials.

The documentation of the skeletons was admittedly incomplete by modern standards, yet only within the past ten years have scholars begun publishing detailed descriptions of eighteenth- or early-nineteenth-century military cemeteries. Once Gifford finished his work, the bones of the dead soldiers remained on view to the public within the temporary log building. In fact, the bones continued to be on display as a major tourist attraction for the next forty years; hundreds of thousands of visitors to the resort community of Lake George viewed the skeletons in the cemetery. And because this display was located outside the walls of the reconstructed fort, the bones were the only exhibit no one had to pay to see—the teaser that drew tourists through the gate.

Artifacts Found in the 1950s

Gifford recovered tens of thousands of artifacts from the ashes of Fort William Henry, but we no longer know precisely where most of them were found, and few have ever received any conservation treatment. However, we know from 1950s newspaper accounts of the excavation, and from the artifacts that remain, that Gifford's team uncovered a great many armaments, especially in the northwest bastion: mortars split from use, dozens of cannon balls, eight-inch mortar shells, hundreds of pieces of grape shot, gunflints, musket parts, sword blades, bayonets, and bushels of musket balls. He found artifacts that pertain to the kitchen and foodways, including knives, spoons, pottery sherds, tin canteens, and great numbers of wine bottles. More per-

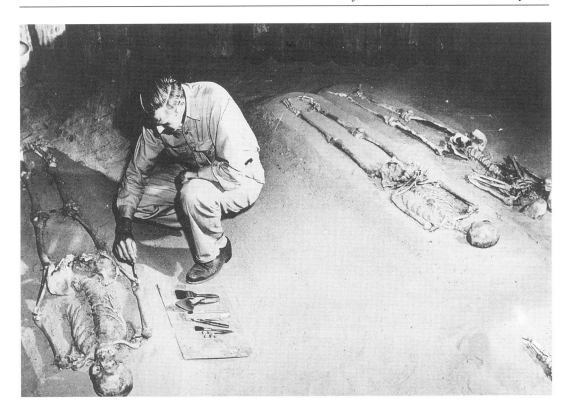

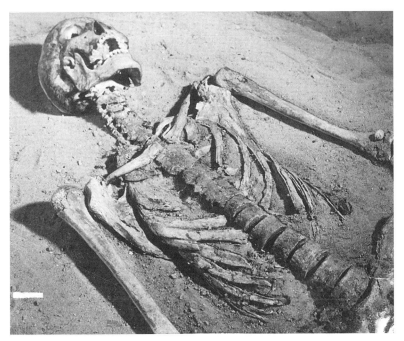

FIG. 4-6. (Top.) Soldiers' skeletons exposed inside the British Military Cemetery in 1954. Courtesy of the Fort William Henry Corporation.

FIG. 4-7. (Left.) This skeleton in the military cemetery has a musket ball embedded at the distal end of the left humerus. Courtesy of the Fort William Henry Corporation.

sonal artifacts, those worn by soldiers and officers, included shoe buckles, cuff links, buttons, a halfmoon-shaped metal gorget, and a pewter signet ring. Everywhere Gifford found pieces of the fort itself: charred wood beams and thousands of hand-wrought nails, spikes, and bricks. A unique artifact was part of a charred blanket that was found in a powder magazine under the northeast bastion of the fort. But much more common were great quantities of butchered bone fragments, tobacco pipes, Spanish, British, and French coins, axes, hoes, spades, candle snuffers, padlocks, and chisels. And underlying all of these were thousands of prehistoric projectile points, pottery sherds, and ground stone tools from Native American occupations from about 6000 b.c. (the Early Archaic period), and through until the soldiers arrived. Several hundred of these artifacts are presently on display at the fort, some have been stolen over the years, while others reside in a storage room.

These are certainly the artifact categories that we expect to find at a frontier fort, albeit in exceptionally large quantities because of the large scale of Gifford's excavation. Thousands of tobacco pipe fragments lay in the dry moat that surrounded the fort, and wine bottles were so numerous that Gifford once wrote, with tongue in cheek, "that the archaeologists came to the conclusion that the war was fought by each side throwing rum bottles rather than firing their muskets."

One of Gifford's most spectacular finds came in 1955 when he unearthed a live eight-inch mortar shell inside the ruins of the East Barracks building. It was still loaded with black powder, and he summoned a demolition squad from Fort Jay to deactivate it. He had already discovered an unexploded mortar shell inside a barracks building in late 1954, and he found the remains of a human scalp with black hair embedded on the surface of that shell (figure 4-8). The most likely explanation is that the mortar shell had been lobbed into the fort and bounced off the head of one of the fort's defenders, tearing off part of his scalp in the process. Still, this is one of those enigmatic artifacts whose origin will always be a mystery. Unfortunately, the scalp was destroyed during the 1967 fire, so it cannot be viewed or subjected to DNA analysis today.

The Reanalysis of the Human Skeletons

For many visitors, it was exciting to see the soldiers' skeletons at Fort William Henry. For most, this was the last opportunity to see human bones on display anywhere in the eastern United States. I personally found it very moving and sad to see the bones lying on display deep inside the recent cemetery building and in the crypt (the casemate room under the East Barracks); I was one of many who did not feel it was respectful to display these

FIG. 4-8. A mortar shell was discovered inside the ruins of a barracks building in October 1954. The shell had not exploded; it appears that when it was fired into the fort, it landed upside down in sand, extinguishing its fuse. A human scalp with black hair was found embedded on the surface of the shell, suggesting that on impact it had peeled the scalp from the head of one of the defenders of the fort. Courtesy of the Fort William Henry Corporation.

remains. Part of this feeling came from the knowledge that these soldiers had been real people, the settlers of our frontier, some of whom were the ancestors of people who live in the region today. However, when I looked down at their bones, all I could see was forty years of dirt and spiders stuck to them and coins thrown in by tourists. One of the skeletons was badly burned from vandals who had poured lighter fluid over it and dropped down a match. And then there was the infamous "head-hunter" who stole one of the skulls and, when caught at the Canadian border, told police that he liked to collect skulls! When this exhibit first opened in the 1950s, it was still common to display human bones in museums, but by the 1990s such displays had pretty much ended everywhere because of changing attitudes toward the dead.

In the spring of 1993 the Fort William Henry Corporation wisely decided that the time had come to rebury and honor its dead. In April and May 1993 they offered to let the forensic anthropologists Maria Liston and Brenda Baker examine the skeletons before removing them from display. After all, Gifford's specialty was not forensics, and tremendous advances had occurred since the 1950s in the interpretation of the human skeleton.

Liston and Baker began by remapping the skeletons in the cemetery and then removed the coating of liquid plastic preservative (alvar) that had been applied to the bones in the 1950s and 1960s to stabilize them. This was no easy task because the alvar had become as hard as rock! It required repeated soaking with acetone to remove the dirt-encrusted plastic. They then reassembled many of the more fragmentary remains so that measurements could be taken on complete bones. They found this to be time-consuming as well, especially because summer staff at the fort had been shifting and mixing bones from body to body for years.

Liston and Baker then began to study how each soldier died and what his age was at death, and they have X-rayed the bones and examined them for signs of chronic stress, pathologies, infections, traumas, and amputations. For the past five years, they have revealed an amazing range of evidence. For example, they found many herniated discs, which demonstrate that the men were carrying loads so heavy that the cartilage discs between the vertebrae were creating depressions in the bone. One skull showed cut marks along the hair line, suggesting that scalping had occurred. Another individual must have been anemic because there was much pitting in his skull bones. There was evidence for tuberculosis and arthritis, and one soldier died of long-term infection throughout his body. The left leg of one soldier had been amputated below the knee, and another probably died before his amputation was finished. There were signs of trauma everywhere, including one individual who may have been hit with cannister shot, breaking his ribs inward and perhaps puncturing his lungs. Cut marks in the abdominal area of several skeletons suggest possible disembowelment, and several kneecaps had been shot out, suggesting the possibility of torture. Liston and Baker's work is revealing graphic evidence both for disease and violent death, and they are beginning to illuminate the problems that afflicted soldiers during the French and Indian War.

After the skeletons were removed from exhibit areas in May 1993, the cemetery exhibit building was modified, and it now displays not the bones themselves but photographs of the skeletons and the 1953 and 1993 projects (figure 4-9). A memorial service was held at Fort William Henry's Military Cemetery on May 30, 1993. Just before the service, three of the skeletons were reburied in the cemetery, and the rest were taken by the anthropologists for further analysis. One of the chiefs of the Onondaga Nation joined representatives of New York State government, the British Consulate, the British military, and the Fort William Henry Corporation in eulogizing the dead and in placing a wreath over their remains.

Since that time, Baker and Liston have conducted an excavation of their own within the cemetery, in November 1995, and uncovered an additional eight grave shafts. Three of these were excavated, revealing one skeleton whose facial measurements suggest he was African-American, and a second that appears to be of mixed ancestry. Baker subsequently analyzed these at the New York State Museum, along with the buttons and textiles she found with the burials. Her most surprising discovery thus far is the remains of lice within the soldiers' buttons.

FIG. 4-9. The log exhibit building that was created to house the ten skeletons excavated in the military cemetery. This reflects the modern appearance of the display structure, as modified in mid-1993 once the skeletons were removed from view. The building is located just south of the reconstructed fort, and it covers only a small corner of the extensive cemetery that now lies under the modern parking lot.

The 1997 Excavations

I wanted to dig at Fort William Henry for a very long time before the opportunity presented itself in the summer of 1997. As a schoolboy, I had run through the reconstructed fort with my classmates, but archeology was not on my mind then. Still, I had grown up with people who had seen the 1950s dig, and many of them had already come to see my digs at other military sites in the region.

The fort is small compared to Fort Edward or Ticonderoga, yet that does not diminish its mystique as the site that spawned a bloody siege and then a terrible massacre. When the Fort William Henry Corporation approached me in 1996 to ask if I would direct an excavation there, I did not know whether Gifford had left behind anything worth digging; I knew only that I had to find out for myself whether portions of the fort were still intact and whether anything new could be learned about life in this frontier garrison.

We selected seven areas to dig. The first was the edge of the cemetery, where several early bifurcate base projectile points had been discovered in

1995 next to the grave shafts. I had no intention of exposing more graves—after all, it had taken years to get just a few of the previously exposed skeletons reburied. Unfortunately, instead of discovering a Native American site from 6000 B.C., our team kept finding Stanley Gifford's filled-in trenches, probably the same ones he had used to locate the cemetery in 1953.

Our second site was equally depressing, the southeast corner of the parade ground inside the fort, where we discovered that Gifford had turned over the soil to a depth of at least seven or eight feet. Contrary to what is printed in archeology textbooks, archeologists do *not* appreciate finding negative evidence! Still, even when we weren't finding much, visitors to the fort—and there were up to four thousand a day—seemed to appreciate what we were doing. One day, one of our diggers overheard one tourist tell another that we were so careful that we almost looked like "real" archeologists —they believed that we were reenactors pretending we were archeologists, just as the guides at the fort dressed up in uniforms and pretended they were eighteenth-century soldiers!

Our next site was much more intact; it was the original entranceway into the fort at its southeast corner, just outside the parade ground. There we found a rich scatter of animal bones, tobacco pipes and pottery sherds, and even the occasional gunflint and musket ball, all within two feet of the present ground level. This was our first evidence that the living surface of the fort might be very shallow, perhaps because Gifford or the Albany developers had removed much of the overburden from the surface of the fort when they began reconstruction.

Just outside this entranceway was one of the best surprises of the season, an unbelievably rich trash dump only about ten feet east of the outermost wall of the reconstructed fort. I did not know whether Gifford had sought out dumps beyond the immediate limits of the fort, but we discovered there an undisturbed column of trash that showed no signs of stopping at eight feet down. In fact, when we took small core samples out of the bottom of these pits, the artifacts were still continuing at a depth of eleven feet. It is amazing to find such a dump at a fort that had been occupied for only two years. We were finding thousands of butchered animal bones, and it was unquestionably a dump for kitchen garbage, but we also had well-preserved burned timbers from the fort, many buttons, tobacco pipes, musket balls, and more. Most important, in the deeper soil layers we found nothing mixed in from the nineteenth or twentieth centuries. Even though our sandy pit walls constantly caved in, requiring frequent shoring with plywood and two-by-fours, we are unlikely ever to find a better dump around the edges of the fort. Still, we need to carefully compare the artifacts from the bottom of this column to those from the top to make absolutely sure that none date from the revolutionary war encampments located nearby some twenty years later.

Our fifth and sixth sites were at the northeast corner and in the north-center of the parade ground, on either side of the fort's well. From photographs of Gifford's excavation, we knew these were areas he had never seriously disturbed, and so we expected them to be the richest pits of the summer. In the northeast corner, we did find that the first five to six feet were rich in artifacts (including a 1730 British half-penny), but with artifacts from many time periods mixed together. However, below that depth we discovered burned timbers that were probably from the north end of the East Barracks, and great numbers of early bricks that we believe were from a destroyed fireplace (figure 4-10). The artifacts included the complete head from a felling ax and exploded pieces of mortar shells, most likely from the siege in 1757. Still, our efforts to shore up the walls did little good, and we finally abandoned this site because we could not protect our diggers from the waves of sand that increasingly fell in upon them without warning. In fact, the northern wall of the trench collapsed one day under the weight of one of our veteran diggers, who tumbled on top of two others who were working six feet below him. And if our excavation had grown any larger, it would have collapsed one of the fort's full-size reproduction cannons into the trench. (We rather relished the thought that future archeologists would be able to expose a complete cannon if they ever dug in this spot again.)

FIG. 4-10. Excavations at the northeast corner of the parade ground in the summer of 1997 (the north end of the East Barracks).

FIG. 4-11. The surface of the fort's 1756 well, with the reconstructed North Barracks in the background.

The north-center of the parade provided some of our greatest surprises, not just by virtue of its richness, but because we were finding exceptional prehistoric and eighteenth-century artifacts virtually side by side and within a few inches of the modern surface. Gifford must certainly have removed some of the overburden there, stopping within a hair's breadth of the time period he sought. We found no traces of buildings, although we had anticipated that temporary shelters would have been erected there at the time of the final siege, as civilians moved inside the protective walls of the fort. But we did find the most wonderful mix of artifacts in the parade ground, including coins, exploded mortar shell fragments, the ubiquitous musket balls and gunflints, tobacco pipes, and more. And next to and underneath them were many sherds of prehistoric pottery, projectile points, and even a very intact Native American firepit. We removed only the first eighteen or so inches there but will soon attempt to go deeper.

The most dramatic focus of the 1997 dig was the fort's well, positioned at the north end of the parade and dating to 1756 when it was constructed by Rogers' Rangers (figure 4-11). We were not the first to plumb its depths and knew that the fort's staff had attempted to reach the bottom in 1959–1960.

FIG. 4-12. Inserting a section of culvert into the top of the fort's original 1756 well, before excavation began in 1997.

For them, the lure of the well had turned to frustration when they hit the water table at about twenty-three feet down. But they were also forced to stop because the well was incredibly unstable, "floating" in a terrace of fine beach sand. Wood planking was the only protection they had as they attempted to brace the walls against a cave-in. Newspaper accounts suggest that they reached Civil War levels in the well before they gave up, but they left behind no excavation records and no photographs.

An added problem was that since 1960 the well had been the center of attention for every school child who visited the fort, and their thousands of "contributions" to the well had refilled it to within thirteen feet of the surface. We had to remove twelve feet of post-1960 tourist rubbish and coins just to return to the point where our predecessors had stopped. While modern material culture studies are quite popular in some quarters, such as the Tucson Garbage Project at the University of Arizona, we nevertheless were neophytes at that sort of thing. All the same, we purchased an electric hoist, constructed a massive cross beam above the well, purchased thirty- and thirty-six-inch-diameter sections of steel culvert with which to line the well, and started down (figure 4-12).

FIG. 4-13. Buckets of coins found in the well.

Although I easily could have found volunteers willing to go into the well from among my staff and crew, I decided to be the one in the bottom because I was the only one who could not sue myself if something went wrong! Within the first twelve feet of tourist rubbish, I sent buckets up to the surface that contained literally tens of thousands of coins, discovering very quickly that American children in the 1990s still enjoy the thrill of throwing money into a well (figure 4-13). The uppermost deposits contained great quantities of dimes, quarters, and half-dollars (even Susan B. Anthony dollars!), while children in the 1970s and 1960s had thrown only pennies into this "wishing well." Many thousands with no money, or perhaps with better judgment, had instead thrown a handful of crushed rock from the parade ground into the well. In this fashion, one handful at a time, debris in the well had built up at the rate of about four inches per year, with soda cans, sunglasses, toy cars, flashbulbs, and flashcubes sometimes accelerating the pace. Also, starting at about nineteen feet down, there was no end to the wads of chewing gum from the sixties and seventies, right in the middle of what a garbologist would probably call the "flashcube era."

At twenty-three and one half feet down I hit the water table; between twenty-four and twenty-five feet the recent tourist trash finally ended. At this same depth I began finding boards, no doubt what was left of the wood that shored up the walls during the 1960 excavation. I cannot help admiring what the earlier well-diggers had accomplished: there I was safely surrounded by steel culvert, on the end of a safety line, and wearing a hard hat, and at twenty-five feet I could easily imagine the utter helplessness they must have felt whenever a stone fell from above.

While digging the well I was totally dependent on my helpers at the surface to provide supplies and to lift me out. I knew that it would be difficult to survive a cave-in. Starting at twenty-four feet, we needed submersible pumps running at all times, and these often became clogged with sand and failed, or lost power when the circuit breaker flipped. This sometimes left me standing in water up to my armpits, wondering when, or if, I would be hoisted to safety. At such times I would crawl up into the lowermost culvert, bracing my hands and feet against the sides, waiting for help. But one of the most difficult aspects of digging the well was the fact that I was always on camera, for my chief helper, Gerald Bradfield, had installed a video camera within the well shaft ten feet above me, recording my every motion and word. This signal was simultaneously broadcast to two monitors in the reconstructed North Barracks so that visitors could watch everything I was doing some twenty-five to thirty feet below them. For long hours I didn't dare scratch myself or say a word as buckets of water and mud splashed down upon me.

At twenty-five feet the nature of the fill inside the well changed, and instead of digging through broken Coke bottles, pennies, and crushed rock, I was now working in fine sand and silt. I had gone deeper than they had in 1960, but now I had ground water constantly rushing at me from all sides, and it was rather like standing among six or eight faucets with the cold water turned on all the way. As it became darker in the bottom, I added a safety light, but my safety harness was so restrictive that I could barely move. No matter what the temperature was above me in the parade ground, the air temperature at the bottom of the well was a constant 52 degrees Fahrenheit. The water itself felt somewhat colder, and I usually found myself standing in at least six to eight inches of it. Condensation also covered every surface, especially the culverts. On the positive side, voices traveled easily up and down the culvert, so I never had to raise my voice to talk with the crew that was hoisting buckets of dirt above my head (figure 4-14). But working inside the well and the culverts was so cramped that by night I was invariably aching and wishing the job was over.

The deeper we went, the harder it became to keep the pumps running, but the contents of the well were becoming more interesting. I found the complete skeleton of a goose at twenty-six and a half feet and the wood end of a barrel or keg at twenty-seven and a half feet. I also found several pockets of pine cones and branches from the many years that the well had stood open, between the time of the massacre and when hotels began to be built nearby. But most important, there was evidence for how the well had been lined at its bottom with vertical wood planks, creating a watertight barrel shape that prevented silt from washing in. I discovered the tops of these planks at about twenty-six feet, nine inches, and each was three inches thick and from six to twelve and a half inches wide. Massive and tightly joined, the planks were waterlogged and swollen, and ground water could flow into

FIG. 4-14. A view looking up the culvert that now lines the fort's 1756 well. Members of the archeology team are looking down from the top, and a video camera is positioned partway up the shaft. The outlet hose from the submersible pump is in the center.

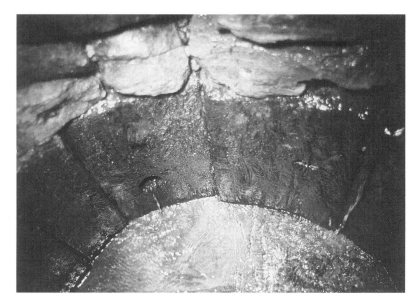

FIG. 4-15. The barrel lining at the bottom of the 1756 well, positioned underneath the massive, dry-laid stones of the well shaft. The sand in the middle was later taken down another two feet below this level.

the well only by running over the tops of the planks or through knot holes (figure 4-15).

Inside the barrel lining, there were many small finds, but nothing to suggest that the well had been deliberately filled in or contaminated at the time of the massacre. The well was abandoned and slowly filled itself in until the influx of twentieth-century tourists. The diameter at the top of the well is about forty-two inches, but at the bottom, the wood lining forms an oval of roughly thirty by thirty-five inches. Because several modern dams have raised the level of water in Lake George, I have no doubt that when the barrel lining was added by Rogers' Rangers, the depth of the water table (and of Lake George) must have been several feet lower than it is today. Otherwise, the torrents of water washing in upon the soldiers as they dug the well would have been overwhelming.

At the very bottom of the well, working with a two-horsepower submersible pump, we exposed about twenty-seven inches of the barrel lining and reached a depth of nearly thirty feet, but waves of sand kept gushing up from *underneath* the surface where I was working. As I removed gravel and stones, sand came bubbling up to take its place. Forcing a steel probe

FIG. 4-16. Some of the artifacts found at the bottom of the 1756 well. From left to right, top row: French gunflints, tobacco pipe fragments; middle row: a corner of a case bottle, an iron ring that reinforced a tent peg, musket balls; bottom row: melted glass, pieces of cut lead shot.

down through the sand, I found that the barrel was still continuing downward at five feet, nine inches, so the height of the wood lining must surely be six feet or more. But reaching that depth had now become impossible because everything was turning to quicksand, and both the pump and I were being pulled down.

While this was going on, there was a constant rain of sand and small stones from above. The culverts provided superb protection most of the time, but finally the ground water began washing in too much sand from the surrounding terrace. In fact, over the course of our excavation, the entire thirty-foot-high well shaft—weighing many tons—literally sank nearly three feet into the sand. The well was now sinking faster than we could possibly keep up with; it was time to stop. Gerry hoisted me out, even as sand from above, from every side, and from below filled in the shaft that we had reopened after 240 years.

Our effort was worth it, though: inside the wood lining at the bottom of the well we recovered about a dozen lead musket balls, four French gunflints, a few dozen small pieces of lead (cut shot), many small butchered bones, the bones from five different frogs, several sherds of pottery and porcelain, twenty to thirty pieces of window glass, and the corner from a square-sided case bottle (figure 4-16). Contrary to local lore, the well did *not* contain the fort's payroll, nor any bodies of female massacre victims, but instead there was a representative range of small, everyday objects from the 1750s. Most of these artifacts I removed from a layer of gravel that had probably been the original lining at the bottom of the well.

Conclusions

While our efforts to triumph over the well have been a definite high point of the new research at Fort William Henry, our renewed excavations inside the fort have not yet revealed anything directly pertaining to the massacre. Still, the ubiquitous mortar shell fragments and musket balls are firm evidence of the final days in August 1757 when Fort William Henry came under siege. Besides, historical sources provide reasonably good documentation for the massacre itself, but we know far less than we should about the many months of difficult frontier life that preceded the final siege. Perhaps our most important discoveries, then, have been the undisturbed parts of the parade ground and the exceptionally deep dump that lies outside the eastern wall of the fort. As archeology proceeds in these areas, we hope to uncover some of the most rewarding, and informative, caches of French and Indian War artifacts ever discovered. We also anticipate finding traces of the later revolutionary war units that were camped nearby. Some evidence for this appeared in 1997 when we found a button from a uniform of the 2nd Battalion,

Pennsylvania Continental Line, a battalion that was in the Lake George area in 1776.

Clearly Gifford dug just enough of Fort William Henry to permit the 1950s reconstruction, and in the years ahead up-to-date archeological techniques will continue to bring the old fort back to life. We cannot discover the remains of the fictional Hawkeye or his Mohican friend Chingachgook, but the small personal effects of the soldiers and officers, along with food remains and construction debris, will form the basis for a host of new exhibits and interpretations. In a way, those killed in the massacre and the others who lived in the fort will be brought back to life again and again, not only as innocent victims, but as real people who have stories to tell to the thousands who visit each year.

Further Reading

Calver, William Louis, and Reginald Pelham Bolton. 1950. *History Written with Pick and Shovel*. New York: The New-York Historical Society.

Cooper, James Fenimore. [1826] 1980. *The Last of the Mohicans*. New York: Penguin Books.

Cuneo, John R. 1988. *Robert Rogers of the Rangers*. Ticonderoga, N.Y.: Fort Ticonderoga Museum.

Gifford, Stanley M. 1955. *Fort Wm. Henry—A History*. Lake George, N.Y.: Fort William Henry.

Kochan, James L. (ed.). 1993. Joseph Frye's Journal and Map of the Siege of Fort William Henry, 1757. *The Bulletin of the Fort Ticonderoga Museum* 15 (5):339–61.

Liston, Maria A., and Brenda J. Baker. 1994. Military Burials at Fort William Henry. In *Military Sites of the Hudson River, Lake George, and Lake Champlain Corridor*, edited by David R. Starbuck, 11–16. Queensbury, N.Y.: Adirondack Community College.

———. 1995. Reconstructing the Massacre at Fort William Henry, New York. *International Journal of Osteoarchaeology* 6:28–41.

Lossing, Benson J. 1851. *The Pictorial Field-Book of the Revolution*. 2 vols. New York: Harper & Brothers.

Magee, James A. 1965. A Brief Outline of the Military Events which Took Place at Lake George during the Colonial and Revolutionary Period. Manuscript on file, Fort William Henry, Lake George, N.Y.

Starbuck, David R. 1991. A Retrospective on Archaeology at Fort William Henry, 1952–1993: Retelling the Tale of *The Last of the Mohicans*. *Northeast Historical Archaeology* 20:8–26.

———. 1993. Anatomy of a Massacre. *Archaeology* 46 (6):42–46.

Steegmann, A. T., Jr., and P. A. Haseley. 1988. Stature Variation in the British American Colonies: French and Indian War Records, 1755–1763. *American Journal of Physical Anthropology* 75:413–21.

Steele, Ian K. 1990. *Betrayals: Fort William Henry & the "Massacre"*. New York: Oxford University Press.

Thwaites, Reuben Gold, (ed.). 1896–1901. *The Jesuit Relations and Allied Documents: Travels and Explorations of the Jesuit Missionaries in New France. 1610–1791.* 73 vols. Cleveland: The Burrows Brothers Co.

Todish, Timothy J. 1988. *America's First First World War: The French & Indian War. 1754–1763.* Ogden, Utah: Eagle's View Publishing Company.

Chapter 5

After the Massacre:
The Village of Lake George

*T*HE MODERN VILLAGE of Lake George, positioned at the south end of the lake, is one of the prettiest resort communities in America. Hundreds of thousands of tourists visit each summer, drawn by this narrow band of clear water, which sweeps north for thirty-two miles, the dense evergreens on the heights at the south end of the village, and the proximity of the Adirondack Mountains on the north and west. Yet underneath and surrounding the modern houses there are traces of the French, British, and provincial camps that blanketed this town throughout the military campaigns in the second half of the eighteenth century. While Fort William Henry has always received the most attention from scholars and the general public, this should not take away from the importance of the many other archeological sites in the village. Few places in America have such a rich variety of military sites, including four forts, one battlefield, innumerable hut sites and siege camps, and many sunken bateaux just offshore.

But even before the soldiers arrived, Native Americans had left numerous campsites around the shores of Lake George, and Early Archaic (ca. 7000 to 6000 B.C.) and Late Archaic sites (ca. 4000 to 1000 B.C.) are especially common. The people who lived from the southern end of Lake Champlain down to the Catskills and east into the Berkshires at the beginning of the historical period were the Mohican, and approximately three to five thousand of them lived either here or in the eastern Adirondacks. While they did not die off, they became increasingly marginalized as other peoples moved into the region. The first European to reach the foot of Lake George was the French Jesuit and missionary, Father Isaac Jogues, who arrived around 1646 and gave the name "Lac du Saint Sacrement" to this body of water. Jogues claimed the waterway for France, but much later, in September of 1755, Major General (Sir) William Johnson claimed the lake for the British and renamed it "Lake George" after King George II.

The stage was thus set for conflict, and French and British forces clashed on September 8 of that year in what became known as the "Battle of Lake

George" (figure 1-2). About fifteen hundred soldiers were on each side, and the fighting occurred on the heights at the south end of the lake (within what is now Lake George Battlefield Park). The day-long battle actually consisted of three separate engagements, but at the conclusion, Johnson and his Mohawk allies had defeated the French and Native American force led by Baron Dieskau. However, the British suffered significant losses of their own, and during the first part of the Battle of Lake George, now called the "Early Morning Scout," King Hendrick, chief of the Mohawks, was killed, as was Colonel Ephriam Williams, leader of the Massachusetts troops. Several miles south of the village of Lake George, a monument honoring Colonel Williams still stands a few hundred feet east of Route 9, down in the ravine where he was killed. Williams had come here from Deerfield, Massachusetts; his will provided for the founding of Williams College.

The main part of the Battle of Lake George occurred when Dieskau's army attacked Johnson's camp overlooking the south end of Lake George, and the French and Native Americans were pushed back. Later, during the third part of the battle, colonial reinforcements coming along the military road from Fort Edward surrounded and surprised a party of French and Native Americans about two miles south of Lake George Village. They fired upon and killed as many as two hundred of them. In perhaps the most memorable event of the engagement, the provincials threw the bodies of their victims into an adjacent pond, where the water was stained red for weeks afterward. This body of water has been known ever since as Bloody Pond, a

FIG. 5-2. "Bloody Pond." However, this is the modern pond created by the Town of Lake George on the east side of Route 9 (October 1997). The original "Bloody Pond" was located further to the east.

fitting name certainly, yet the pond that presently lies on the eastern side of Route 9 was created in recent times by the Town of Lake George and is one hundred feet or more west of the historical site (figures 5-1 and 5-2). There is a modest stream to the east that most likely was the original site of the ambush; "Bloody Pond" was probably a pool created as the stream flowed through a large depression.

Newspaper accounts describe skeletons that were found there early in the twentieth century, but I have generally resisted the urging by others to conduct an excavation to verify whether this is, in fact, the spot. In effect, we would be digging in an area where native skeletons are known to be buried, and this would certainly be unwise, even if not necessarily illegal. It also would be pointless to begin because New York State law as it pertains to the remains of Native Americans requires that we would have to stop immediately if any human remains were found. While forensic information obtained by studying French victims of the slaughter would be useful, the possibility that native remains might be buried alongside them means we probably would not be allowed to finish what we had started.

Later in September of 1755, Johnson ordered his chief engineer, Captain William Eyre, to construct Fort William Henry, the first log fort at the southern end of Lake George. This fort, as we know, was intended to keep

French forces from expanding south and to guard the portage between Lake George and the Hudson River from French attack. The British had now established a foothold in land claimed by France, and this escalation of the British presence in the region led, two years later, to the French and Native American attack upon Fort William Henry and the subsequent massacre. While waging the 1757 siege against the fort, Montcalm's forces created an extensive camp within what is now the village of Lake George, near the Lake George High School, and the French artillery shelled the British into submission. To do this, the French dug an 890-yard-long entrenchment running toward the fort in order to move their guns closer. With the fort burned, the French returned to Fort Carillon and Canada. The British chose during subsequent campaigns never to rebuild on the same spot, and Fort William Henry vanished from sight until the excavations of the 1950s.

In retaliation for the attack, General James Abercromby created an extensive camp nearby in June and July 1758 as he gathered an army of fifteen to sixteen thousand British regulars and American provincials to attack Fort Carillon. From this stopping-off point, soldiers who had come up the Hudson River from Albany to Fort Edward, and then portaged to Lake George, now left Lake George on July 5 in hundreds of bateaux and whale boats and traveled north to assail Fort Carillon. Their zeal was short-lived, however, and on July 8 their attack upon the French lines at Carillon ended in disaster as great numbers of the Scottish Black Watch and others were killed. The British force had been far superior in size; Abercromby's utter incompetence —he threw his men against a well-entrenched position—had caused their defeat. The survivors who returned to Lake George retrenched, but also began preparations for future campaigns against the French.

Fort Gage

One of the first steps the British took toward consolidating their forward position was to construct Fort Gage in July 1758. This was a small fort located on high ground about a mile south of where Fort William Henry had been. It overlooked the military road running toward Fort Edward, and the construction was carried out by Connecticut troops, provincial light infantry from Abercromby's army. This outpost was occupied briefly that year, and then it was probably abandoned, although some use during the revolution is certainly possible.

The remains of Fort Gage survived amazingly intact until 1975 when developers proposed the construction of a Ramada Inn in this location. In the nightmare that followed, business and preservation interests clashed, and the site was destroyed forever. The Inn was at first designed to contain over one hundred rooms, making the proposed development subject to the restrictions of the Adirondack Park Agency (APA). The APA asked the New

FIG. 5-3. Two views of archeologists working at the site of Fort Gage in May 1975. Courtesy of Paul Huey and the Bureau of Historic Sites, New York State Office of Parks, Recreation and Historic Preservation.

York State Bureau of Historic Sites to determine whether Fort Gage was still intact, which it was, so the developer subsequently down-sized the motel to ninety-nine units and started bulldozing.

Archeologists across New York State were furious at this deliberate destruction of a major historical site, while the developers felt that they had been unfairly slowed down and their costs were mounting because of delays. The only possible compromise was for Lois Feister and Paul Huey of the

FIG. 5-4. Logs discovered in trench 2 during the 1975 excavation of Fort Gage. These horizontal timbers were buried in the bottom of a moat and apparently served to brace vertical posts. Courtesy of Paul Huey and the Bureau of Historic Sites, New York State Office of Parks, Recreation and Historic Preservation.

FIG. 5-5. A tin plate discovered in pit 6 at the site of Fort Gage. The scale is marked in inches. Courtesy of Paul Huey and the Bureau of Historic Sites, New York State Office of Parks, Recreation and Historic Preservation.

New York State Bureau of Historic Sites, aided by the Auringer-Seelye chapter of the New York State Archaeological Association and the Lake George Institute of History, Art and Science, to conduct a brief salvage excavation at Fort Gage (figure 5-3). Huey and Feister visited the site once before, in 1972, at which time they saw well-preserved earthworks and the northwest bastion of the fort. They had even discovered a moat in the woods that circled around the ruins of the fort. But after the 1975 dig was over, all remains of the fort were razed during the earth-grading and construction of the Inn.

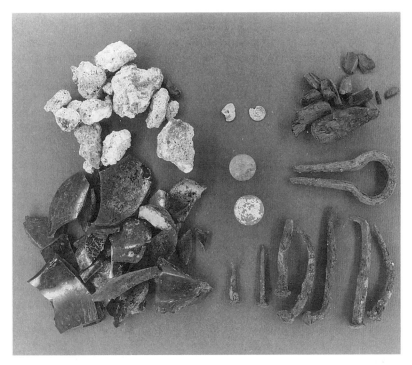

FIG. 5-6. Some of the artifacts found in feature 3 at the site of Fort Gage, including green bottle fragments, lime mortar fragments, wood, hand-wrought nails, and a Jew's harp. Courtesy of Paul Huey and the Bureau of Historic Sites, New York State Office of Parks, Recreation and Historic Preservation.

The archeological results, especially given the short duration of the dig, were spectacular, but this makes the destruction of Fort Gage that much more disturbing. Feister and Huey excavated a variety of features, including the south moat from the fort (figure 5-4), hearths, the breastwork, lime kilns, and even the foundation stones from a probable blockhouse that stood within the fort. They also found an impressive range of artifacts, including a great variety of food remains, musket balls, gunflints, melted lead sprue, a tin-plated serving dish, canteen fragments, dark green bottle glass, a pewter spoon handle, clay tobacco pipes, buttons, and even a Jew's harp (see figures 5-5, 5-6, 5-7, 5-8 and 5-9).

The problems that led to the loss of this site *probably* would not occur today because more recent preservation laws now provide for the identification of such sites well in advance, and a site of this magnitude would either be preserved completely, or the project would not be allowed to proceed unless adequate funding and time were provided to the archeologists. Nevertheless, the site of Fort Gage has now been lost, and the archeologists had enough time to learn only a fraction of what the site had to offer.

This grim story of archeological loss continues, because the vicinity of Fort Gage has now become the most severely looted part of Lake George. I am contacted once or twice each year with new reports of diggers with metal detectors ranging through the woods near Fort Gage. Outside the fort proper there were extensive military camps running north on the high

FIG. 5-7. A closeup of the Jew's harp. Courtesy of Paul Huey and the Bureau of Historic Sites, New York State Office of Parks, Recreation and Historic Preservation.

FIG. 5-8. The flat top of a
canteen with the neck still
attached, found in pit 21 at
Fort Gage. Courtesy of Paul
Huey and the Bureau of Historic
Sites, New York State Office of
Parks, Recreation and Historic
Preservation.

ground overlooking Lake George, and most of this land is privately owned.
The amount of looting that is being done, in most cases without permission
from property owners, guarantees that a major portion of Lake George Village will not be available for serious archeological research in the years to
come.

In Lake George, too often the looter or the developer has won the battle
with the archeologist, and unless there is a loud public outcry, one of the
most historic eighteenth-century communities in America will soon have
nothing left but modern motels and gift shops.

FIG. 5-9. A plain, hollow,
two-piece button found in
pit N10W40 at the site of
Fort Gage. Courtesy of Paul
Huey and the Bureau of Historic
Sites, New York State Office of
Parks, Recreation and Historic
Preservation.

Fort William

In the same year that Fort Gage was built, another, still smaller fort was
raised a few miles south of Lake George, very close to the strip of factory
outlet stores that is known as the Million Dollar Half Mile. This fort, sometimes called Fort William, but also known as "Three-Mile-Post," was one of
the stockaded posts that General Amherst constructed every three or four
miles along the military road between Fort Edward and Lake George. Completed on June 21, 1759, Fort William contained at least one cannon, but the
site was abandoned on July 20. It thus represents a very thin slice of time, the
sort of site that we archeologists dearly love to find because we don't have to
worry about disturbances from later occupations.

Fort William is now heavily overgrown with trees, but there are still signs
of the entrenchment here, chiefly some mounding of earth, coupled with de-

pressions. Over the last several years, treasure hunters have begun digging into the site, and developers have proposed expansions of the factory outlet stores and the access roads around them. Fort William may be lost before research is ever conducted there.

Fort George

In 1759, the year after Abercromby's disastrous defeat outside Fort Carillon, it was by no means certain that there would ever be a victory over the French. But that July, General Jeffery Amherst authorized construction of a new fort on the high ground overlooking the south end of Lake George (figure 5-10). Colonel James Montresor of The Royal Engineers began work on the pentagonal-shaped fort (figure 5-11), which the British named Fort George after King George II. We know from historical sources that only the southwest bastion of this stone fort was ever completed, but nevertheless, a wooden stockade of three bastions was constructed to the north, along with barracks, hospitals, storehouses, and other buildings. Covering many acres, Fort George was, of course, intended to replace Fort William Henry—to be the principal new base from which to attack the French.

FIG. 5-10. View of the south end of Lake George from the heights in Lake George Battlefield Park (October 1997).

A. Fort shewing what was finished 1. Officers Barracks 2. Soldiers Barracks 3. Powder Magazine B. Stockaded Fort erected to serve during the time the other was Building   Guard Room   the Kitchin   6 6 Saw houses 7. Saw Mill in the Swamp to the south westward.

Scale 200 Feet to an Inch.

PART OF LAKE GEORGE

PLAN
of
PART OF FORT GEORGE,
with the Barracks &c
Erected in the Year 1759.

Situated Lat. 43. 30. Long 73. 30

FIG. 5-11. "Plan of Part of Fort George, with the Barracks &c. Erected in the Year 1759." Courtesy of Fort William Henry Corporation.

While Montresor was erecting Fort George, Amherst assembled a new army of about eleven thousand British and provincial soldiers; they departed that July to attack Carillon. This time, the small French garrison blew up the powder magazine (and thus the fort) and retreated to Canada. Given the success of this mission, the British renamed the captured French fort Ticonderoga; it remained in British hands until 1775. During the same campaign, Amherst also captured Fort St. Frederic from the French and began constructing the English fort at Crown Point, which became the northernmost point of British expansion.

Given the British victory and the creation of new bases in the north, Amherst stopped the construction of Fort George, but a small British garrison remained there throughout the 1760s and until the next war. In May 1775 American forces under Captain Bernard Romans captured Fort George in one of the easier American victories of the war: the British garrison had been reduced to a solitary man, a Captain John Nordberg. That July, General Philip Schuyler went to Fort George, established regulations for the American soldiers, and built vessels on Lake George. Later, extensive smallpox hospitals were constructed at Fort George, and in 1776 this had become the largest concentration of smallpox hospitals and patients in America. Between two and three thousand soldiers were sent here, many of whom had contracted smallpox during the disastrous American invasion of Canada at the end of 1775.

The following year, in July 1777, the patriots stationed at Fort George and their leader, Major Christopher Yates, were threatened by attack from British forces under General John Burgoyne. Their response was to burn Fort George and retreat to Fort Edward, after which the British garrisoned Fort George with two companies of men. Fort George thus became one of the necessary supply points that linked Burgoyne with Canada, but his defeat in October caused the fort to revert to the Americans.

The fort was to change hands yet again in October of 1780 when Captain Thomas Sill and a small group of Vermonters who held Fort George came under attack by a British raiding party under Major Christopher Carleton. The Vermonters were forced to surrender, and Carleton burned the fort. That ended the use of Fort George as a military base, and for much of the time since then, the grounds of the fort and its outlying building sites have been lightly forested. Fort George has never been built upon since then, and the New York State Department of Environmental Conservation (DEC) now manages the remains of the fort within its Lake George Battlefield Park, a pleasant campground and picnic area. Unfortunately, the fort is under

FIG. 5-12. The one surviving corner bastion of Fort George. Its appearance reflects the restoration work done here in the 1950s (October 1997).

FIG. 5-13. A 1932 historical marker denoting one of the hospitals in Lake George Battlefield Park (October 1997). This is on the edge of a large depression, but we do not know what type of building once stood here.

constant attack from treasure hunters, and it is an especially vulnerable site because the soil is very thin on the hilltop—the whole eighteenth-century military occupation is contained within the first foot or so of soil.

In the summer of 1994, with permission from the DEC, I directed a surface inventory and topographic mapping project that documented portions of Fort George. We first plotted features in between the ruins of the fort and a foundation that the DEC had long ago identified as a hospital (figures 5-12 and 5-13). We mapped the southwest bastion of the fort, which is still about fifteen to twenty feet high, and several scatters of foundation stones, but this was just the beginning. In the future, we would like to complete the huge task of surface mapping the entire Battlefield Park and all of its visible foundations, depressions, and earthworks.

Perhaps, with the mapping done, we can seriously discuss with the DEC how best to use archeology within the park in order to begin identifying its many buried features. This is a truly spectacular site, most likely the most unspoiled major British site of the French and Indian War, and the only British site on Lake George that spanned the revolution as well. With such a high level of integrity, and a much longer history than most frontier military outposts, New York State wants to ensure that Fort George receives the most careful treatment possible.

Later Developments

After the colonial wars ended in Lake George, settlers rapidly moved into the region, and even the earliest tourists often came specifically to see the remains of one or more of the old fort sites. Portions of Fort George, in particular, continued to be visible into the nineteenth century, and travelers often stayed in its remaining buildings. Among the many visitors were General George Washington in 1783, James Madison and Thomas Jefferson in 1791, and Benjamin Silliman in 1819. Still, with the colonial wars over, Fort George had become unnecessary, and its structures were gradually robbed of building materials and thus it vanished.

The tourism industry later in the nineteenth century and throughout the twentieth century has often paid little attention to the military history of the town, although there are a modest number of historical markers and monuments to the colonial wars (figures 5-14 and 5-15). It is unfortunate that for many visitors Lake George is simply a pretty little town at the end of a beautiful body of water, with souvenir shops, motels, restaurants, and the recreated Fort William Henry in the middle. Much more should be done to make the colonial wars become the centerpiece of modern tourism here. After all, only one or two other communities in America have a military past as rich as that of Lake George.

Further Reading

Bellico, Russell. 1996. Historical Proposal for Fort George. *The Chronicle* 17 (660): 1, 6.

Bellico, Russell P., Bob Benway, Tim Cordell, John Farrell, Scott Padeni, and Joseph W. Zarzynski. 1996. Colonial Wars of Lake George Self-Guided Tour. Brochure prepared by Bateaux Below, Inc.

De Angelo, Gordon C. 1995. Interim Report: Fort George. Surface Inventory and Topographic Mapping, Adirondack Community College 1994 Field School. Privately printed.

Feister, Lois M., and Paul R. Huey. 1985. Archaeological Testing at Fort Gage, a Provincial Redoubt of 1758 at Lake George, New York. *The Bulletin and Journal of Archaeology for New York State* 90:40–59.

Lake George Chamber of Commerce. n.d. Historical Sites and State Markers in the Lake George Region, Warren County, N.Y. Brochure prepared by the Lake George Chamber of Commerce and funded by the Warren County Tourism Department.

Padeni, Scott A. 1994. A Review of Potential Sites for the Archaeological Study of Military Life at Lake George's Southern End during the French and Indian War and American Revolution. Manuscript on file at Empire State College.

Steele, Ian K. 1990. *Betrayals: Fort William Henry & the "Massacre."* New York: Oxford University Press.

Zaboly, Gary S. 1993. A Royal Artillery Officer with Amherst: The Journal of Captain-Lieutenant Henry Skinner 1 May–28 July 1759. *The Bulletin of the Fort Ticonderoga Museum* 15 (5): 363–88.

FIG. 5-14. (Top left.) The 1903 monument to the Battle of Lake George located within Lake George Battlefield Park (October 1997). The figures portrayed on the monument are General William Johnson and King Hendrick of the Mohawks.

FIG. 5-15. (Top right.) The 1921 Indian Monument located in Lake George Battlefield Park (October 1997). A life-sized Native American, cast from bronze, is cupping his hand to drink water from a spring.

Chapter 6

The Most Intact Revolutionary War Site in America: Mount Independence

*M*ount Independence in Orwell, Vermont, is the largest military fortification in the North built specifically for the American Revolution. Even today "the Mount" is a formidable peninsula as it thrusts its way into Lake Champlain, with cliffs dropping fifty to one hundred feet to the lake below, and with easy access only at its southern end (figure 6-1). I have never seen another military site, short of Masada in the State of Israel, so well positioned to repel attackers. Its great historical significance derives from events in October of 1776 when between twelve and thirteen thousand Continental soldiers and militia manned the sites of Fort Ticonderoga and Mount Independence in order to prevent a British fleet from passing south on Lake Champlain. The Americans came from the colonies of New Hampshire, Massachusetts, Connecticut, New Jersey, and Pennsylvania, and many had no prior military experience. Some had taken part in the ill-fated invasion of Canada at the end of 1775 and witnessed the death of their leader, Richard Montgomery, on the outskirts of Quebec City.

In a bold move to prevent an attack from Canada, on the orders of General Philip Schuyler, American soldiers in mid-1776 reoccupied the former French site of Fort Carillon—now called Ticonderoga—on the New York side of the lake. They then created a three-hundred-acre encampment on a wooded mountaintop on the Vermont shore. The lake is only a quarter-mile wide at this point, and an American army in control of both sides of the lake could easily prevent a British fleet from passing through the channel (figure 6-2). The soldiers received news of the Declaration of Independence on July 18, 1776, and when the text was read to the soldiers on July 28, they proudly christened their rocky, hilltop fortress "Mount Independence" and continued to prepare for the British attack.

Most of the Continental soldiers had enlisted for one year, but state militia might sign up for any length of time, often just two or three months (earning them the nickname of "three months men"). This resulted in con-

FIG. 6-1. Map of Mount Independence and Fort Ticonderoga prepared for Major General St. Clair's court martial proceedings in 1778. "X" represents a floating bridge across Lake Champlain, "3" is the star-shaped fort on Mount Independence, "A" is Fort Ticonderoga, and "Y," "Z," and "6" all represent batteries on Mount Independence. Mount Defiance, while not identified here, is located in the left-center of the drawing. *Collections of the New-York Historical Society for the Year 1880.*

FIG. 6-2. The northern end of the Horseshoe Battery on Mount Independence. Fort Ticonderoga is located in the center on the far side of Lake Champlain.

stant changes in troop strength as regiments came and went. Regional differences were often a problem, and only a common hatred for British authority kept the garrison united. Soldiers from Pennsylvania had little use for those from the New England colonies, and fights were common. A ghoulish example of this type of conflict was reported by Ebenezer Elmer in February 1777: soldiers from the 3rd New Jersey Regiment had dug graves for two of their deceased comrades, but once the holes were open, they had to fight off soldiers from Pennsylvania who attempted to place their own dead in the graves.

Soldiers were crowded into rows of thin tents and small log cabins; officers lived in rough plank houses, sometimes with windows. A soldier's day began when a cannon was fired at headquarters, and then the camp drums beat reveille. The soldiers rose and went to their alarm posts, after which they had breakfast, went to the parade ground, and received their assignments for the day. Those might consist of standing at a guard post or going with a scouting party to watch for enemy movements—or, just as often, cutting firewood, drilling, or repairing equipment.

When scheduled to appear on the parade ground, soldiers were to be clean and freshly shaved, with their hair tied and well powdered, and they were instructed to save fat and grease in order to groom their hair. The men were ordered to place their latrines on the edges of cliffs, and the American commander of the winter garrison, Colonel Anthony Wayne, announced that if his soldiers committed any "nastiness" elsewhere in the camp, they "shall upon sight receive 40 lashes well laid on." History does not record how many wives, camp followers, or children lived on Mount Independence, but Wayne's daily orderly book insisted that "Any Woman . . . who shall refuse to wash for the Men, shall be immediately drumm'd out of the Regt, as they are [here] . . . to keep them clean and decent."

This rather spartan existence came to a head on October 28, 1776, when the two armies sighted each other. Fresh from a victory over Benedict Arnold and a fledgling American navy at the Battle of Valcour Island on October 11, the British hoped to push through to Albany before the onset of winter, effectively cutting the northern colonies in two. On October 28 the Governor-General of Canada, Sir Guy Carleton, sailed a fleet of ships with eight thousand British soldiers to within three miles of Mount Independence and Fort Ticonderoga. But as they approached the heavily armed fortresses, the British witnessed the thousands of American troops, the great numbers of cannons and howitzers, flags flying on both shores, and realized that a prolonged siege would be impossible. Because it was so late in the year, Carleton was forced to return to Canada for the winter. It had been an easy American victory, and the defense of Mount Independence and Fort Ticonderoga delayed the British advance for nearly a year. The British effort to divide the northern colonies had stalled.

Many of the American soldiers went home to their farms in November and December of 1776. Of the fewer than three thousand who remained in barracks through the winter, as many as seven or eight froze to death each night. During October a footbridge was constructed across Lake Champlain, connecting the two forts, but in December a violent wind destroyed the bridge, and then the lake froze over. One soldier sent a letter home to Pennsylvania on December 4 complaining that no more than nine hundred pairs of shoes had been received by the men, such that "one-third at least of the poor Wretches is now barefoot, and in this Condition obliged to do Duty." Even before winter set in, the chief American engineer, Colonel Jeduthan Baldwin, expressed his disgust about life on Mount Independence when he wrote in his daily journal, "I am heartily tired of this Retreating, Raged, Starved, lousey, thevish, Pockey Army in this unhealthy Country." Baldwin had good reason to be upset for some of his own men had just stolen much of his clothing!

With the arrival of spring, a newly formed army of eight thousand British and German soldiers left Canada under the command of General John Burgoyne. Burgoyne's forces were well equipped with cannons in order to lay siege to Mount Independence and Ticonderoga, which were considered to be the only serious obstacles between Canada and Albany. The diminished American garrison was ill-prepared to withstand the onslaught. At the re-

★ Fort Ticonderoga

I have visited Fort Ticonderoga almost every year of my life; it is the favorite military site of countless reenactors and others. The history of the battles at Ticonderoga is deservedly famous, and modern-day interpreters love to tell the story of how three times the fort was attacked and held, and three times it was attacked and fell. The original fort was constructed by the Marquis de Lotbiniere, a Canadian, in 1755, and in addition to its barracks it contained such things as a cistern (still in use today), a bakery, a powder magazine, stables, and storerooms. The fort proper held only a small garrison, and most of the troops were in tents in the open. Since most fighting was done in the summer, many of the French troops then moved back to Canada for the winter. Little archeology has been done here in order to learn more about the daily lives of the soldiers, but life here was no doubt challenging, given the frequency with which the fort came under attack.

The ruins of the fort were purchased by William Ferris Pell in 1820, and the Pell family has owned and interpreted this site ever since. The fort's restoration was carried out in the early twentieth cen-

A marker indicating "The French Lines" alongside the tour road at Fort Ticonderoga.

A corner of the reconstructed Fort Ticonderoga, with a Canadian flag flying over it.

A marker commemorating the actions of "The Black Watch" who fell at Ticonderoga on July 8, 1758, during Abercromby's disastrous attack.

A marker on the tour road at Fort Ticonderoga, honoring General Henry Knox and the Americans who removed the cannons from the fort in the winter of 1775–1776 and transported them to Cambridge, Massachusetts, to end the siege of Boston.

tury by Stephen H. P. Pell, and President Taft was present when Stephen Pell first opened part of the fort to the public in 1909. Many photographs and postcards have survived that show the fort before the restoration, and millions of visitors have passed through the gate since then. The architect in charge of the restoration was Alfred C. Bossom, and his workmen dug around the original foundations and saved the artifacts they found. The human bones they encountered were reinterred in the military burying ground at the fort.

Fort Ticonderoga holds attractions of interest for every visitor. The fort's collections of original paintings, maps, diaries, weapons, powder horns, drums, and even uniforms are most impressive, and the recently created Thompson-Pell Research Center is a first-class, modern storage facility available to serious scholars for research. However, what impresses many visitors the most is probably the fort's superb fife and drum corps, and the cannon and mortar demonstrations.

Some of the earthworks surviving from the French Lines at Ticonderoga.

The grounds of Fort Ticonderoga contain a wealth of archeological sites, and any visitor who drives down the long entrance road can read the signs and monuments along the way that identify some of these. Huts and tent sites were manned successively by French, British, and then American soldiers, and innumerable earthworks and depressions still bear testimony to the presence of the encampments. Though artifact collectors have sometimes invaded these grounds with metal detectors, the fort has been extremely vigilant—and quite successful—in protecting its sites and prosecuting such looters. After all, Fort Ticonderoga has fought to maintain the integrity of its grounds for 180 years, and the fort today has the distinction of owning the best-preserved French sites in the United States, along with extensive British and provincial remains as well.

A historic marker at Fort Ticonderoga indicating the location of "Hut Sites" erected there by American forces during the Revolution.

Further Reading

Bossom, Alfred C. 1958. The Restoration of Fort Ticonderoga. *The Bulletin of the Fort Ticonderoga Museum* 10 (2): 124–31.

Campbell, Lt. Col. J. Duncan. 1958. Investigations at the French Village 1957. *The Bulletin of the Fort Ticonderoga Museum* 10 (2): 143–55.

Coolidge, Guy Omeron. [1938] 1979. *The French Occupation of the Champlain Valley from 1609 to 1759.* Harrison, N.Y.: Harbor Hill Books.

Hamilton, Edward P. 1964. *Fort Ticonderoga.* Boston and Toronto: Little, Brown and Co.

Pell, Stephen H. P. [1935] 1990. *Fort Ticonderoga: A Short History.* Ticonderoga, N.Y.: Fort Ticonderoga Museum.

quest of the American command, Colonel Baldwin used the winter and spring of 1777 to construct a more permanent floating bridge, 1,600 feet long, across Lake Champlain, as well as a 250-foot-long general hospital to handle the anticipated casualties. Congress did send a new commander to the Mount, General Arthur St. Clair, but few additional troops, and the situation became increasingly hopeless.

In early July, British and German troops landed on the New York and Vermont shores of Lake Champlain and began to encircle the two forts. At the last moment, St. Clair ordered his men to leave their positions, and Fort Ticonderoga was abandoned, followed by Mount Independence. The British advance guard entered Fort Ticonderoga and then charged across the bridge to the Vermont shore. Four Americans had been left behind at Mount Independence, in the Horseshoe Battery overlooking the bridge, and they had orders to fire a cannon upon the British when they started across. Had they obeyed their instructions, the outcome might have been truly heroic. Instead they broke into some of the supplies abandoned by their fleeing comrades, and as the British officer Thomas Anburey later reported, "we found them dead drunk by a cask of Madeira." The British easily swept after the retreating Americans, and the next day the British advance guard fiercely clashed with the American rear guard in Hubbardton, Vermont. Fortunately, many of the Americans were able to escape and lived to fight again in the major battles at Bennington and Saratoga (see the box "The Hubbardton Battlefield").

Burgoyne left a small garrison on Mount Independence to prevent the Americans from returning, but when news of his subsequent defeat at Saratoga reached them that November, the last German and British soldiers burned hundreds of buildings and then retreated to Canada. A superb map drawn by Michel Capitaine du Chesnoy, the marquis de Lafayette's cartographer, shows many of the buildings atop Mount Independence in October 1777, just before the soldiers departed, and even indicates how many German soldiers were stationed in each part of the Mount.

With the war now over in the northern colonies, Mount Independence was quickly forgotten, even by many historians who increasingly thought of the Mount as merely an outlier of Fort Ticonderoga, rather than as a major site in its own right. In the years that followed, most of Mount Independence was used for pasturage, while portions of it grew over with forest. The integrity of the site was clearly evident, however, for collapsed fireplaces and chimneys, and the remains of houses, barracks, blockhouses, shops, lookout posts, and artillery batteries were visible everywhere atop the wooded promontory. Mount Independence had become an unusually pristine archeological site.

Archeological Research

In the late 1960s, three Middlebury College students, Chester Bowie, David Robinson, and Erik Borg, spent their summers camped on Mount Independence and prepared a detailed surface map and descriptions of 142 possible archeological sites. Their work was done under the auspices of a newly formed group of local history enthusiasts who called themselves the Mount Independence Associates, and while they conducted no excavations, the thorough research by these Middlebury students was unquestionably the beginning of modern research efforts on the Mount.

However, it was not until 1975, during the fervor of the United States Bicentennial, that the state of Vermont decided to build a visitors' center at the southwest corner of the Mount that they had recently acquired. On a mounded rock pile at the approximate center of this proposed facility, one of the members of the Mount Independence Associates, William Murphy, led a small group of students and avocational archeologists as they established a nine-by-nine-foot grid. Over two weeks in July of 1975, the team troweled shallow pits and found rosehead nails, a few pieces of pottery, and a musket ball. Based on these few items, the state decided to construct the center in a different location. Unfortunately, nothing was built, chiefly because of lack of funding.

Eleven years later Murphy convinced me and a group of my diggers from the Saratoga Battlefield to visit the Mount. Though I had been born within a few miles of there, I had never even heard of Mount Independence, let alone walked its trails. I had never imagined that Vermont had a major military site, yet here was an immense, superbly well-preserved site that told a wonderful story of heroism, struggle, and failure. Right away, I knew that I had to find a way to do archeology at the Mount, partly because the site was so important to Vermonters and to historians around the country, but also because it had lain unheralded for too long. It was time to wake up Vermonters to this wonderful historical resource, and archeology would be a great way to do it. Attempts to keep the site a secret had done nothing to keep out artifact collectors—many of whom had dug there repeatedly—instead it was the history-conscious public that was being denied the opportunity to view and appreciate this site.

When I phoned Giovanna Peebles, the Vermont State Archeologist, a few days later, I was amazed to learn that a program entitled "Heritage '91," just approved by the state of Vermont, would allow for historical and archeological research as a prelude to the construction of the first visitors' center on the Mount. I directed the first archeological field school at Mount Independence in 1989, and after three years of mapping and digging, we succeeded in discovering the remains of nearly thirty cabins and houses, five

★ The Hubbardton Battlefield

The only battlefield located in the State of Vermont is in East Hubbardton, just north of Castleton, where American forces retreating from Mount Independence fought a rear guard action against over one thousand British and Brunswick troops led by Brig. General Simon Fraser and Major General Baron von Riedesel. In an effort to slow the British advance, about one thousand American soldiers formed lines in Hubbardton to permit the escape of the main American force, led by Arthur St. Clair. When the pursuing British troops caught up to them, it was July 7, 1777, and the American units consisted of Green Mountain Boys from Vermont, led by Colonel Seth Warner, Massachusetts militia, led by Colonel Ebenezer Francis, and the 2nd New Hampshire Continental Regiment, led by Colonel Nathan Hale.

The battle was relatively brief but fierce, with high casualties on both sides, and the outcome could easily have gone either way. The Americans established their primary position atop Monument Hill and suffered repeated attacks before they were able to disengage and follow after St. Clair's main force. Colonel Francis was mortally wounded, and many other Americans were killed or captured, but it was an American success in that the British were not able or willing to continue pursuit after the rest of St. Clair's army. Many of the Americans were, in fact, able to fight later in the Battles of Saratoga, so the sacrifices made in Hubbardton definitely accomplished their objective.

Much later, a monument was constructed at the battlefield, in 1859, in the spot where Colonel Fran-

Excavating in 1989 next to the visitors' center at the Hubbardton Battlefield.

The 1989 excavation at the Selleck Cabin site at the Hubbardton Battlefield. The visitors' center is at the top of the hill in the rear.

cis was reported to have been buried. More recently, a visitors' center was built there in 1970, and visitors are able to walk to the top of the hill believed to have been the American position. The fields and hills that comprise the battlefield are unusually beautiful, and when peering down from the hilltop, one can imagine some of the feelings of the Americans as wave after wave of British regulars came running up toward them.

The battle occurred on the farm of John Selleck and his family, who had moved there in 1775 from Connecticut. Southeast of the battlefield and at the base of Monument Hill is a cellar hole, measuring twenty-six by twenty-four feet, which is either the remains of the original Selleck cabin or of a later Selleck house that replaced it. In 1977 Beth Anne Bower excavated here for the Vermont Division for Historic Preservation and found numerous artifacts, although many were from the early nineteenth century.

I knew all of this in 1989 when I was hired to do excavations north of the visitors' center where rest rooms were about to be built. Over a period of four days, my crew and I found virtually nothing from the time of the battle, making us wonder whether this was even the right hill where the battle had been fought! We also dug three pits just west of the Selleck cabin cellar hole, hoping to find material there from the 1770s. But once again, all we found were nineteenth-century artifacts (circa 1800 to 1840). Many eighteenth-century battlefields have few surviving artifacts, perhaps because of illegal digging by collectors, but this is a case where archeology has totally failed to establish that this was even the site of a battle!

Further Reading

Bower, Beth Anne. 1978. Excavations at the Selleck Cabin Site, Hubbardton Battlefield, East Hubbardton, Vermont, Vt-RU-39. Manuscript prepared for The Division of Historic Preservation, State of Vermont.

Williams, John. 1988. *The Battle of Hubbardton*. The American Rebels Stem the Tide. Montpelier, Vt.: The Vermont Division for Historic Preservation.

FIG. 6-3. Powderhorn carved by New Hampshire soldier John Calfe while atop Mount Independence in April 1777. It is inscribed: "What I contain shall freely go to bring a haughty tyrant low." Courtesy of New Hampshire Historical Society/# 1922.3.

lookout posts, several barracks buildings, one blockhouse, a battery, a large dump, and a storehouse. For all of our archeology students and volunteers, it was an exciting time.

Among our goals was to determine the layout of an American camp *early* in the revolutionary war, before military regulations and construction methods were standardized. We wanted to know how well supplied this frontier outpost was, and how the day-to-day life of the soldiers compared to the dry official records kept in officers' orderly books. Were the men eating salt beef, salt pork, and dried vegetables, or were they eating fresh game too? Would any of the artifacts reveal that women and children were living there? And could individual soldiers be identified from artifacts found at the site, or would the thousands of soldiers seem remote and unrecognizable to visitors today?

No more than about twenty of the primary fortifications and barracks at Mount Independence had ever been drawn on maps of the 1770s, and these were major buildings and earthworks designed by military engineers such as Jeduthan Baldwin. (One of the few exceptions is the map drawn on a powderhorn by John Calfe in April 1777; see figures 6-3 and 6-4.) In contrast, we were finding the remains of cabins and lookout posts, the more modest structures built by the soldiers themselves. We focused especially on the cabins that were constructed at the southwestern corner of Mount Independence, an area that John Trumbull's map of 1776 identifies as the site of the 2nd Brigade. This cantonment was composed of regiments from New Hampshire, New York, and Massachusetts, and was commanded by Colonel James Reed of the 2nd New Hampshire Continental.

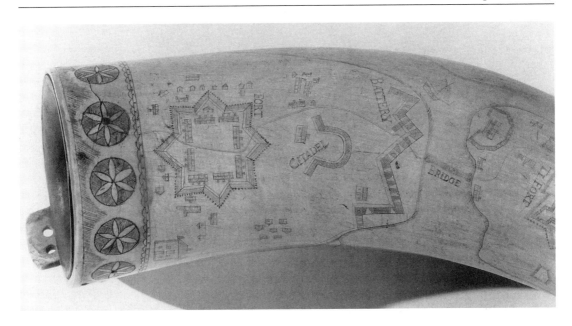

We dug small numbers of pits into these hut sites in 1989 and 1990 (figure 6-5) and found that the 2nd Brigade dwellings had been small, and most lacked windows. They probably stank from soldiers who rarely washed, and all that remains today are dozens of low earth and stone mounds, each about fifteen feet across and evenly spaced in long rows. The cabins do not appear to have had foundations, and only the stones remain from fireplaces and chimneys that have been scattered by tree roots and collectors.

FIG. 6-4. Map of Mount Independence engraved on the John Calfe Powderhorn. This shows the star-shaped fort (left), and an assortment of barracks buildings, huts, batteries, artificers' shops, and a blockhouse. Courtesy of New Hampshire Historical Society/# 1922.3.

FIG. 6-5. Students uncovering the remains of a soldiers' cabin in the Second Brigade area.

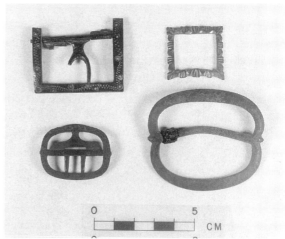

FIG. 6-6. (Top left.) Sherds from a white salt-glazed stoneware plate, with barley pattern, discovered inside a hut in the 2nd Brigade. Now reassembled, this is on display in the visitors' center at the Mount.

FIG. 6-7. (Top right.) Assorted buckles found on Mount Independence.

FIG. 6-8. (Bottom.) Pair of cuff links found in a hut site (site 77) in the 2nd Brigade area.

In the soil around each building we found large numbers of rosehead nails, glass from many wine bottles, sherds of unrefined stoneware, tin-glazed earthenware, creamware, and white salt-glazed stoneware (figure 6-6), as well as cow, sheep, and pig bones, and bones from fish caught in Lake Champlain. We discovered several regimental buttons during the cabin excavations, including ones from the British 40th and 47th Regiments and the American 5th, 12th, 22nd, and 25th Regiments. Other finds in the house dumps included musket balls, gunflints, an occasional gun part, non-military buttons, buckles (figure 6-7), and, less frequently, wine glasses and window glass. These last two artifact categories suggested that sometimes we were digging into the remains of more substantial houses that were built as officers' quarters, in several of which we found attractive sets of cuff links (figure 6-8).

Something that never failed to amuse us was the presence of so many wine bottles, and we liked to joke about how it appeared that soldiers have *always* drunk too much. But in the eighteenth century, wine was prescribed for soldiers in many situations, especially when it was cold or wet, and alcohol was believed to promote good health. So the bottles did not surprise us, and neither did the fish bones, because historical sources indicate that the men had been borrowing boats and going fishing. Because the boats were never available when needed, the leadership finally banned the use of boats in fishing.

On the western edge of the 2nd Brigade area, we discovered an extensive, shallow dump that contained artifacts that had all been burned. Small pieces of bone, wine bottles, and tin-glazed earthenware were scattered over a slope too steep to build upon. I was pretty sure that the floors of cabins, and especially fireplaces, had been swept clean and the trash dumped there. In fact, later, in the laboratory, I was actually able to fit a case bottle fragment from the dump to a second fragment from a cabin site five hundred feet away, establishing beyond question the source of the trash found in this dump. Of special interest was a Spanish silver coin that I found in the dump, a one-half real piece ("cob" money) minted before 1760. Coins were extremely rare at this outpost, where there was probably little to buy, but British, Spanish, and French coins were all legal tender in the colonies.

Elsewhere, along the eastern side of Mount Independence, our surface walk-overs and archeological testing located the remains of at least one hundred lookout posts, spread out for a distance of nearly a mile. These were on high ground, overlooking East Creek, probably manned by American soldiers as they watched for approaching British forces. We excavated just five of these small, three-sided structures and found thousands of wine bottle fragments along with musket balls and gunflints, suggesting that drinking was common among solders on duty.

In 1989 I picked Bill Murphy to head up a team that was going to expose the foundation of a blockhouse that had been occupied by British or German soldiers after they seized the site in July 1777. Its thick foundation walls formed a thirty-foot square, and in the exact center Murphy excavated a large fireplace that opened on two sides (see figures 6-9 and 6-10). Like other blockhouses of that period, this stoutly built structure would have stood two stories tall, with ports for one or more cannons. While we found no artifacts that were clearly of British or German origin inside the foundation, we did find large nails and spikes used in the building's construction,

FIG. 6-9. The remains of a fireplace exposed in the center of a blockhouse (site 105) on the White Trail (facing southwest).

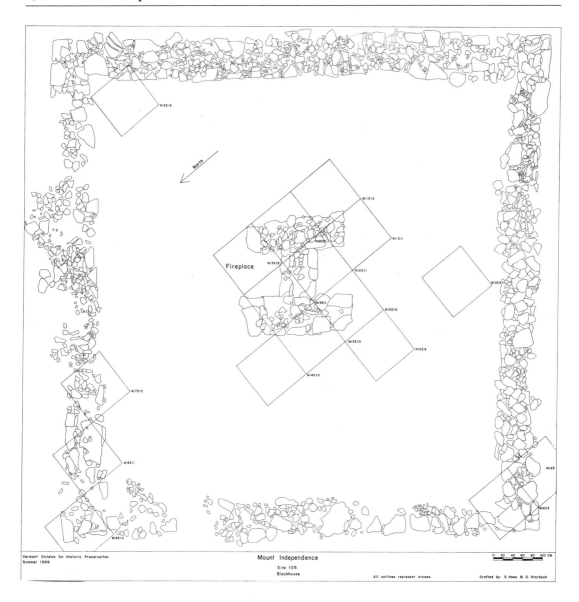

Vermont Division for Historic Preservation
Summer 1989

Mount Independence

Site 105
Blockhouse

All outlines represent stones.

0 20 40 60 80 100 CM.

Drafted by: S. Howe & D. Starbuck

FIG. 6-10. Plan view of the blockhouse in figure 6-9.

along with a lead clock or sash weight, a gunflint, and a single piece of cast-iron shot. This combination of artifacts—building materials, munitions, and few personal belongings—suggests a structure where soldiers stood on sentry duty, but where they did not actually live.

In 1992 we excavated inside and around the foundation of a possible storehouse, one of very few to have been excavated from this period. Since then, nearly ten thousand bone fragments from the dumps surrounding this building have been analyzed by one of our volunteers, Bruce Hedin, who has given us a great deal of information about butchering practices and beef and

FIG. 6-11. Prehistoric projectile points discovered inside a possible storehouse.

pork consumption. And once again, we discovered large numbers of fish bones. A curious feature of this foundation was that inside it we found four complete prehistoric projectile points, perhaps souvenirs acquired by some of the soldiers (figure 6-11).

Also in 1992, we excavated five huts and one dump within what is known as the Southern Battery on the White Trail, at the southeastern corner of the Mount (figure 6-12). The battery and its cannons had been strategically po-

FIG. 6-12. The Southern Battery on the White Trail, looking south.

FIG. 6-13. Site 122, an excavated hut in the Southern Battery.

sitioned to protect the southern flank of the Mount and the supply road from the south. The Americans constructed this just sixteen days before they were driven out by the British, after which the British occupied this area for as much as four months. We really did not know, however, which army's artifacts would be better represented there.

All of the huts in the Southern Battery had been built against a natural stone outcrop on the northern side of the battery, and in the easternmost of these huts, site 122, we found a wealth of material (figure 6-13). Right away we discovered the remains of a brick fireplace against the northern wall of the hut, but inside the foundation we recovered a truly exceptional range of artifacts: 3 musket balls, 2 lead net sinkers (figure 6-14), 7 fragments of lead sprue (from casting musket balls), 22 tin canteen fragments from two kidney-shaped canteens (figure 6-15), 1 iron pot hook, 2 metal buttons, 160 nails, 85 wine bottle fragments, 176 butchered bone fragments from cow, pig, and sheep, 3 nut shells of hickory and butternut, 169 sherds from a single slip-decorated earthenware mug, and 1 sherd of delft. Given the richness of artifacts in this hut, and its positioning at the far eastern end of a row of huts, this must have been an officer's, or senior non-commissioned officer's, quarters.

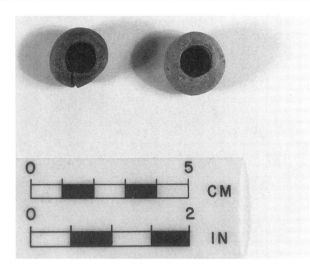

FIG. 6-14. (Top.) Lead net sinkers recovered from site 122.

FIG. 6-15. (Bottom.) Top and bottom of a kidney-shaped canteen found in site 122.

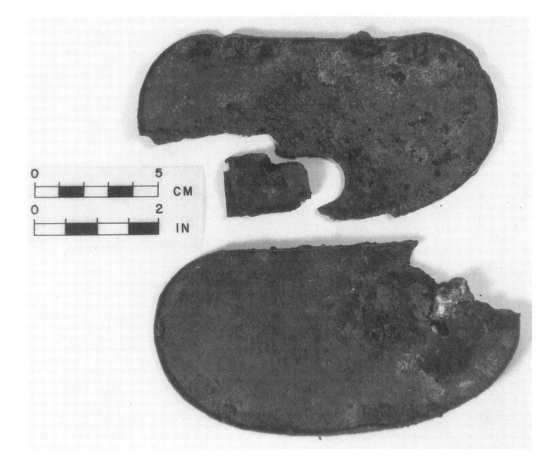

FIG. 6-16. Drawing of the
"James Hill 1777" wine bottle found in site 122. Bottle
is dark green and has in-
scribed lettering. Drawing by
Sarah Kinsella Waite.

Dark Green Bottle
with Inscribed Lettering

FIG. 6-16. Drawing of the "James Hill 1777" wine bottle found in site 122. Bottle is dark green and has inscribed lettering. Drawing by Sarah Kinsella Waite.

But the greatest find inside this hut was totally unexpected: the fragments from a nearly complete wine bottle that bore the name and date "James Hill 1777" scratched into two sides (figure 6-16). We had not noticed any of the lettering while in the field, and it wasn't until later, in the laboratory, that a thorough washing of the glass began revealing letters and sent us excitedly looking for the missing pieces. This bottle is the only clearly personalized artifact ever found at Mount Independence, but we never discovered for sure whether James Hill was the builder or the occupier of this hut, or whether he was British or American. However, one of our students systematically tracked down every available signature from every "James Hill" known to have lived on the Mount, and concluded that our James Hill was an American from Charlotte, Vermont, and I tend to agree.

Hospitals on Mount Independence

When the Northern Army attacked Quebec City at the end of 1775, General Richard Montgomery was killed, Benedict Arnold was wounded, and smallpox took a fearsome toll of both soldiers and officers. Many of the soldiers had battle injuries, and poor provisioning left many soldiers destitute. The men who subsequently retreated to Crown Point and Fort Ticonderoga in

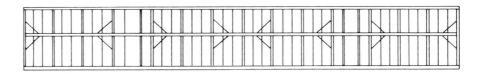

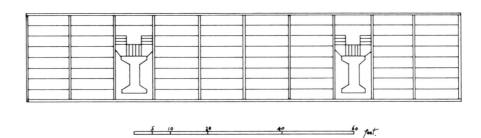

early 1776 needed intensive hospitalization, and regimental hospitals were established on Mount Independence and at Fort Ticonderoga to deal with the sick and injured. Smallpox cases, however, were considered too contagious and were shipped off to the general hospital at Fort George. We do not know how many hospitals existed on the Mount during that first year, although a set of plans for one of them has survived in the Philip J. Schuyler papers in the New York Public Library (figure 6-17). This early hospital was 120 feet long and 24 feet wide, but we never discovered its exact location. However, a letter has survived by a sick soldier who was probably residing within this hospital. In it, Matthew Kennedy, of Goffstown, New Hampshire, wrote on October 11, 1776, to his brother, Robert Kennedy:

FIG. 6-17. The end, front (or side), and floor plan "of one of the Hospitals on Mount Independence. 120 feet Long, 24 feet Wide." Redrawn from a diagram in the Philip J. Schuyler papers at the New York Public Library and dated 1776.

Loving Brother, I inform you that I am and have been in a low state of health for some time past and don't imagine I shall get well very soon. Wherefore I earnestly intreat you not to delay coming for me or if you can't come yourself. Send a man that you can confide in and a horse for me; let whoever comes; bring some butter and Indian meal with him to serve me on the way home. I can get discharged as soon as one comes for me; but am as frail at present that I could not venture home alone. P.S. There is hardly any sustenance to be had for man or horse between this place and [Fort] No. 4 so I advise you to bring some provender. Excuse the meanness of the paper.

Unfortunately, though Matthew Kennedy's family *did* travel to Mount Independence to get him, he had already died by the time they arrived.

In another reference to this early hospital, Colonel Anthony Wayne, a Pennsylvanian who commanded the winter garrison at Independence and Ticonderoga in 1776–1777, observed:

> our hospital, or rather house of carnage, beggars all description, and shocks humanity to visit. . . . no medicine or regimen on the ground suitable for the sick; no beds or straw to lay on; no covering to keep them warm, other than their own thin wretched clothing.

In the late fall of 1776, the threat of attack from Canada lessened because the British could not mount a successful siege during the winter, and the American leadership allowed many regiments to go home. Unfortunately for the two to three thousand troops who remained, warm clothing was scarce, and many men froze to death in their tents during the winter of 1776–1777. Still, health conditions on Mount Independence improved greatly in 1777: the army was smaller but better provisioned, and smallpox had almost ceased to be a problem. All the same, in early 1777, in anticipation of a British invasion from Canada during the summer, Congress authorized the establishment of a large general hospital on the Mount.

We do not know whether any previous hospital served as the model for the one about to be built on Mount Independence, although Dr. John Morgan, Director General of Hospitals for the Continental Army, prepared a set of specifications for a general hospital on November 20, 1776. In response to a query about a proposed hospital at Peekskill, New York, he wrote that hospital buildings

> ought to be floored above, so as to make two stories each, and to have a stack of chimneys carried up the middle. . . . It is further required that bed bunks be made, and straw be always in readiness, for the sick, and a carpenter or two to be employed solely in the business of the general hospital in making coffins, tables, and utensils of various kinds.

As plans were made for the Mount Independence hospital, Dr. Jonathan Potts, a 1768 graduate of the new Philadelphia Medical College, was placed in charge of the health care to be given there. Potts had received his M.D. in 1771 and had studied with Dr. Benjamin Rush, considered during his lifetime to be the most able physician in America. Although we cannot be sure which of his staff were based at the Mount Independence hospital, and which were at the Albany or Fort George hospitals, we do know that in April 1777 Potts had under his command a total of five general officers, six senior surgeons, six second surgeons, six surgeons' mates, four men in the commissary, and one steward. Potts was ordered to report to the Mount Independence hospital on April 14, 1777:

> You will Proceed with all possible Dispatch, I believe we shall have some few patients Ready against your arrival it will not be amiss however for you to come with your sleeves Rolled up and your Amputating Instruments, etc., etc., placed in proper Order.

Beginning shortly before Potts's arrival, the chief engineer for Mount Independence, Colonel Jeduthan Baldwin, oversaw construction of the hospital building. Baldwin's *Revolutionary Journal* states that the plans were drawn on March 12; his men began to cut timber for the hospital on March 13; they finished getting timber on March 31; they "laid out the ground for the Hospital" on May 5; and they "Raisd the Hospital N. side" on May 27. On June 9 and June 20, Baldwin referred to dining with the doctors at the hospital. Although Baldwin's journal would suggest that the hospital was essentially complete by June 9, 1777, a letter sent from Major General Philip Schuyler to Congress on June 25, 1777, complained that "not one single room [in the hospital] . . . is yet finished, nor will it soon be in condition to receive a considerable number of sick."

While Schuyler's letter raises the issue of whether the hospital ever held many soldiers, Baldwin's occasional references to dining leave little doubt that the general hospital saw frequent use as a large dining hall during the weeks leading up to General John Burgoyne's attack in July 1777. While we have never found contemporary plans that present a detailed view of the hospital, a small outline of the hospital *does* appear on a map prepared in 1777 by Lieutenant Charles Wintersmith, Assistant Engineer to the British army. Wintersmith's drawing convincingly places the hospital in the exact position where we conducted excavations in 1990.

Several historical references have survived that describe the provisioning of the general hospital. Perhaps the best of these is a letter from "Jon[n] Potts, Director Gen[l]. Hospital," dated June 19th, 1777, and addressed to "John Brown, Steward to the Gen[l]. Hospital":

> You will delay no time in procuring for the General Hospital 200 Sheep & 20 good Milk Cows with as many fat Cattle as you can procure, the 500[wt.] Butter. find Men to assist you in driving them to this place—if you cannot get that Number purchase as many as you can. . . . If you have not Money sufficient I will pay the moment the Cattle arrive for them.

Later, when the abandonment of the Mount caused St. Clair to be tried in court martial proceedings, a Mr. Yancey, who superintended the Issuing

Commissary's Department at Ticonderoga and Mount Independence, testified under oath that "The general hospital was sometimes supplied by my magazine, but not steadily." And, when asked where else the general hospital might have received provisions, he responded, "I do not know from any place with respect to fresh provision, unless they sent out and purchased it. The salt provision and flour could be got from me only."

When British and German troops stormed Mount Independence on July 5 & 6, the general hospital was unquestionably the largest building on the Mount, but it had few patients relative to its size. A year later it was reported that "There were very few [patients] in the hospital, not above 100; a great proportion of them wounded." All medical supplies and all but four of the sick were removed from the hospital just before Burgoyne's attack. One of the surgeons' mates, James Thacher, later reported that he was ordered "to collect the sick and wounded, and as much of the hospital stores as possible, and assist in embarking them on board the batteaux and boats at the shore." Thacher further recalled that, "among the hospital stores we found many dozen bottles of choice wine, and breaking off their necks, we cheered our hearts with the nectareous contents."

The Excavation of the Mount Independence General Hospital

When I first saw the foundation of the Mount Independence General Hospital in 1987, all I could see was a rectangular outline of dry-laid field stones, extending for 250 feet east-west and 25 feet north-south. Covered with cedar trees, the foundation walls are well defined in some spots and invisible in others. The building stood on what is now the western edge of the Red Trail, one of the modern-day walking trails maintained for visitors by the Vermont Division for Historic Preservation. Given its size, the hospital foundation is the most visible survival within that part of the site that was occupied by the 2nd Brigade. From the first moment I saw it, I knew that this was the site atop Mount Independence that I *most* wanted to explore.

From the above historical sources, I knew that the general hospital building was originally two stories high, of wood frame construction, and large enough to hold six hundred men. A sizable wing was still being added to the western end of the building when the British arrived, and this would have turned the hospital into an L-shaped structure (with the original building as the long leg of the "L"). However, there had not been sufficient time to complete the new wing, and the short leg of the "L" now has the appearance of a large cellar hole (figure 6-18).

Early military hospitals in the American colonies have sometimes been researched by archeologists and historians, yet many encampments did not have general hospitals, and many were located in urban settings where hos-

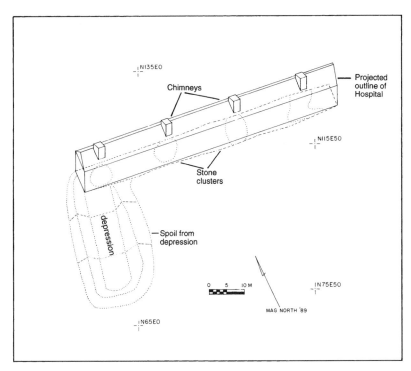

Chimneys

Projected outline of Hospital

N135E0

N115E50

Stone clusters

depression

Spoil from depression

0 5 10 M

MAG NORTH '89

N75E50

N65E0

FIG. 6-18. Schematic reconstruction of the general hospital on Mount Independence, including the clusters of surface stone thought to represent fireplace bases. The "depression" on the left is the cellar hole for the new wing that was never completed. Drawing by Gordon DeAngelo.

pital sites have not survived to the present day. The isolation of the general hospital at Mount Independence, on the other hand, resulted in the excellent preservation of its foundation walls. Some collecting has occurred there, and a Vermont game warden, Thomas Daniels, excavated within the foundation in 1958–1959. His collection was subsequently donated to the state of Vermont, and his finds included five medicine cups of white salt-glazed stoneware, a white salt-glazed bowl, a white salt-glazed saucer with scratch blue decoration, several knife blades, and numerous fragments of glass medicine bottles and stoppers (figure 6-19). Given the rarity of professional excavations at other eighteenth-century hospitals, this small artifact assemblage is perhaps the most distinctive and important collection yet recovered from Mount Independence.

Because of its very brief occupation (only one to two months), the removal of medical supplies by Potts and Thacher, and the frequent disturbance by collectors, I knew that artifacts would be scattered thinly within the hospital, and that the most common remains would be architectural. Still, when we started to dig there in 1990, I hoped that we could establish the locations of fireplaces, doorways, and dumps, and that enough might have survived to determine the locations of different rooms within the building. I was especially curious to learn whether British troops had used the hospital after capturing it from American forces. We did not know whether

FIG. 6-19. Artifacts excavated from within the Mount Independence general hospital in 1958–1959. These consist of medicine cups of white salt-glazed stoneware (upper left), a saucer with "scratch blue" decoration (lower left), a "worm" used to clean the bore of a musket (upper right), and small glass medicine bottles or vials (lower right).

the British advance guard, under Brig. General Simon Fraser, had brought casualties to this hospital after the nearby Battle of Hubbardton on July 7, but that seemed quite likely. And this raised the concern that any artifacts we found within the ruins of the hospital could just as easily be British as American.

During the summer of 1990, we placed a total of sixty-seven one-meter-square test pits within the remains of the Mount Independence general hospital. All excavation was done with trowels, and all features, stones, and most artifacts were mapped *in situ*. In confirmation of historical sources, we discovered few recognizable medical supplies within the hospital, although we found a small trash pit just outside the northern wall of the hospital foundation. This pit contained butchered cow bones, as well as a delft ointment jar, an extremely ornate lid from a creamware bowl (figure 6-20), tobacco pipe fragments, a knife blade, numerous nails, a few buttons, and one cuff link. (All artifacts from the hospital are summarized in table 6-1.)

We recovered nearly one thousand nails throughout the foundation of the hospital, ranging in size from small one-inch shingle nails to spikes over three inches long. The types included rose head, L-head, and T-head nails (see table 6-1), and our preliminary observations suggested that all of the

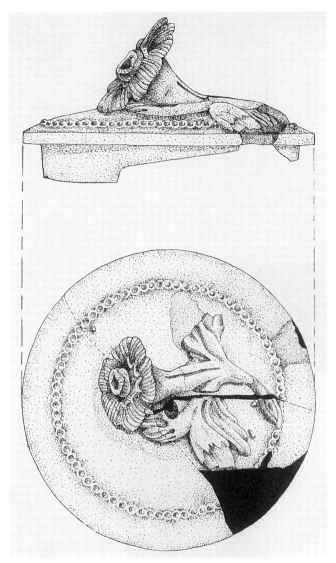

FIG. 6-20. Lid from a creamware bowl, two inches in diameter; English, Leeds. Found in a trash pit on the northern edge of the general hospital. Drawing by Ellen Pawelczak.

nails longer than two inches were located near the foundation stones, while nails two inches or shorter in length were distributed fairly evenly throughout the excavations. Our analysis of the nail collection suggests that the structure had been completed beyond framing to include board walls, possibly floors, and a shingled roof. Still, the building may have had a rather unfinished appearance because we found virtually no fragments of window glass: probably no window sashes had been installed.

The hospital must have contained several fireplaces because there were four large concentrations of stone evenly spaced along the length of the foun-

Table 6-1
General Hospital: Artifact Classes and Groups Excavated in 1990

Kitchen artifact group	
Creamware sherds	26
Tin-glazed earthenware (delft) sherds	23
Soft-paste porcelain sherds	1
White salt-glazed stoneware sherds	11
Gray salt-glazed stoneware sherds	1
Unrefined stoneware sherds	4
Unidentifiable pottery sherds (burned)	35
Wine bottle fragments	139
Burned wine bottle fragments	279
Glass tableware/vial fragments	50
Burned/melted glass fragments	195
Knife blade (4⅛" long)	1

Bone group	
Cow bones (chiefly foot bones)	23
Pig tooth (left P₃)	1
Sheep bones (right radius & left tarsal)	2
Deer tooth (3 fragments of 1 molar)	1
Bird bone (tarsometatarsus)	1
Total Animal Bone Fragments:	513 (111 burned, 402 unburned)

Architectural group	
Rose head nails/spikes	984
Hand-wrought nails (unident. heads)	190
T-head nails	16
L-head nails	17

Arms group	
Gunflints (gray, English)	3
Musket balls (.64 cal. & .69 cal.)	2
Lead sprue fragments	4
Cast iron shot (1.17" dia.)	1
Cleaning jag for a musket	1
Hammer fragment from a pistol	1

Clothing group	
Iron buckle	1
British 20th Regiment button	1
Metal buttons	3
Bone button	1
Cuff link (blue stone in center)	1

Tobacco pipe group	
Tobacco pipestem fragments (4/64" bore)	1
Tobacco pipestem fragments (5/64" bore)	2
Tobacco pipe bowl fragments	5

dation. Our excavation in the westernmost concentration of stone rubble revealed only a few brick fragments, suggesting that the chimneys may still have been under construction when the building was destroyed (although large quantities of brick may also have been carried off by collectors). Alternatively, fireplaces and chimneys may have been constructed solely of stone.

We discovered over four hundred fragments of wine bottles, often melted or burned (see table 6-1), scattered throughout the entire foundation of the hospital. Needless to say, I was delighted to have this corroboration for James Thacher's statement about sampling the "ample stores" of choice wine taken from the hospital. I have little doubt that these wine bottles were melted during the burning of the general hospital by British forces in November 1777.

Other artifacts we recovered within the hospital foundation included a cleaning jag for a musket, two musket balls, one piece of cast-iron shot, a buckle, several tobacco pipestems, three gunflints, a few buttons, and numerous butchered animal bones. Artifacts such as these are identical to the classes of artifacts found in the surrounding 2nd Brigade hut sites, suggesting that, until the retreat on July 6, the principal use of the hospital space was as living quarters. One of the buttons is especially interesting because it was left by the British 20th Regiment of Foot. The 20th was one of the units led by Brig. General Simon Fraser as he pursued the retreating Americans on July 6, en route to Hubbardton, and I like to think that this button came from the uniform of a British soldier who was injured in the fighting at Hubbardton.

But an even more interesting find lay nearby. About 150 feet north of the hospital foundation, on the northern edge of an isolated cabin site (site 65), we found hundreds of butchered cow bones inside a large trash pit (figure 6-21). I wish I could say that my brilliant archeological detective work helped us discover this pit, but in fact the credit goes to Dennis Howe, the field supervisor there. He had noticed a slight depression behind the mound of rocks at site 65. While I assumed that it was nothing but a recent disturbance, Howe correctly guessed that this was an early feature, and almost immediately his pits were exposing masses of bone. Given the universal interest in human remains, it was all we could do to convince visitors that they were, in fact, looking at the remains of cows, rather than the skeletons of soldiers carried there from the hospital.

From this evidence, coupled with the large numbers of wine bottles and Jeduthan Baldwin's references to dining in the hospital, feeding the sick seems to have been a primary activity in the general hospital during its brief period of use. The 513 bone fragments found *within* the hospital foundation (see table 6–1) reflect a minimum of just one cow, one pig, one deer, one sheep, and one bird (species unidentified); whereas the cow bone disposal pit behind site 65 contained a total of 726 bones, reflecting a minimum of seven-

FIG. 6-21. Butchered cow bones found about forty-six meters north of the general hospital (site 65).

teen cows (based on seventeen left metatarsals and seventeen left metacarpals). The bone pit also contained one fish bone (species unidentified), but otherwise the bones consisted of cow metapodials, phalanges, carpals, and tarsals, a total of sixty-four articulated lower legs. The deposit represented body parts with little food value, and I believe these were probably the first parts to be discarded during large-scale butchering, prior to the consumption of fresh beef by men in the hospital or in the 2nd Brigade cabins around the hospital. As our bone specialist Bruce Hedin analyzed these bones for us, he found a single cow vertebra that exhibited saw marks, under magnification, on the distal end above the malleolus. This was the only case where he observed evidence for the use of a saw in butchering out of the many thousands of bones and fragments recovered from Mount Independence.

During the 1990 excavations, we completely exposed the eastern end of the hospital foundation, but elsewhere we kept the scale of the digging very modest in order to maintain the integrity of the structure. We found numerous soil disturbances, indicating years of digging by collectors, and medical artifacts were extremely rare. The only likely medical artifacts we recovered in 1990 were the knife blade and delft ointment jar we found in the trash pit outside the hospital, and several thin-walled sherds of white salt-glazed stoneware that probably were pieces of medicine cups.

Pottery and porcelain were poorly represented within the collection; and we found no sherds of redware or slipware, only a single sherd of soft-paste porcelain, and very small quantities of creamware, delft, white and gray salt-glazed stoneware, and unrefined stoneware. It was also impossible to identify some thirty-five pottery sherds because they had been burned beyond recognition. Given the extremely fragmentary nature of the collection, we could not determine the minimum number of vessels represented, and the only recognizable vessel was the creamware bowl lid (figure 6-20) found just outside the hospital foundation.

In studying the general hospital on Mount Independence, we were unable to find enough activity-specific artifacts to be able to define the functions and outlines of a single room. This was disappointing, as was the scarcity of medical supplies in the hospital. Still, we recovered enough architectural evidence in 1990 to reveal the nail distribution, the locations of four fireplaces, the absence of glass in the windows, the presence of a shingled roof, and evidence for an unfinished wing that would have given the hospital an L-shaped configuration.

As far as I know, the Mount Independence hospital is, to date, the only eighteenth-century general hospital to have been professionally excavated within the United States. This may seem surprising, given the importance of medicine and surgery at all military sites of the eighteenth century, but most other hospitals have not survived and so cannot be studied archeologically. Nevertheless, this class of structure is so poorly known through historical records that archeologists would do well to seek them out in order to study the evidence they contain for early health care. While the Mount Independence hospital was occupied only briefly and was stripped of supplies by doctors as they left in July 1777, I certainly hope that other, richer, hospital sites will be found. If, for example, the sites of the earlier regimental hospitals on Mount Independence are ever located, they should provide a great deal of information about how casualties were cared for after the invasion of Canada at the end of 1775.

Conclusions

Historical documents reveal much about the events that occurred at Mount Independence, especially when Carleton and his fleet approached in October of 1776 and again when Burgoyne's army arrived in July of 1777. They also provide anecdotal evidence for daily life on the Mount, including clothing shortages, disease, and punishments for infractions. However, history often fails to provide adequate quantitative information about buildings, food-

ways, clothing, and consumption patterns. Archeology need not duplicate what is already known from military history. Rather, the archeological integrity of Mount Independence makes the site itself one of the best documents with which to better understand the daily lives of soldiers during the American Revolution.

The archeology we conducted at Mount Independence has already made a profound difference in the way history is presented to the public because the Vermont Division for Historic Preservation finally opened its long-awaited visitors' center in the summer of 1996. At the foot of the Mount, inside a building shaped like an upside-down bateau, many of the artifacts we excavated are now on display (figure 6-22). More important, many of the story lines in the exhibits are based on our archeological discoveries, and most visitors watch a slide presentation that demonstrates the role archeology played in interpreting the site. Then, as visitors leave the new center and go out on the trails, they can visit the ruins of dozens of huts and barracks, knowing that everything they see is just as it survived from 1777, without reconstructions that would detract from the site's scenic beauty.

Archeology has contributed to the understanding of Mount Independence by revealing for the first time the precise placement of buildings and activities across the Mount, by demonstrating how buildings were constructed, and by highlighting some of the differences in living standards between officers and enlisted men at this remote northern outpost. But basic research and recording are far from complete; we need to continue our mapping and site determinations because literally hundreds of sites have yet to be identified. In many spots, archeology is the only technique that will be able to determine which surface concentrations of stone are natural (broken-up bedrock) and which are cultural.

The soldiers who camped atop Mount Independence left behind only a modest number of journals, so archeology is now one of the best ways to understand the hardships they faced during America's fight for independence. This was the only major revolutionary war fortification ever constructed in Vermont, and traces of the siege of Mount Independence are now richly strewn all across this rocky mountaintop.

Further Reading

Anburey, Thomas. 1789. *Travels Through the Interior Parts of America*. London: Printed for William Lane. Reprinted in 1969 by the New York Times & Arno Press.

Baldwin, Colonel Jeduthan. 1906. *The Revolutionary Journal of Col. Jeduthan Baldwin 1775–1778*. Bangor, Maine: Printed for the De Burians.

Blanco, Richard L. 1979. *Physician of the American Revolution: Jonathan Potts*. New York: Garland Publishing Inc.

Bowie, Chester W. 1966. Mount Independence Summer 1966. Manuscript submitted to the Mount Independence Associates, Inc. and the Vermont Board of Historic Sites, Montpelier, Vt.

Cohen, Paul E. 1998. Michel Capitaine du Chesnoy, the marquis de Lafayette's Cartographer. *Antiques* 153 (1): 170–77.

Collections of the New-York Historical Society for the Year 1879. 1880. Proceedings of a General Court Martial, Held at Major General Lincoln's Quarters, near Quaker-Hill, in the State of New-York, by Order of His Excellency General Washington, Commander in Chief of the Army of the United States of America, for the Trial of Major General Schuyler, October 1, 1778. Major General Lincoln, President. New York: Printed for the Society.

Collections of the New-York Historical Society for the Year 1880. 1881. Proceedings of a General Court Martial, Held at White Plains, in the State of New-York, By Order of His Excellency General Washington, Commander in Chief of the Army of the United States of America, for the Trial of Major General St. Clair, August 25, 1778. Major General Lincoln, President. New York: Printed for the Society.

Elmer, Ebenezer. 1848. Journal [of service in the Third New Jersey Regiment, winter 1776–1777]. *New Jersey Historical Society Proceedings*, vol. 3.

Frese, Joseph R., S.J. 1971. A Trumbull Map of Fort Ticonderoga Rediscovered. *The Bulletin of the Fort Ticonderoga Museum* 13 (2): 129–36.

Furcron, Thomas B. 1954. Mount Independence, 1776–1777. *The Bulletin of the Fort Ticonderoga Museum* 9:230–48.

Howe, Dennis E. 1991. The Archeology of a 1776 Cantonment of New Hampshire Regiments. *The New Hampshire Archeologist* 32 (1): 1–25.

———. 1996. *This Ragged, Starved, Lousy, Pocky Army*. Concord, N.H.: The Printed Word, Inc.

Howe, Dennis E., Marjorie Robbins, and William C. Murphy. 1994. The South Battery at Mount Independence. *The Journal of Vermont Archaeology* 1:127–40.

Kennedy, Matthew. 1776. Letter from "Camp at Mount Independence 11th Octr 1776" to "Mr. Robert Kennedy In Goffstown [N.H.]." Kennedy family documents, Special Collections, University of Vermont.

Krueger, John William. 1974. A Gentleman of Zeal and Character in the Public Service: Doctor Jonathan Potts and the Northern Medical Department. Masters Thesis, University of Vermont.

———. 1981. *Troop Life at the Champlain Valley Forts during the American Revolution.* Ph.D. Dissertation, Dept. of History, State University of New York at Albany.

Lossing, Benson J. 1851. *The Pictorial Field-Book of the Revolution.* New York: Harper & Brothers.

Munsell, Joel. 1859. *Orderly Book of the Northern Army at Ticonderoga and Mt. Independence from October 17, 1776 to January 8, 1777 with biographical and explanatory notes and an appendix.* Albany, N.Y.: self-published.

Neill, Rev. Edward D. 1864. Biographical Sketch of Doctor Jonathan Potts. [January 1864]. *New England Genealogical and Historical Society Register,* 21–36.

Potts, Jonathan. *The Potts Papers.* 1766–1777. Microfilm, Volume 1. The Historical Society of Pennsylvania.

Robinson, David E. 1968. Mount Independence 1968. Manuscript submitted to the Mount Independence Associates, Inc., and the Vermont Board of Historic Sites, Montpelier, Vt.

Saffron, Morris H. 1982. The Northern Medical Department 1776–1777. *The Bulletin of the Fort Ticonderoga Museum* 14 (2): 81–120.

Schuyler, Philip. n.d. The Philip J. Schuyler Papers. New York Public Library. (Available on microfilm.)

Sgorbati, Steve. 1993. A Hill of a Wine Bottle on a Mound Called Independence. Unpublished manuscript prepared for Sociology 397 (Fall 1992), Castleton State College.

Starbuck, David R. 1990. The General Hospital at Mount Independence: 18th Century Health Care at a Revolutionary War Cantonment. *Northeast Historical Archaeology* 19:50–68.

———. 1993. Building Independence on Lake Champlain. *Archaeology* 46 (5): 60–63.

———. 1993. Mount Independence. In *The American Revolution, 1775–1783: An Encyclopedia,* edited by Richard L. Blanco, Vol. I, 1128–29. New York: Garland Publishing, Inc.

———. 1993. Mount Independence: Teaching Respect for Our Heritage. *Castleton Alumni Review* 10 (1): 11–12.

Starbuck, David R., and William C. Murphy. 1994. Archaeology at Mount Independence: An Introduction. *The Journal of Vermont Archaeology* 1:115–26.

Thacher, James, M.D. 1862. *Military Journal of the American Revolution To Which Has Been Added the Life of Washington.* Hartford, Conn.: Hurlbut, Williams & Company.

Torres-Reyes, Ricardo. 1971. *Morristown National Historical Park, 1779–80 Encampment: A Study of Medical Services.* Washington, D.C.: Office of History and Historic Architecture, Eastern Service Center, National Park Service.

The Wayne Orderly Book. 1963, 1964. The Wayne Orderly Book. In three parts. *The Bulletin of the Fort Ticonderoga Museum* 11 (2): 93–112; 11 (3): 125–34; 11 (4): 177–205.

Wickman, Donald H. 1993. Built with Spirit, Deserted in Darkness: the American Occupation of Mount Independence, 1776–1777. Master's Thesis, University of Vermont.

Williams, John A. 1967. Mount Independence in Time of War, 1776–1783. *Vermont History* 35 (2): 89–108.

———. 1988. *The Battle of Hubbardton*. Montpelier: Vermont Division for Historic Preservation.

Wintersmith, Lt. Charles. 1777. Map prepared by Lt. Charles Wintersmith by order of Lt. Twiss, Burgoyne's chief engineer, July 1777. "Plan of Carillon or Ticonderoga which was quitted by the Americans in the nigth [*sic*] from the 5th to the 6th of July 1777." The original is in the Public Archives of Canada, and copies are held by Special Collections, the University of Vermont, and the Fort Ticonderoga Museum.

Wolkomir, Joyce Rogers. 1990. The Spirit of Mount Independence. *Vermont Life* 44 (4): 24–28.

Chapter 7

The Largest Fortification of Them All: Crown Point

FIG. 7-1. (Opposite, top.) Fort St. Frederic from the air (April 1986). The New York end of the Lake Champlain Bridge is on the left. Courtesy of Paul Huey and the Bureau of Historic Sites, New York State Office of Parks, Recreation and Historic Preservation.

FIG. 7-2. (Opposite, bottom.) The English fort at Crown Point from the air (April 1986). Courtesy of Paul Huey and the Bureau of Historic Sites, New York State Office of Parks, Recreation and Historic Preservation.

*I*FIRST VISITED the forts at Crown Point (figures 7-1 and 7-2) in the late summer of 1976. I knew that I would find unbelievably rich French and British military remains dating from 1731 until 1777, but I did not know how much of the original forts had actually survived. Most of all, though, I was eager to walk through the ruins of the largest British fortification in North America. The English and provincial soldiers who lived at Crown Point between 1759 and 1773 must have enjoyed their superb view of Lake Champlain, and visitors to the site today cannot fail to appreciate the arch of the adjacent Lake Champlain Bridge that has crossed over the lake into Vermont since 1929. Since my first visit, I have been impressed every time I have gone to Crown Point and looked up at the massive earthworks and walked into the parade ground to see the soldiers' barracks and the officers' barracks. And the best part is that everything that stands there today is original—this is not a twentieth-century interpretation of the past. Virtually every group of students I have taken to Crown Point over the years has told me that this is their favorite fort site because of its integrity and its beautiful, mist-shrouded setting as it overlooks the lake. This National Historic Landmark is gigantic and truly inspiring (figures 7-3, 7-4, and 7-5).

But in 1976 I was especially fortunate to arrive at a time when a Bureau of Historic Sites team was there from the New York State Office of Parks, Recreation and Historic Preservation. Most of the archeologists were digging around the foundations of the officers' and soldiers' barracks (figures 7-6 and 7-7), but there, in the middle of the parade ground, a solitary archeologist was digging a very small but deep hole and identifying the tiny pottery sherds as they came out of the ground. It was Paul Huey, one of the leading experts on Crown Point, and his crew was digging as a prelude to creating better drainage around the barracks' buildings. I watched him pull one small sherd after another out of the hole, and I could not help being impressed by the extreme care that Paul, and the State of New York, have given this site in recent years.

FIG. 7-3. A modern view of the interior of Crown Point (October 1997). The officers' barracks is on the left, with a British flag flying over it, and the soldiers' barracks is on the right.

FIG. 7-4. A view of the parade ground inside Crown Point, looking toward Lake Champlain in the distance (October 1997). The officers' barracks is on the left, and the soldiers' barracks is on the right.

FIG. 7-5. The point at which the modern tour road enters Crown Point, looking toward Lake Champlain at the rear.

FIG. 7-6. The excavation around the base of the officers' barracks at Crown Point (1976). Courtesy of Paul Huey and the Bureau of Historic Sites, New York State Office of Parks, Recreation and Historic Preservation.

FIG. 7-7. Excavating inside
the soldiers' barracks (1976).
Courtesy of Paul Huey and the Bureau of Historic Sites, New York
State Office of Parks, Recreation
and Historic Preservation.

Background History

Even earlier, before "His Majesty's Fort at Crown Point" was constructed by
the British, this peninsula that juts into Lake Champlain was the site of a
French fortress, Fort St. Frederic, built at what the French called "Pointe à la
Chevelure." The French settlement had begun in 1731 with just twenty men
inside a stockaded fort on the east side of the lake, and in 1734 they began to
build Fort St. Frederic on the New York side of the lake, which would be the
first prominent fortification in the region. The fort now marked the southernmost advance of French forces along The Great Warpath, and as such it
caused a great deal of consternation among British settlers in the colony of
New York. It was an ideal spot for a fortification because at this point Lake
Champlain is only about a quarter-mile wide, and from Fort St. Frederic it
was possible for the French to control all trade up and down the Champlain
Valley.

It took the French three years to complete Fort St. Frederic. Its strong
point was a four-story-high tower, or citadel, with thick masonry walls, and
it contained quarters for the commander, cannons, a powder magazine, an
armory, a bakery, and more. The citadel and about a dozen other buildings
were surrounded by an outer stone parapet wall that was nearly square and
had six corner bastions, the entire fortification covering about one acre. The

garrison usually consisted of eighty to one hundred men, and a windmill constructed nearby provided flour to the settlers and soldiers. Even the windmill was well fortified, with six swivel cannons. Fort St. Frederic became the launching point for French attacks in 1746 upon Fort Massachusetts and Deerfield, Massachusetts, and Fort Number 4 in New Hampshire, as well as Fort William Henry in 1757. This last raid, and the resulting massacre, was clearly the last straw for the British. Two years later, on July 31, 1759, the garrison of two hundred French soldiers was forced to blow up the citadel and windmill at Fort St. Frederic, retreating just before the arrival of a twelve-thousand-man British and provincial army led by General Jeffery Amherst. The British had long wanted to dislodge the French from this position which had blocked their own expansion plans in northern New York, and Amherst immediately created a hospital and quarters inside Fort St. Frederic.

Rather than repair Fort St. Frederic, General Amherst decided to build a new fort, and in three years his troops constructed a stone and timber fort half a mile in circumference and shaped like a giant pentagon with five corner bastions. Nearby, they built roads and three satellite redoubts—small forts—also of stone and timber, and four miles to the south they added a line of blockhouses. Inside the fort, the great parade ground covered six acres and contained three stone barracks buildings (one was never finished), a guard house, and an armory. Each barracks had the appearance of four two-story Georgian mansions, all strung together, and each barracks room had a fireplace, two windows facing the parade ground, and just one window on the back wall. The forty-foot-high outer wall that ran around the parade ground was built of limestone and wood, was twenty-two feet thick, and rested on bedrock. The ramparts were made from squared timbers filled with earth, with stone footings, using an immense amount of fill. All together, this vast complex grew into the greatest British military installation ever raised in North America.

By this time, though, the French and Indian War was drawing to a close, for during the taking of Ticonderoga and St. Frederic in 1759, a British army led by Major General James Wolfe was in the process of capturing Quebec. Still, the English fort at Crown Point played a small part in concluding the war because it was the launching point for one of the British armies, led by Colonel William Haviland, that brought about the surrender of Montreal in 1760. We know that life at Crown Point that year could not have been pleasant, however, because Major Skene found it necessary to burn the huts of the Rangers who had smallpox. Still, improvements continued to be made to the fortifications until the war ended in 1763.

With the arrival of peace, the British army reduced its garrison at Crown Point, but British settlers were now moving into the Champlain Valley, and many veterans who had fought under Amherst received grants of land and settled there. The civilian community contained such amenities as a black-smith shop, tavern, and store, and became the principal stopping point be-tween Albany and Canada. Meanwhile, a disaster struck Crown Point on April 21, 1773: soldiers' wives set fire to a dirty barracks chimney, and the sparks were carried upward by the wind. The pine shingles of various build-ings were set on fire, and even the ramparts of the fort—framed timbers that were covered with tar and oakum—were ignited. After an hour of burning through the outer walls, the bastions and the buildings, the fire reached the powder magazine. One hundred barrels of powder ignited, there was an in-credible explosion, and most of the fort was destroyed. Flying timbers in-jured some of those present, but the remaining soldiers moved into store-houses or to Fort Ticonderoga. Local residents subsequently carried off what they could salvage, and the fort was temporarily abandoned. It is diffi-cult to imagine a more ignominious end to a spectacular fortification.

Although Crown Point had been rendered useless, the community of set-tlers remained. However, perhaps because they were no longer protected by the fort, the British settlement began to be harassed by the Green Mountain Boys during the border disputes between New Hampshire and New York. These actions escalated until May 11, 1775, when Seth Warner and some of the Green Mountain Boys captured Crown Point and its garrison of nine British soldiers. This was just one day after Ethan Allen, Benedict Arnold, and others had captured the British garrison at Fort Ticonderoga. The Americans took possession of a total of 111 artillery pieces at Crown Point, and Henry Knox transported 29 of the cannons to Boston in order to lift the British siege. With the fall of Crown Point and Ticonderoga, Lake Cham-plain was now firmly in American hands.

Later in 1775, Crown Point became the launching point for General Richard Montgomery's ill-fated invasion of Canada, which sought to bring a prompt end to the war. After a disastrous defeat, with Montgomery dead and Benedict Arnold wounded, the "Army of Canada" straggled back to Crown Point in June of 1776 where they lay in makeshift hospitals. At the end of August, Arnold and the fledgling American navy set sail from Crown Point to prevent the British from advancing up the lake. However, after Arnold was defeated at the Battle of Valcour Island that October, he burned everything at Crown Point, and the peninsula was abandoned altogether. Consequently, General John Burgoyne's army encountered no resistance when it occupied Crown Point in the summer of 1777. Burgoyne created a hospital and a supplies magazine at Crown Point but left behind only a small force of about two hundred men. The peninsula remained in British hands until 1784 and the conclusion of the war.

After the Armies Left

The Treaty of Paris, which ended the revolutionary war, ensured that the ruins of both Fort St. Frederic and Crown Point would never again be needed for defensive purposes. And so they became little more than sources of quarry stone, frequently raided for building material. In 1801 New York State donated the remains of the forts to Columbia and Union colleges, along with the surrounding land. Union transferred its deed to Columbia in 1812, and Columbia sold its deed to Sylvester Churchill in 1828. After that, the forts changed hands several times until 1910, when Witherbee, Sherman and Company of Port Henry decided to donate the property back to the state of New York in order to guarantee its long-term preservation.

The New York State Legislature promptly authorized the removal of much of the rubble from Fort St. Frederic, repaired the walls in 1915, unearthed the bake ovens in 1916, and conducted excavations inside the citadel in 1922. This early work recovered many artifacts, including a breech-loading swivel cannon in 1924.

Since that time, New York State has done an outstanding job of maintaining the ruins, interpreting them, and keeping treasure hunters out. The National Park Service designated as National Historic Landmarks Fort St. Frederic in 1961 and Crown Point in 1968. To provide the public with meaningful interpretation, the state erected the first museum-type structure at Crown Point around 1914, and opened a small but excellent visitor center on that same site in 1976. This new building has tastefully presented exhibits and artifacts representing the French, British, and American periods of occupation (figure 7-8). Also, since 1975, the Bureau of Historic Sites, New

FIG. 7-8. The modern visitors' center at Crown Point State Historic Site.

York State Office of Parks, Recreation and Historic Preservation, has done much cleaning and repointing (replacing with fresh mortar) of the walls, has added drains, and conducted many professional, but small-scale, archeological excavations.

Recent Archeology

Modern archeology began at Crown Point in 1956, when several house sites were excavated on privately owned land. These were believed to have been the homes of former British officers (overlying earlier French houses) outside the walls of the fort. A small regional museum also dug here in 1958 and found lots of musket balls, sherds of delft and creamware, salt-glazed stoneware cups decorated with scratch blue, wine glasses, wine bottles, a pewter spoon imprinted with the name "Grenfill," barrel hoops, tobacco pipes, an ice creeper, padlocks and keys, the brass escutcheon plate from a British 17th Regiment Brown Bess musket, and even a pewter button of the 60th British Regiment. Unfortunately, no excavation records exist from these projects, or from the many years of relic hunting that went on before.

Excavation on a much larger scale occurred in 1968 when New York State sponsored a dig with Roland Robbins as project archeologist. Robbins, a self-taught amateur whom the media fondly termed "the pick and shovel archeologist," was hired because of his reputation for digging—and then reconstructing—many famous early American houses and industries. Robbins was a colorful character who had little use for professional archeologists, who, in turn, considered his methods to be crude and unacceptable. I met Robbins only once, in 1977, at an archeological conference at which he refused to sit through the talks of any of the other speakers. Even now, years after his death, I still love to tell my students stories about Robbins and his distinctive brand of archeology.

It was close to the end of his career when Robbins was hired to clear out portions of Fort St. Frederic and to expose walls at the Light Infantry Redoubt. During the 1968 project, he found military dumps, two breech-loading cannon, a pair of moccasins, and a great number of personal artifacts. In the process, his team discovered a stratified British dump (1760s to 1770s) inside the moat of the citadel at Fort St. Frederic. But while Robbins's work was originally intended to be long-term, the state terminated it almost immediately, partly because New York had just begun to hire its first professional historical archeologists. Unfortunately, few records survive from the 1968 excavation, and many of the artifacts—stored by New York State at Peebles Island in Waterford—have yet to be conserved. Robbins's excavations were filled with clean sand in 1975; since then, all further archeology at Crown Point has been professionally conducted by historical archeologists

FIG. 7-9. Buttons and cuff links excavated from the soldiers' barracks (1976). Courtesy of Paul Huey and the Bureau of Historic Sites, New York State Office of Parks, Recreation and Historic Preservation.

from the New York State Office of Parks, Recreation and Historic Preservation and by the Department of Environmental Conservation.

The first scientific archeology by the Bureau of Historic Sites was conducted at Crown Point in 1975 and 1976, partly to ensure that nothing of significance would be destroyed during construction of the modern visitor center. During my first visit to Crown Point in 1976, I observed the bureau's archeologists installing new drain tile in a trench along the back wall of the soldiers' barracks. Their results were decidedly mixed—an early-twentieth-century drain along the back wall of the barracks had already destroyed much of the archeological information. Still, they were finding great quantities of garbage from the military occupation, including fish bones, buttons and cuff links, and sherds of Chinese export porcelain, white salt-glazed stoneware, delft, and creamware (figure 7-9).

The Bureau of Historic Sites conducted many small excavations, including work inside the southeast bastion of Fort St. Frederic, the Bastion de Moulin, in 1977, and they tested along the route of a new storm drain between the visitor center and Fort St. Frederic in 1979–1980. Excavations inside some of the rooms in the soldiers' and officers' barracks in 1982 proved especially revealing because the bureau's Lois Feister uncovered very different flooring materials inside the officers' barracks from that in the soldiers'

FIG. 7-10. A brick floor exposed inside the soldiers' barracks (1982). Courtesy of Paul Huey and the Bureau of Historic Sites, New York State Office of Parks, Recreation and Historic Preservation.

barracks (figure 7-10). She found that officers' rooms were more nicely finished, with square, dry-laid, red tile floors, whereas the soldiers' rooms had dry-laid, red brick floors. In fact, it would have been five times as expensive to build the officers' flooring, which Feister believes helped reinforce publicly the higher status of the officers. She also has observed that fireplaces were more expensively built in the officers' barracks because the upper part of each fireplace was constructed of red brick, as opposed to the large, cut, limestone blocks for the soldiers' fireplaces. This is the type of status distinction that historical archeologists always hope to find but rarely do.

After Feister's work, some of the best discoveries were made between 1985

FIG. 7-11. The excavation of a provincial hut site at Crown Point (1988). Courtesy of Paul Huey and the Bureau of Historic Sites, New York State Office of Parks, Recreation and Historic Preservation.

FIG. 7-12. The completed excavation of a provincial hut site (1988). Courtesy of Paul Huey and the Bureau of Historic Sites, New York State Office of Parks, Recreation and Historic Preservation.

and 1988 when Charles Fisher, also with the Bureau of Historic Sites, excavated the sites of three provincial officers' huts (figures 7-11 and 7-12). These dated to 1759 when the English fort at Crown Point was first being constructed. Based on his finds in these rough structures, Fisher has reasoned convincingly that this temporary housing actually proves that the provincials had a very clean, orderly camp, nothing like the chaotic camp life that British officers usually attributed to the provincials. In fact, he believes that archeology here has proven that the provincials had become quite professional or "British" in the way they conducted themselves. Fisher has also shown that huts varied considerably in size, the larger habitations reflecting the additional space allocated to officers. Perhaps most important of all, Fisher discovered in the Crown Point officers' huts artifacts that reflect the social world of the officer class, including saucers (for tea drinking), a punch bowl, wine glasses, a gray salt-glazed stoneware chamber pot, clay tobacco pipes, and a pistol-sized lead ball. All of these would have helped the officers maintain their social distance from the enlisted men. Fisher argues persuasively that artifacts that suggest privacy and individualism reflect the behavior of officers and suggest social boundaries, whereas the enlisted men were living more communally in smaller spaces, with tents and huts placed closer together; they ate out of cast-iron pots, and used group latrines.

Conclusions

The ongoing investigations at Crown Point have been immensely helpful in raising new questions about military life and construction techniques at the biggest and best-preserved fortress on The Great Warpath. The Bureau of Historic Sites has done, and continues to do, excellent research at Fort St. Frederic and Crown Point. In the years ahead, much more can be done at both forts, and the potential for archeology inside the ruins of the British village (outside the fort) is immense. Many cellar holes still mark where the village once existed between 1760 and 1776, and future archeological research holds tremendous promise for bringing back the many aspects of daily life in this incredibly pristine community. I have been to Crown Point many times since 1976, and I will keep going back because it gives me the truest sense of what it is like to enter into a genuine eighteenth-century fort.

Further Reading

Feister, Lois M. 1984. Building Material Indicative of Status Differentiation at the Crown Point Barracks. *Historical Archaeology* 18 (1) :103–107.

————. 1984. Material Culture of the British Soldier at 'His Majesty's Fort of Crown Point' on Lake Champlain, New York, 1759–1783. *The Journal of Field Archaeology* 11 (2): 123–32.

Fisher, Charles L. 1991. *A Report on the 1977 Archaeological Test Excavations at Fort St. Frederic, Crown Point State Historic Site, Essex County, New York*. New York State Office of Parks, Recreation and Historic Preservation, Bureau of Historic Sites, Peebles Island, Waterford.

———. 1995. The Archaeology of Provincial Officers' Huts at Crown Point State Historic Site. *Northeast Historical Archaeology* 24:65–86.

Furness, Gregory, and Timothy Titus. 1985. *Master Plan for Crown Point State Historic Site.* New York State Office of Parks, Recreation and Historic Preservation, Bureau of Historic Sites, Peebles Island, Waterford.

Hagerty, Gilbert W. 1983. Crown Point's Secret. *Adirondack Bits 'n' Pieces* 1 (3): 15–20.

Hopkins, Arthur S. 1962. Old Fort St. Frederic—French Relic at Crown Point. *The Conservationist*, August-September: 13–15.

Huey, Paul R. 1959. *New Discoveries at Crown Point, N.Y.* Troy: Rensselaer County Junior Museum.

Kravic, Frank J. 1971. Colonial Crown Point and Its Artifacts. *Northeast Historical Archaeology* 1 (1): 70–71.

Titus, Timothy D. 1994. *An Illustrated History of Crown Point State Historic Site.* New York State Office of Parks, Recreation and Historic Preservation, Bureau of Historic Sites, Peebles Island, Waterford.

Chapter 8

Archeology Beneath the Water: Lake George and Lake Champlain

*T*HE MILITARY SITES that grew up along The Great Warpath protected the long north-south waterway and allowed movement and trade between the colony of New York and the French settlements that were both north and south of the St. Lawrence. This strategically important region had Indian paths but few roads; the Hudson River, Lake George, Lake Champlain, the Richelieu River, and all of their tributaries provided the only convenient means of travel for native people, European traders, and a handful of settlers (see the box "The Ferris Site in Panton, Vermont"). Later, when the armies of the eighteenth century attempted each summer to determine the destiny of the region, these same waterways facilitated the movement of bateaux, whaleboats, sloops, row galleys, and larger watercraft back and forth between the two great colonial empires. Thousands of bateaux—short (eighteen to fifty feet), flat-bottomed, double-ended boats—were rowed or poled along inland waterways, and it was so easy to construct the bateaux that they became a favorite for military use. The Lake Champlain Maritime Museum in Basin Harbor, Vermont, created a superb reproduction bateau in 1987, using traditional shipbuilding methods, and every summer the staff row it around Lake Champlain to the delight of sightseers.

The remains of eighteenth-century vessels now rest along the bottom of each waterway, exceptionally well preserved in the cold water where salvors and sport divers have long observed them and sometimes brought them to the surface. New York State owns title to historic shipwrecks in the Hudson River and Lake George, whereas wreck sites within Lake Champlain are jointly administered by New York and Vermont. Both states are responsible for identifying and evaluating these sites, and allow their disturbance or artifact removal only by permit. Unfortunately, professional underwater archeology, which requires intensive training and sizeable budgets, has been practiced along The Great Warpath since only the early 1980s. Underwater archeology in the region has thus been fairly rare, and the emphasis has usually been upon *in situ* preservation, rather than on subjecting artifacts and timbers to the rapid deterioration that occurs when exposed to the air.

Before 1980, many well-intentioned salvage efforts in Lake Champlain and Lake George too often resulted in the raising of ships that were put on display, only to dry out and be destroyed from little or no conservation. Certainly the most experienced diver during those early years was the late Lorenzo Hagglund, whose raising of the revolutionary war gunboat the *Philadelphia* in 1935 garnered a great deal of publicity. The *Philadelphia* was one of the ships that Benedict Arnold had constructed in Whitehall, New York, in 1776, and it sank about one hour after the fighting ended on October 11 at the Battle of Valcour Island. Hagglund always used hardhat gear—it was before scuba equipment had even been invented—and he found the *Philadelphia* in about sixty feet of water between Valcour Island and the New York side of the lake. The ship was in amazing condition, right down to the British cannon ball that had originally sunk her and was still embedded in her side. On board, Hagglund found human bones and teeth, a shoe that still contained a skeletalized foot, great numbers of artifacts and kettles, a twelve-pound cannon on the bow, two nine-pounders on the sides, and even stacks of cannon balls.

After removing the cannon, Hagglund raised the fifty-four-foot ship and put her on display in a barge shed near Willsboro. After years of being shown to the public for a fee, with virtually no conservation of the oak hull, the *Philadelphia* was finally sold and moved to the Smithsonian Institution after Hagglund's death. There she was soaked with polyethylene glycol and other preservatives, and the *Philadelphia* survives today as one of the finest vessels ever taken from Lake Champlain or any other lake in the United States (figure 8-1). Unfortunately, the several other shipwrecks that Hagglund raised from Lake Champlain never received proper conservation and have all been lost.

The techniques of underwater exploration have advanced a great deal since that time, and the group known as Bateaux Below, Inc., has spearheaded modern research on Lake George, while on Lake Champlain the leader has been the Lake Champlain Maritime Museum (formerly the Basin Harbor Maritime Museum). While underwater archeology elsewhere in the world has a reputation, or notoriety, for huge budgets and for being shaped by "cowboys" rather than scholars, the work on Lake George and Lake Champlain is guided by the professional approaches and personalities of the leaders of these two organizations. Bateaux Below, Inc., was formed in 1987 by a small group of historians and divers, led by Joe Zarzynski, a dynamic seventh-grade social studies teacher from Wilton, New York. Working with D. K. Abbass, a professional underwater archeologist, his primary goal has been to preserve historic shipwrecks in Lake George, and together they have systematically drawn and photographed vessels and artifacts on the lake's

★ The Ferris Site in Panton, Vermont

In 1984–1985 an underwater archeology team headed by Arthur Cohn, director of what was then the Basin Harbor Maritime Museum, examined Arnold's Bay for evidence of the fleet that Benedict Arnold had scuttled after the Battle of Valcour Island. They discovered a stone foundation eroding out of a bluff overlooking the bay. Upon closer investigation, they concluded that this was what had survived of Peter Ferris's house, one of the earliest dwellings constructed on the Vermont side of Lake Champlain. Peter Ferris was a farmer and probably a Quaker, and he built a log cabin in 1765 in what is now the town of Panton, Vermont. Later accounts tell us that his fields were among the most fertile on Lake Champlain.

There were few English travelers on Lake Champlain at that time, but during the spring of 1776, the Continental Congress sent a delegation of three men, including Benjamin Franklin, north to review the progress of the American military expedition against Quebec. The group stayed at the Ferris home on the night of April 24 while en route to Canada. Some six months later, Benedict Arnold and a British fleet clashed north of here at the Battle of Valcour Island, and two days later the British caught up to Arnold's five rearmost ships. The two forces engaged in a two-and-a-half-hour running gun battle just north of Ferris Bay (later to be renamed "Arnold's Bay") and within sight of the Ferris home. In order to save his force of roughly two hundred men, Arnold ran his ships (one galley and four gondolas) aground in the bay, dumped his cannons overboard, and ordered the ships scuttled. The retreating Americans dashed ashore while receiving fire from British ships located just outside the bay.

Arnold rallied his men at the Ferris cabin, which reportedly received several grapeshot in its walls. Arnold's men and the Ferris family then retreated south to Crown Point, about fifteen miles away. The British, under the command of Sir Guy Carleton, Governor General of Canada, subsequently burned Ferris's crops, cut down his orchard, killed his farm animals, and buried the bodies of those American sailors who washed ashore over the following days. The Ferrises later returned and continued to farm their lands until 1778 when Major Christopher Carleton raided the town, burned the Ferris farm buildings, and captured Peter Ferris and his son, Squire Ferris. The next three years and eight months saw Peter and Squire imprisoned in Quebec, but in 1782 they returned to Panton, rebuilt the farm, and subsequently established a ferry on Lake Champlain, taking travelers between the Vermont and New York shores. The farm was abandoned much later, probably in the 1840s.

While Art Cohn's team was in the area to do underwater research, they discovered that at least two-thirds of the foundation of the 1782 Ferris house had already fallen off the bluff onto the beach below (and into Lake Champlain). They decided then that it was necessary to conduct a salvage excavation, and they hired me to direct the project for four weeks during the summer of 1988. We dug some forty-eight one-meter-square pits and exposed the surviving portion of the Ferris cellar hole, the surrounding yards, and some debris that had already slid down the bank into Arnold's Bay. Because of the fragile nature of the surviving foundation walls, which were poised to collapse into the bay at any moment, we kept excavations inside the foundation as limited as possible. We drew the stone foundation walls and revealed the remains of a house that had been approximately fifteen feet wide. Everything else, though, had already fallen into the bay.

While we found great quantities of pottery, glass, and bone, the most interesting result of our excavation was the discovery of five lead balls and eight pieces of grape or cannister shot. The pieces of cast iron shot were scattered in the field just south of the Ferris house foundation and on the beach below. We can only guess that these pieces of shot landed there as the British were firing upon Arnold's retreating forces in October 1776. Their presence here is the one hopeful sign that the original Ferris house stood very close to the second house foundation, and it is certainly possible that both houses stood upon the same foundation that we recorded in 1988. While this was "only" a farm site, the Ferris house was nevertheless at the center of some of the most dramatic events ever to occur on Lake Champlain, and its steady loss to erosion is most unfortunate.

Further Reading

Cohn, Arthur. 1987. An Incident Not Known to History: Squire Ferris and Benedict Arnold at Ferris Bay, October 13, 1776. *Vermont History* 55 (2):1–17.

Starbuck, David R. 1989. *The Ferris Site on Arnold's Bay*. Basin Harbor, Vt.: Lake Champlain Maritime Museum.

floor *without* bringing anything up. In cooperation with the New York State Department of Environmental Conservation, they have also created three Submerged Heritage Preserves within the lake, permitting sport divers to visit and learn from a cluster of 1758 bateaux, a seven-sided warship known as a radeau, and a 1906 gasoline-powered launch.

The Lake Champlain Maritime Museum also takes a non-destructive approach and, in cooperation with the Vermont Division for Historic Preservation, has created several outstanding underwater preserves. But the museum has somewhat higher visibility thanks to its fast-growing museum

FIG. 8-1. The *Philadelphia* on display at the National Museum of American History, Smithsonian Institution, where she has long been one of the most popular exhibits. The British cannon ball that sank her is visible on the left.

complex on the grounds of the Basin Harbor Club in Basin Harbor, Vermont. The museum has succeeded in attracting both funding from state and federal sources, and visits from large numbers of school groups and others every summer.

Both Bateaux Below, Inc., and the Lake Champlain Maritime Museum have capitalized on the immense popularity of underwater archeology, and have been able to conduct their research in relatively clear freshwater lakes that have been little disturbed over the past two hundred years. However, both lakes have seen some deterioration of wreck sites because of the actions of treasure hunters and sport divers, and Lake Champlain is also faced with heavy encrustations of zebra mussels that cling to its wreck sites. The museum has therefore increased its underwater recording, seeking to document wrecks before they are totally obscured, and no doubt more wrecks will be excavated before they are lost forever.

FIG. 8-2. Conjectural view of the British Army ships on Lake Champlain in the fall of 1759, sloop *Boscawen* on left and brig *Duke of Cumberland* on right. Drawing by Kevin J. Crisman.

Lake Champlain: The French and Indian War Period

Easily the most significant French and Indian War vessel ever found in Lake Champlain is the *Boscawen*, a 115-ton, sixteen-gun English sloop that was built in the King's Shipyard at Fort Ticonderoga. She was constructed at the orders of General Amherst in 1759, to help destroy the French fleet on the

FIG. 8-3. Section of the *Boscawen* wreck slightly forward of
the stern. Note the shallow depth of water (six feet), the grid
suspended over the hull, and the depth of sediments within
the wreck. The diver is removing sediment with a water
dredge. Drawing by Kevin J. Crisman.

FIG. 8-4. One of two
twenty-five-foot-square
grids, subdivided into five-
foot-square excavation
units, is readied for placement over the wreck site.
Courtesy of Kevin J. Crisman.

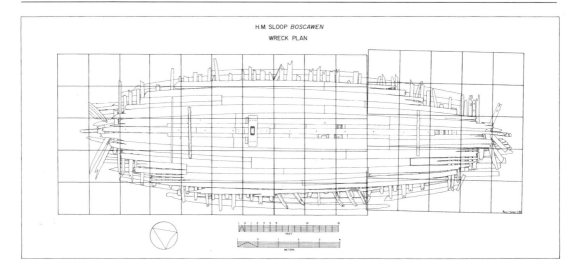

H.M. SLOOP *BOSCAWEN*
WRECK PLAN

FEET

METERS

FIG. 8-5. Plan of the British sloop *Boscawen*, as excavated in 1984–1985. Drawing by Kevin J. Crisman.

lake. After the war, the eighty-foot *Boscawen* was probably allowed to rot and sink at her mooring; she was rediscovered in 1983 by the Champlain Maritime Society, as it conducted a survey of the waters around the Great Bridge that had connected Mount Independence with Fort Ticonderoga. During the summers of 1984 and 1985, the Champlain Maritime Society, the Fort Ticonderoga Museum, and New York State sponsored an excavation of the King's Shipyard, which included intensive mapping and excavations at the hull of the *Boscawen*. Roughly one-half of her remaining timbers were exposed by the archeologists, who also discovered and conserved well-pre-

FIG. 8-6. Conservator Peggy Zak cleans an oaken mast cap recovered from the wreck of the *Boscawen*. Courtesy of Kevin J. Crisman.

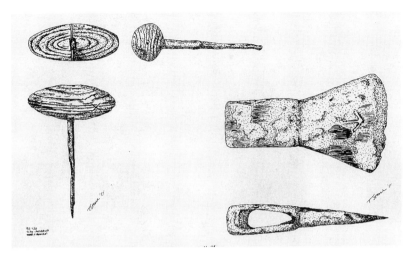

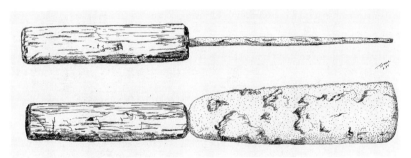

FIG. 8-7. Tools from the wreck of the *Boscawen*: an awl or punch with a wooden handle and iron point, and a small iron hatchet head with a broad arrow stamp. The awl is 10.4 cm long; the hatchet is 12.7 cm long. Drawings by Theresa Stone. Courtesy of Kevin J. Crisman.

FIG. 8-8. Brush knife from the wreck of the *Boscawen*, with its original pine handle. Knife is 43.7 cm long overall. Drawing by Theresa Stone. Courtesy of Kevin J. Crisman.

served pulley blocks, rope, shoes, buttons, tools, coins, a Jew's harp, a hand grenade, and much more. While much of the wood of the *Boscawen* did not survive, there was enough left to demonstrate that the ship had been large and heavily built, one of the most formidable eighteenth-century ships on Lake Champlain (see figures 8-2 to 8-8). Kevin Crisman has conducted exhaustive and continuing research on the *Boscawen*, noting that there is evidence of shortcuts made during her construction, including the use of green, unseasoned wood. This surely reflected the speed with which the British wanted to drive the French from the lake.

Lake Champlain: The American Revolution

The most memorable vessels to be found in Lake Champlain from the time of the American Revolution are certainly those that were constructed in 1776 by Benedict Arnold's shipwrights in Skenesborough (now Whitehall), New York. The hastily built American fleet is popularly referred to within the re-

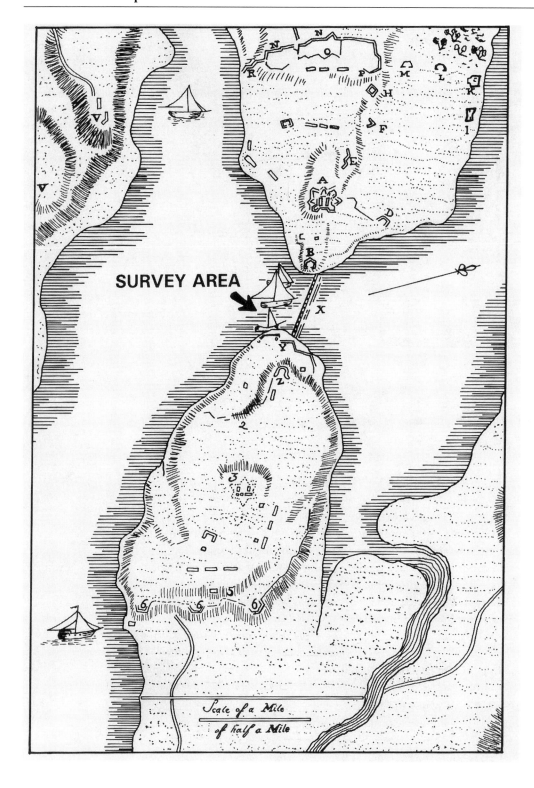

SURVEY AREA

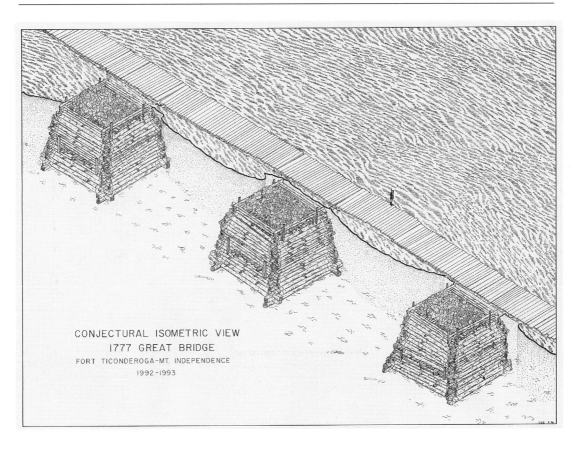

CONJECTURAL ISOMETRIC VIEW
1777 GREAT BRIDGE
FORT TICONDEROGA-MT. INDEPENDENCE
1992-1993

gion as "America's First Navy," and when they challenged the British fleet for supremacy over Lake Champlain that October, the American "navy" consisted of just fifteen vessels, including eight gunboats and four row galleys. I have already mentioned that one of these, the *Philadelphia*, was promptly sunk at the Battle of Valcour Island but was later recovered by Lorenzo Hagglund. Using the dimensions of the original vessel, the Lake Champlain Maritime Museum recently reproduced the *Philadelphia*, launched it in 1991, and sails this superb replica among the various ports on Lake Champlain each summer.

Actively seeking Arnold's other ships on the bottom of Lake Champlain, the Lake Champlain Maritime Museum found, in June 1997, an exceptionally intact gunboat once commanded by Benedict Arnold. When located with side-scan sonar, the vessel was still sitting upright with its mast standing over fifty feet high. Either abandoned or scuttled by the Americans as they retreated after the Battle of Valcour Island, this new gunboat, as one of eleven of Arnold's boats lost during or after the battle, cannot be identified precisely. But the bow cannon is still in place, and the ship appears as fully intact as the *Philadelphia*. No decision has yet been made about whether to

FIG. 8-9. (Opposite.) Location of the Great Bridge across Lake Champlain between Mount Independence and Fort Ticonderoga. Traced from a plan from the General St. Clair court martial proceedings by Scott A. McLaughlin.

FIG. 8-10. (Top.) A conjectural isometric view of the 1777 Great Bridge. Drawing by Joseph Cozzi. Courtesy of the Lake Champlain Maritime Museum and the Vermont Division for Historic Preservation.

FIG. 8-11. Caisson 2 of the
1777 Great Bridge. Drawing by
Joseph Cozzi. Courtesy of the Lake
Champlain Maritime Museum and
the Vermont Division for Historic
Preservation.

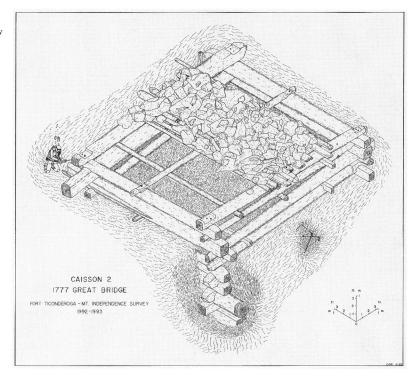

FIG. 8-12. Feature 7C, an
ammunition scatter, from
the Mount Independence
Shoreline Survey, June 1993.
Drawing by Scott A. McLaughlin.
Courtesy of the Lake Champlain
Maritime Museum and the Vermont Division for Historic Preservation.

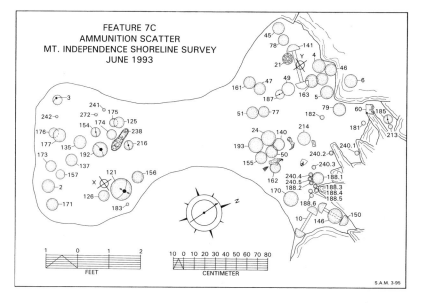

leave the ship where it is or to bring it up, but its hull is clearly in even better shape than the *Philadelphia*'s and, if it ever does come out of the water, modern conservation methods will be used to stabilize it.

Important revolutionary war discoveries in Lake Champlain are not limited to shipwrecks. One of the most important military features constructed during the war was the 1777 Great Bridge that spanned the lake from Mount Independence to Fort Ticonderoga (figures 8-9 to 8-11). Art Cohn and his colleagues began documenting this bridge during their underwater survey in 1983 and finally obtained sufficient funding to do an extensive underwater project during the summer of 1992. Using side-scan sonar, over the course of many dives, Cohn's team discovered twenty-two complete spades and shovels, pickaxes, a broadaxe, nine bar shot, wine bottles, a musket, two bayonets, a cannon, thirty-three mortar bombs, nine anchors, cast-iron pots, and much more, all scattered around the sides of the bridge and lying on the lake bottom (figures 8-12 to 8-14). This is the richest and best-preserved collection of revolutionary war military artifacts ever found. Because treasure

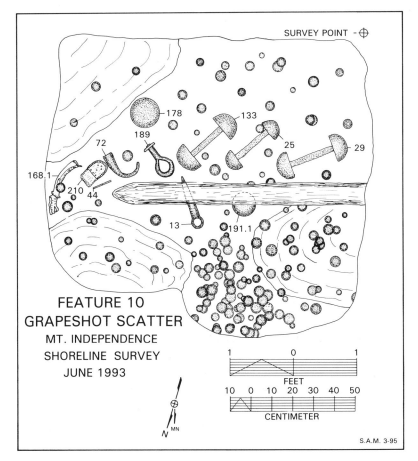

FIG. 8-13. Feature 10, a grapeshot scatter, from the Mount Independence Shoreline Survey, June 1993. Drawing by Scott A. McLaughlin. Courtesy of the Lake Champlain Maritime Museum and the Vermont Division for Historic Preservation.

FIG. 8-14. A twelve-pounder iron cannon, found during the Mount Independence Shoreline Survey, 1992–1993. Drawing by Scott A. McLaughlin. Courtesy of the Lake Champlain Maritime Museum and the Vermont Division for Historic Preservation.

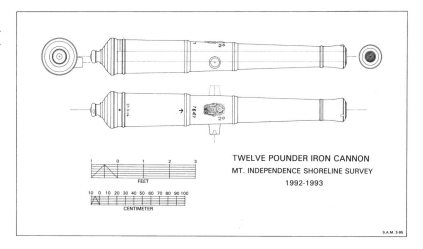

TWELVE POUNDER IRON CANNON
MT. INDEPENDENCE SHORELINE SURVEY
1992-1993

S.A.M. 3-95

hunters have frequently vandalized sites in Lake Champlain, the maritime museum, funded by the State of Vermont, was later forced to remove all of these artifacts from the lake in order to conserve them at the museum. Many were then moved to the new visitors' center at Mount Independence where they are some of the most impressive artifacts on display.

Just as important, Cohn and his colleagues documented the remains of the bridge itself, some twenty-one timber caissons that had been built in the winter of 1776–1777 and pushed out onto the ice. The American engineer who accomplished this feat, Colonel Jeduthan Baldwin, had filled the caissons with rocks, and the cribs sank to the bottom of the lake as the ice melted in the spring. A wooden roadway was chained together on top of the caissons, and soldiers were thus able to walk back and forth on the water between Mount Independence and Fort Ticonderoga. Recording the underwater caissons in the murky, silt-filled waters of Lake Champlain was a daunting task for Cohn and his team, but they managed to draw the remains of the bridge and the artifact scatters lying nearby on the bottom of the lake, often with a visibility of only inches.

Lake George: The French and Indian War

In 1758 and 1759, vast fleets of ships were needed to carry British and provincial soldiers from the south end of Lake George to Fort Carillon (Ticonderoga) where they assaulted the French positions. A bateau could carry up to 23 men, along with provisions, and some 900 bateaux and 135 whaleboats were assembled in 1758 as troop carriers during General James Abercromby's failed expedition. Later that year, after they had returned to the south end of the lake, 260 bateaux, plus other vessels, were deliberately sunk by the

FIG. 8-15. Maritime historian Mark Peckham's drawing of a colonial bateau. Bateaux were common on Lake George during the French and Indian War. They were pointed at bow and stern, made of pine and oak wood, could be rowed using oars or poled in shallow waters, and had an oar off the stern for steering. Seven 1758 bateaux sunk in Lake George, called the Wiawaka bateaux after the nearby Wiawaka Holiday House, were studied by Bateaux Below, Inc., and were then listed on the National Register of Historic Places in 1992. Courtesy of Mark Peckham.

British so that the French could not capture them, and these now lie in less than fifty feet of water. The lower part of each hull has survived and is buried in lake sediment, and most of them lie perpendicular to the shoreline.

From 1960, divers have often sought out these bateaux; several were raised then and taken to the Adirondack Museum and the New York State Museum for curation or display. Later, in 1963–1964, the first systematic survey of Lake George was conducted by the Adirondack Museum, which found many additional bateaux. The New York State Police scuba team found still more in 1965, but the next thorough study did not occur until between 1987 and 1991. It was then that Bateaux Below, Inc. (then called the Lake George Bateaux Research Team), mapped one cluster of wrecks, known as the "Wiawaka bateaux." While no artifacts were found on board the Wiawaka bateaux, concentrations of rocks were discovered that had probably been used to sink the vessels. These seven military bateaux, lying between twenty and forty-five feet below the surface of the lake, were subsequently listed on the National Register of Historic Places (see figures 8-15, 8-16, and 8-17).

In 1990, Bateaux Below, Inc., used Klein side-scan sonar to find an even more significant wreck, an intact radeau named the *Land Tortoise*, built in 1758 as part of the effort to take Ticonderoga. This rather unusual category of vessel was essentially a large, flat-bottomed raft, 52 feet long, 18 feet wide, and seven-sided. Built with its sides pierced for seven cannons, the *Land Tortoise* was probably never completed before the British sank her in the autumn in 1758 in order to hide her from the French. While they no doubt planned to raise and rig her when they returned the following year, Zarzynski and his colleagues believe that the *Land Tortoise* must have drifted into deeper water—she was found in 107 feet of water—where she could not be

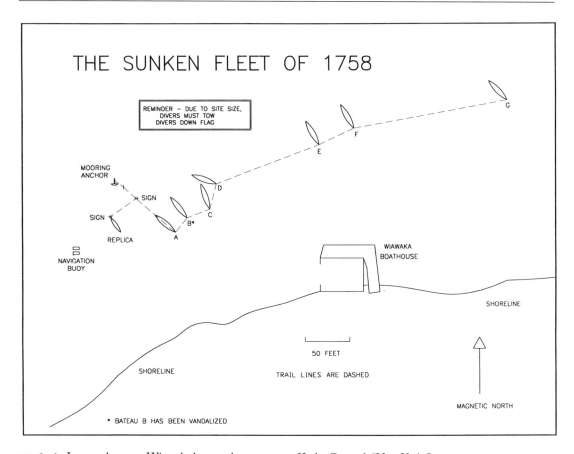

THE SUNKEN FLEET OF 1758

REMINDER — DUE TO SITE SIZE, DIVERS MUST TOW DIVERS DOWN FLAG

G

F

E

MOORING ANCHOR

SIGN

D

SIGN

C

B*

REPLICA

A

NAVIGATION BUOY

WIAWAKA BOATHOUSE

SHORELINE

50 FEET

SHORELINE

TRAIL LINES ARE DASHED

MAGNETIC NORTH

* BATEAU B HAS BEEN VANDALIZED

FIG. 8-16. In 1993 the seven Wiawaka bateaux became part of Lake George's "New York State Submerged Heritage Preserves," a shipwreck preserve for visiting scuba divers. One of the preserves was named "The Sunken Fleet of 1758." In 1997, a twenty-three-foot-long replica bateau was sunk south of the site so divers could examine what an intact bateau would look like. This map shows the seven approximately thirty-foot-long colonial bateaux, designated A to G, with the nearby replica bateau. Trail lines and signs guide divers along so they can view the sunken warships. Courtesy of Joseph W. Zarzynski and Bateaux Below, Inc.

FIG. 8-17. Surviving hull of one of two Lake George bateaux recovered in 1960. This example, now on display at the Adirondack Museum, dates to the war of 1756–1760, and is probably a relic of the campaigns of 1758 or 1759. Drawing by Kevin J. Crisman.

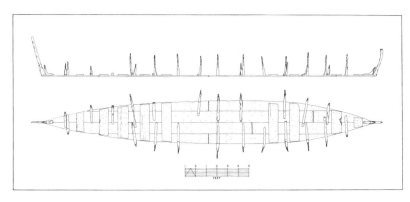

FIG. 8-18. Silhouette of what the 1758 *Land Tortoise* radeau may have looked like fully rigged for sail. Many radeaux were designed for both rowing and sailing. This radeau was deliberately sunk by the British forces to keep it out of French hands before it was ever completely rigged for sailing. Courtesy of Joseph W. Zarzynski and Bateaux Below, Inc.

FIG. 8-19. Plan of the *Land Tortoise* radeau. Courtesy of Joseph W. Zarzynski and Bateaux Below, Inc.

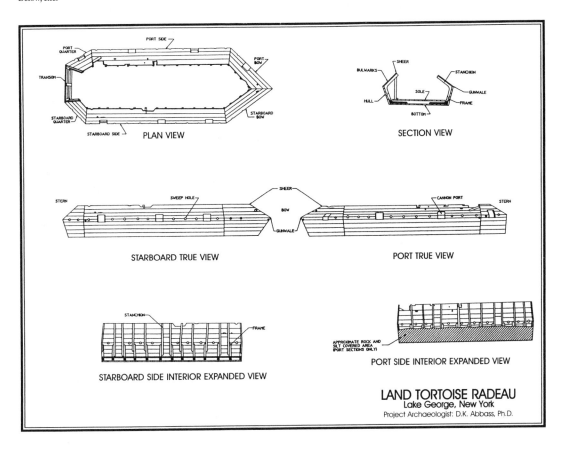

FIG. 8-20. A Bateaux Below, Inc., diver measuring the bow section of the *Land Tortoise* radeau, lying in 107 feet of water. Courtesy of Russell Bellico and Bateaux Below, Inc.

FIG. 8-21. The starboard side cannon port of the *Land Tortoise* radeau. This vessel was a seven-sided floating gun battery. Courtesy of Russell Bellico and Bateaux Below, Inc.

retrieved. Members of Bateaux Below, Inc., mapped and photographed the *Land Tortoise* between 1991 and 1993 and even prepared a photomosaic of the upper part of the vessel, funded with a grant from the Lake Champlain Basin Program. Because only a few radeaux were ever built, and this is the only one discovered archeologically, the *Land Tortoise* was listed on the National Register of Historic Places in 1995 and was declared a National Historic Landmark in 1998. It has been described as "North America's oldest intact warship" and may now be viewed as one of the Submerged Heritage Preserves at the bottom of Lake George (see figures 8-18 through 8-21).

Conclusions

The discoveries made by underwater archeologists along The Great Warpath have been truly exciting, and many of the wrecks found in Lake Champlain and Lake George are remarkably well preserved—reflecting the very instant that a ship sank during battle, as in the case of the *Philadelphia* and Benedict Arnold's gunboat. It is an incredible thrill to view *in situ* the original ships, the rich scatters of complete artifacts, and even the log caissons from the 1777 Great Bridge across Lake Champlain.

While it is infinitely better to leave these sites undisturbed on the bottom of each waterway, at the same time the public is often eager to have the better artifacts retrieved and displayed. Since the cost of artifact conservation for underwater sites can be enormous, priorities need to be weighed carefully, keeping in mind that no fort or military feature on land has survived with the same integrity, and that it is far more exciting to see an intact site under water than a wooden replica on land. As underwater technology improves, perhaps the final compromise will be to develop new types of interactive exhibits, in which visitors within museums on land can see and interact with vessels that are under water, using remote cameras and rovers to travel through each wreck site. The costs would be high, but there is no substitute for the feeling of actually being there.

Further Reading

Abbass, D. K., Robert Cembrola, and Joseph W. Zarzynski. 1992. The Lake George *Radeau*: An Intact Vessel of 1758. In *Underwater Archaeology Proceedings from the Society for Historical Archaeology Conference*, edited by Donald H. Keith and Toni L. Carroll, 142–47. Washington, D.C.: Society for Historical Archaeology.

Bellico, Russell P. 1992. Radeau Below. North America's Oldest Intact Warship. *Sea History* 63:18–19.

———. 1992. *Sails and Steam in the Mountains—A Maritime and Military History of Lake George and Lake Champlain.* Fleischmanns, N.Y.: Purple Mountain Press.

———. 1995. *Chronicles of Lake George—Journeys in War and Peace.* Fleischmanns, N.Y.: Purple Mountain Press.

Crisman, Kevin J. 1986. *Of Sailing Ships and Sidewheelers: The History and Nautical Archaeology of Lake Champlain.* Montpelier, Vermont: The Division for Historic Preservation, Agency of Development and Community Affairs, State of Vermont.

————. 1996. Struggle for a Continent: Naval Battles of the French and Indian Wars. In *Ships and Shipwrecks of the Americas*, edited by George F. Bass, 129–148. London: Thames and Hudson Ltd.

Crisman, Kevin J., and Arthur B. Cohn. 1994. Lake Champlain Nautical Archaeology Since 1980. *The Journal of Vermont Archaeology* 1:153–66.

Crockett, Walter Hill. 1909. *A History of Lake Champlain, 1609–1909*. Burlington, Vt.: Hobart J. Shanley.

Fowler, Barney. 1982. *Adirondack Album*. Schenectady, N.Y.: Outdoor Associates. See the chapter "So Proudly We Sailed."

Hill, Ralph Nading. 1995. *Lake Champlain: Key to Liberty*. Woodstock, Vt.: Countryman Press.

Krueger, John W., Arthur B. Cohn, Kevin J. Crisman, Heidi Miksch, and Jane M. Lape. 1985. *The Bulletin of the Fort Ticonderoga Museum* 14 (6). Thematic issue devoted to the Fort Ticonderoga King's Shipyard excavation.

Lundeberg, Philip K. 1966. *The Continental Gunboat* Philadelphia. Washington, D.C.: Smithsonian Institution.

Van de Water, Frederic F. 1946. *Lake Champlain and Lake George*. Indianapolis and New York: The Bobbs-Merrill Company, Publishers.

Zarzynski, Joseph W., and John Farrell. 1994. Recent Underwater Archaeological Surveys at Lake George, New York. In *Military Sites of the Hudson River, Lake George, and Lake Champlain Corridor*, edited by David R. Starbuck, 5–9. Queensbury, N.Y.: Adirondack Community College.

Zarzynski, Joseph W., Kendrick B. McMahan, Bob Benway, and Vincent J. Capone. 1995. The 1758 *Land Tortoise Radeau* Shipwreck—Creating a Seamless Photomosaic Using Off-the-Shelf Technology. In *Underwater Archaeology Proceedings from the Society for Historical Archaeology Conference*, edited by Paul Forsythe Johnston, 181–86. Washington, D.C.: Society for Historical Archaeology.

Chapter 9

Some Final Thoughts about The Great Warpath

General Observations

*T*HE MILITARY SITES presented in these chapters reflect the sites that I know best and also those where I have personally worked. When I began planning this book, my choice of chapter topics was based more on those sites along The Great Warpath whose history I knew to be significant and well documented. But as I considered how little professional archeology has occurred at many sites, it was necessary to reduce them to a mere sidebar or to eliminate them altogether. This is, after all, a book about how archeology has aided research at certain military sites, not a summary of the military history of the waterway that runs between New York and Vermont. Thus a site like the Bennington Battlefield is difficult to describe archeologically when little digging has been done, and when the artifacts recovered there by the New York State Museum over ten years ago numbered a grand total of one musket ball. Significant, yes, but not exactly a chapter of a book.

I have eliminated discussion of some lesser known sites along the warpath that are totally unprotected, because it would be unwise to bring attention to them that might result in additional looting. I firmly believe that known sites need to be publicized more so that the public may help protect them. But sites that still enjoy a measure of obscurity should remain secret.

I also want to acknowledge, as I close this book, that my definition of "archeology," and that of most professional archeologists, may differ from that of some people who have dug along The Great Warpath. Professional archeology is not just a matter of keeping the walls of an excavation pit straight, or learning how to fill out recording sheets, and it certainly is not having architects expose some foundations before doing a reconstruction. It is asking questions about the past and systematically using artifacts, features, and sites to try to find out the answers, culminating in the publication of professional-quality reports. It also requires the ability to suspend judgment until *all* information has been collected. No one is more harmful on an archeological dig than the self-professed "expert" who wanders from pit to pit giving instant interpretation to all who will listen.

Archeology ceased to be the simple-minded quest for artifacts a long time ago, and modern archeology has evolved into the deliberate use of the scientific method. When archeology is combined with exacting recording techniques, it helps tell the story of how past people once lived. When used wisely, it can be of greater value in interpreting buried structures than any of the eighteenth-century engineer's drawings that have survived. After all, many contemporary drawings simply show what the military *hoped* to build —not what was actually built. Only archeology *combined* with history can do that.

I have addressed the theme of treasure hunting several times in this book, but not because it is a topic I enjoy writing about. Those who despoil our past view every site and artifact as potentially theirs, something to show off, brag about, display on the mantle, or sell when it suits them. But the past is not a renewable resource, and treasure hunters destroy the past for the rest of us. When the last eighteenth-century military site has been torn up, we will be left to try to imagine life as it was then without the benefit of studying camp layouts, associations among different categories of artifacts (revealing where specific activities occurred), or construction techniques used in building huts and lookout posts. Over the years I have conducted excavations at prehistoric Native American campsites, and at a wide variety of industrial and domestic European-American sites. But nowhere else have I seen the level of looting and selling that goes on with military artifacts. It is *the* dirty secret of modern life along The Great Warpath.

Synthesis and Conclusions

In each chapter I have presented some specific interpretations and thoughts about what still needs to be done at individual military sites along The Great Warpath. But can I draw any overarching conclusions? I'll begin my answer by noting that for me, like many of the visitors to my digs, history has been alternately exciting and boring. Sometimes documents "speak" to me about the experiences of real people in the eighteenth century, and sometimes they are merely facts to be memorized and do not tell stories of interest to us living in the twentieth century with our very different lives and values. I believe that the great strength of archeology lies in its ability to provide a tangible link to the clothing, accoutrements, foodways, weapons, and housing of ordinary people who have been largely forgotten by history. Upon closer examination, they often do seem very much like us, and for many of my diggers, it is the tactile aspect of finding and touching archeological remains, and then describing to others what they have seen and learned first-hand, that finally makes history become real for them.

Starting with the earlier French and Indian War sites along The Great Warpath, this book has presented lots of specific details. I have noted that military ceramics of the 1750s were predominantly unrefined stonewares combined with significant quantities of delft and white salt-glazed stoneware, some porcelain (usually found together with other, high-quality artifacts, suggesting the presence of officers), and only the smallest amounts of redware and buff-bodied slipware. Our discoveries at revolutionary war sites twenty years later show that the stonewares are still common, but the slipware has vanished, the delft has decreased, and creamware has been added in goodly quantities.

It was fairly uncommon for military buttons to be numbered during the French and Indian War, and no numbered buttons from this period were found at Fort William Henry or Fort Edward. In fact, until recently it was believed that numbered buttons were not in regular use until 1767, when standardized dress by the army was adopted. And so we used to believe that if a military site contained no numbered buttons, it had to date to the French and Indian War or earlier; and if such buttons were present, we assumed it must date to the Revolutionary War or later. However, because of the excavation of the seventy-four-gun ship of the line *Invincible* between 1979 and 1990, we now know this simple rule of thumb does not hold true. This warship sank in the Solent in 1758 and contained a cargo of numbered buttons from many different British regiments, proving that numbered buttons can date to either war. Still, that is barely reflected archeologically along The Great Warpath, except at the English fort at Crown Point where buttons numbered "L" and "51" were excavated in 1963 in a French and Indian War context. Much more typically, numbered military buttons—often with quite decorative designs—did not become common along the Warpath until the 1770s.

Food and foodways show very little change between the 1750s and 1770s at the various military sites along The Great Warpath. The design of cutlery was much the same; wine bottles were always present; and considerable use was made of fresh beef and pork at all of these sites. Weaponry appears to have changed very little between the two wars, but interestingly enough, much more coinage, especially Spanish, appears to have been in circulation along the warpath during the French and Indian War. Unfortunately, items that would provide evidence of women and children at the military camps are consistently ambiguous or missing for this entire period.

Archeology has been extremely helpful in revealing information about the types of construction used in huts, barracks, and hospitals, and it is especially good at revealing temporary, post-type buildings. In retrospect, the huts revealed on Rogers Island do not appear significantly different from those at Crown Point or Mount Independence, even though the local building materials available were certainly different from site to site. Evidence for differences in the quality of officers' spaces and enlisted men's spaces is not always apparent, but the study done at Crown Point by Lois Feister shows that the British officers used much better flooring materials and had better fireplaces than did the soldiers. And we did find that some huts had wood floors and better fireplaces on Rogers Island, and some huts at Mount Independence contained window glass and nails, while others did not. This may well represent a difference in status or rank, but it could also represent a different season of occupation or an "early" campsite versus a later, more permanent habitation.

There is little evidence for any change in leisure activities between the two wars. The occasional Jew's harp for making music, the red patches of sand that denote the manufacture of musket balls, the fine sets of cuff links that suggest officers wanted to look their best even in a frontier setting, the soldier who etched his name into the side of a wine bottle at Mount Independence, these are hints of daily life. James Hill's wine bottle at Mount Independence is without doubt the most personalized and truly unique artifact found at any of these military camps, although the human scalp found at Fort William Henry is probably the most dramatic. We found another example of the "human" side of archeology on Rogers Island as we recovered literally dozens of chewed musket balls. My students spent countless hours discussing all of the possible explanations for these, from soldiers' clenching them between their teeth at the whipping post, to "biting the bullet" in a military hospital while being operated upon, to creating dumdum bullets that would spin in flight.

Much of the time, though, archeology does not provide definitive explanations for what people were doing or why. It presents us instead with a set of possibilities, among which the archeologist tries to determine the one that best fits the data. It also provides us with some grand detective stories and, occasionally, brings out aspects of life that history tells us nothing about. Archeology has given rise among my diggers to such endless speculation about the past that I must conclude it is also one of the greatest teaching techniques devised for making history come alive.

It is still possible to tell new stories about the eighteenth-century wars. After all, the men who fought along the Hudson River, Lake George, and Lake Champlain have earned the right to be remembered and honored by all those who come after them, in spite of the passage of time. Archeology, reenactments, and the many facets of public history have all done a great deal to keep early American military history relevant and interesting. For me personally, it has been rewarding beyond measure to conduct archeology at the sites of these forts and battlefields; my hope is that these sites will continue to be carefully managed and studied so that the soldiers and officers will keep coming back to life, telling us all we want to know about the eighteenth century.

Glossary of Terms

Also see "Glossary" in *American Forts* by Willard B. Robinson, 1977, Urbana: University of Illinois Press; and definitions throughout *A Guide to Artifacts of Colonial America* by Ivor Noel Hume, 1970, New York: Alfred A. Knopf and *Collector's Illustrated Encyclopedia of the American Revolution* by George C. Neumann and Frank J. Kravic, 1975, Texarkana: Rebel Publishing Co., Inc.

barracks: Eighteenth-century military barracks for housing soldiers could be either one or two stories high, typically of log construction, with exterior staircases and massive interior fireplaces of brick and/or stone running along the center line of the building.

bar shot: An iron bar with a large ball at either end, capable of rotating during flight when fired from a cannon. These were effective against both personnel and ship's rigging.

bastion: A construction of earth or stone projecting out from the corner of a Vauban-style fortification. It has two faces and two flanks, such that each flank defends the adjacent curtain wall. This effectively catches the attacking force in a crossfire.

battery: A parapet thrown up to protect the gunners and artillery behind it.

camp follower: Wives, sweethearts, and prostitutes who accompanied British and American forces on many of their campaigns. Their rations were only a fraction of that given to the men, but their role as nurses, laundresses, and caregivers was indispensable.

cannister shot: Round, cast-iron shot, loaded into a tinned container, to be fired from a cannon or howitzer. The dozens of balls separated in mid-air and were quite effective in mowing down opposing personnel.

cannon: Field artillery cast of bronze or iron that shoots either solid balls or grapeshot or cannister shot. It is identified according to the weight of the ball, such as "a 6-pound cannon."

case bottle: A straight-sided, square bottle, blown into a mold and typically carried in a compartmented case with other bottles. Used as a container for gin or medicine.

casemate: A bombproof room underneath the ramparts of a fortification. These might be used either for housing cannons that faced out upon the enemy or as quarters to protect the troops and their dependents.

cob money: Small, irregular, Spanish coins cut from a bar of silver.

creamware: A cream-colored earthenware that was developed by Thomas Astbury and Thomas Whieldon in the 1740s and later perfected by Josiah Wedgwood. Sets of dishes manufactured from this ware were immensely popular in the late eighteenth and early nineteenth centuries. Early pieces were a very deep yellow, while later ones became much lighter in color.

delft: The same as tin-glazed earthenware. The lower-cased term "delft" refers to this ware when manufactured in England.

fascine knife: A large knife used for cutting brush. (Fascines were bundles of sticks tied together, hence a fascine knife was used for cutting these to length.)

French drain: A ditch filled with loose stones, which permitted water to flow through it easily.

frog: A scabbard loop used for hanging a sword or bayonet.

grapeshot: Round, cast-iron balls, placed on a wood base and around a center pole, with a cloth bag then tied around it. When fired from a cannon, these were especially effective in tearing down the sails of opposing ships.

gunflint: A wedge- or prism-shaped blade of flint that produced a spark when struck against a steel frizzen, thus firing a flintlock musket. The flints were cushioned with strips of lead as they were inserted into the cock grip of a musket. Those used in the eighteenth century were typically gray or black (of English origin), or brown or honey-colored (of French origin). The French gunflints were much preferred and are more commonly found at military sites.

howitzer: Short-barreled field artillery that shoots explosive shells with a low muzzle velocity much like a mortar, but with a lesser trajectory. Also shoots cannister shot and grapeshot.

Jew's harp: A small, common, musical instrument of iron or brass with a vibrator ("tongue") of steel or brass that vibrates and produces a twanging tone.

moat: A ditch dug around a fortification, typically wide and deep, and sometimes filled with water. The dirt that was removed was raised up to form the ramparts.

modern material culture: Artifacts of the recent past, capable of revealing much information about the consumption habits and preferences of modern society.

mortar: Short-barreled field artillery that fires an explosive shell in a high trajectory. Mortar shells were filled with black powder and employed a hollow wood fuse that was lit just before it was fired from the barrel. These typically were used to land shells inside an opposing fortification or camp that was under siege.

musket ball: A round lead ball, produced in a mold, and placed into a musket cartridge with an appropriate amount of black powder. The diameter of the ball typically is a good indicator of what caliber of musket it was fired from.

palisade: A high fence or defensive wall of vertical posts or logs set in the ground (or in a ditch) about six to nine inches apart.

pearlware: An earthenware that evolved out of creamware in the 1770s but had a whiter glaze. (It appears bluish wherever the glaze buildup is thicker, as on the footring.) It was the most common ware of the early nineteenth century before being fazed out ca. 1820.

picket: A sharpened pole or stake set vertically in the ground. A picket fort is thus one surrounded by an enclosure of poles.

polyethylene glycol (PEG): Wax used as a preservative in the conservation of wood, bone, and other organic materials. Prolonged soaking of an artifact in an aqueous solution of PEG causes the wax gradually to fill the pores and stabilize the material.

posthole/postmold: A posthole is the hole into which a post is placed or driven, whereas a postmold is what remains from the actual post that stood within the hole. On historic sites, the dark stain that survives from the surrounding posthole is usually square in outline (because it was cut with the flat blade of a spade), whereas the inner postmold is most often round and even darker.

provincials: Soldiers raised in the American colonies (as opposed to the regulars or Redcoats who were brought over from Britain).

redoubt: A temporary fortification or breastwork, typically of earth and/or logs, used to secure hilltops, passes, and so on.

redware: A red-bodied earthenware made from local, readily-available red clays, typically used for food preparation or storage. Redwares were in common usage throughout the colonial period and later, but forms were so long-lasting that it is almost impossible to date this ware.

remote sensing: Any of several techniques for predicting scientifically what may lie below the surface of the ground. This includes the use of ground-penetrating radar, resistivity meters, proton magnetometers, and so on, each of which is suited to detecting a certain type of feature (such as fireplaces) in certain types of soil (such as sand or clay). None, however, eliminates the need for digging because one must still expose and verify the anomaly that is detected below the surface, as well as the associated artifacts and inferred activities.

rose head nail: A hand-wrought nail whose head has a distinctive, faceted "rose-head" shape because the blacksmith hit the head five times on an angle.

sallyport: A covered passageway permitting egress from the inner to the outer works of a fortification and permitting the defenders to carry out sorties against the attacking enemy.

scratch blue: Incised decoration added to the surface of white salt-glazed stoneware. Cobalt, when placed within these incisions, leaves a pattern of thin blue lines.

sprue: The waste left after making a musket ball (or any other melted metal) in a mold.

sutler: A private contractor who follows an army in order to sell provisions to the troops.

tin-glazed earthenware: An earthenware popular throughout the seventeenth and eighteenth centuries. The soft body is a pale yellow or pink, and the glaze contains tin oxide that turns the ware white (a "tin enamel"), resembling the appearance of porcelain. The surface was often painted before firing.

unrefined stoneware: Thicker, coarser stonewares, often of unknown origin (but either British or American-made), that are almost ubiquitous on eighteenth-century military sites.

white salt-glazed stoneware: A refined English stoneware (a tableware), manufactured in molds, that was common throughout the eighteenth century. Molds typically added elaborate relief scenes to the rims of plates (such as the "barley" design).

whiteware: A hard white ware (such as "stone china" or "ironstone china") produced after ca. 1810 and still in use throughout much of the twentieth century.

worm: A short, rotating screw used for removing a charge from a musket.

Index

University Press of New England publishes books under its own imprint and is the publisher for Brandeis University Press, Dartmouth College, Middlebury College Press, University of New Hampshire, Tufts University, and Wesleyan University Press.

Library of Congress Cataloging-in-Publication Data
Starbuck, David R.
   The great warpath : British military sites from Albany to Crown
Point / David R. Starbuck.
      p.   cm.
   "Sponsored by the National Society, Daughters of Colonial Wars."
   Includes index.
   ISBN 0–87451–903–9 (alk. paper)
   1. New York (State)—History—Revolution, 1775–1783—Battlefields.
2. Vermont—History—Revolution, 1775–1783—Battlefields. 3. United
States—History—Revolution, 1775–1783—Battlefields. 4. New York
(State)—History—Revolution, 1775–1783—British Forces.
5. Vermont—History—Revolution, 1775–1783—British Forces.
6. United States—History—Revolution, 1775–1783—British Forces.
7. Great Britain. Army—History—18th century. 8. Historic sites—
New York (State) 9. Historic sites—Vermont. I. Daughters of
Colonial Wars. II. Title.
E230.5.N4S7   1999
973.3'3—dc21   98–48378